REDISCOVERING LAFCADIO HEARN

Lafcadio Hearn in his later years
Courtesy Asahi Shimbun

REDISCOVERING
LAFCADIO HEARN

JAPANESE LEGENDS
LIFE & CULTURE

EDITED BY
SUKEHIRO HIRAKAWA

GLOBAL
ORIENTAL

REDISCOVERING LAFCADIO HEARN
JAPANESE LEGENDS, LIFE & CULTURE

Edited by Sukehiro Hirakawa

First published 1997 by
Global Books Ltd

Second Impression 2004 by
GLOBAL ORIENTAL LTD
PO Box 219
Folkestone
Kent CT20 2WP

www.globaloriental.co.uk

British Library Cataloguing in Publication Data
A CIP catalogue entry for this book is available
from the British Library

ISBN 1-86034-014-8

Set in Bembo 12 on 12pt by Bookman, Slough
Printed and bound in England by The Bath Press, Avon

CONTENTS

Publisher's Note

JAPANESE NAMES

The Japanese convention for names is to put the family name first and the given name last, as in Koizumi Yakumo – the name Lafcadio Hearn adopted when he became a naturalized Japanese citizen in 1896. This convention is respected throughout the text, except in the case of the Japanese contributors who, for the sake of consistency with other contributors, are presented according to Western convention.

PREFACE

About a century ago, while lecturing to students at Tokyo University, Lafcadio Hearn, alias Koizumi Yakumo (1850–1904), said:

> Yet after all, the greatest of critics is the public – not the public for a day or a generation, but the public of centuries, the consensus of national opinion or of human opinion about a book that has been subjected to the awful test of time. Reputations are made not by critics, but by the accumulation of human opinion through hundreds of years.

Subjected to this awful test of time, Hearn's reputation as a Japan interpreter seems to have been eclipsed in the West, especially after World War II. However, Japanese opinion, which is based upon feeling rather than upon thinking, continues to say: 'We like Koizumi Yakumo.' If the test of a good book is whether we want to read it only once or more than once, Hearn's *Kwaidan* is without doubt a good book, for his ghost stories have been read not only in English by the Japanese of many generations, but also have been repeatedly translated into Japanese. Moreover, since 1980 there has been a remarkable revival of interest in Lafcadio Hearn in Japan and elsewhere.

Has this Lafcadio Hearn rediscovery something to do with the increase in importance of Japanese traditional culture in the world community? Many Westerners are now deeply attracted to natural Shinto, and many such people turn to Lafcadio Hearn for information. Shinto, the soul of Japan, is peaceful and very different from State Shinto, as manipulated by the militarists and the ultra nationalists during times of war. The fourteen papers collected in this volume entitled *Rediscovering Lafcadio Hearn* hopefully testify to the extent of that renewed interest and concern.

Let me explain how this book has come into existence. Its origin is also indicative of that 'Hearn fever': on 30 August 1990, the Lafcadio Hearn Festival was opened in Matsue, 'the chief city of the province of the gods', where the American-based writer of Irish–Greek origin had arrived a hundred years before, on the same date. Surprisingly, the four-day conference was attended by more than eight hundred enthusiastic Hearn lovers every day. However, among the audience as well as among the panel there were also persons who were very critical of or even inimical to Hearn. That divergence of views made the discussions all the more lively and stimulating. In his lifetime Hearn, who 'had gone native', was a dubious figure among Western residents in Japan, and for many people he still remains very problematic a century after his arrival.

Practically all contributors to this volume, of various opinions and of diverse cultural backgrounds, were invited to attend that centennial meeting. The late Dr Louis Allen from Durham, England; Professor Earl Miner from Princeton, USA; Professor Yuzo Ota from McGill University, Canada; and others from several Japanese universities. Not only our papers but also many other papers of interest written in or translated into Japanese and presented at the symposium have since been printed in Tokyo mainly in issue number 88 of the journal *Mugendai*, 1991; in *Hikaku Bungaku Kenkyū* (Studies of Comparative Literature), number 60, 1991; and especially in the book *Sekai no naka no Rafukadio Haan* (Lafcadio Hearn in worldwide perspective) published by Kawade Co., 1994.

These publications again have generated animated discussions and controversies about Hearn the writer, the Japan interpreter, the teacher and the man. In Japan, many books and the special issues on Hearn from various periodicals have been published in recent years: among them Nishi Masahiko's analytical studies (*Rafukadio Haan no mimi*, Iwanami, 1993) and the monthly *Eureka*'s special number on Hearn (April, 1995) are remarkable achievements.

For this book in English most of the contributions I have selected were originally presented in English. Some of them, like those of Professor George Hughes, Masaru Toda, Yuzo Ota and mine, have been amplified since then; other papers are practically as presented at that conference. Professor Rosen's paper was submitted to another Hearn symposium held at Kumamoto some years later; Mr Paul Murray, author of *A Fantastic Journey: The Life and Literature of Lafcadio Hearn*

(Japan Library, 1993) has written a new article for our volume. As I had been requested to write an Introduction, 'Lafcadio Hearn: Towards an Irish Interpretation', to Mr Murray's book, I was cordially asked, this time again, by its publisher, Mr Paul Norbury of Japan Library and Global Oriental, to edit this book *Rediscovering Lafcadio Hearn*, which, I hope, will communicate to a wider Western audience the results of recent Japanese scholarship on Hearn. I am very grateful to all the contributors for their helpful collaboration and to all the Izumo people who were kind to Hearn, to his family and also to us Hearn readers and scholars.

SUKEHIRO HIRAKAWA
Professor Emeritus, Tokyo University

1

REDISCOVERING LAFCADIO HEARN

Sukehiro Hirakawa

PART I: HEARN VERSUS CHAMBERLAIN

HEARN'S REPUTATION AS A JAPAN INTERPRETER

Among the Western writers and scholars who have come to Japan since the middle of the nineteenth century, none has been better loved by the Japanese than Lafcadio Hearn (1850–1904), who is popular among us and known as Koizumi Yakumo – a name which he adopted when he was naturalized as a Japanese citizen in 1896. While Hearn's reputation as a Japan interpreter was spread far and wide in the first two decades of the twentieth century, his name was later eclipsed by such eminent scholars as Basil Hall Chamberlain, Ruth Benedict, E. H. Norman and Edwin Reischauer. It is true that there has also been a fluctuation of Hearn's reputation in Japan. However, Hearn has always been regarded as preeminent among foreign observers of Japan by the Japanese themselves. Is this because Hearn stood up for the traditional beliefs and practices of the Japanese and described them so lyrically, especially at a time when so much that was native was being swept away by Western influences? Is the most obvious reason for Hearn's appeal to the Japanese, then as today, Hearn's contribution as an apologist for much that

1

was so distinctly Japanese? Is his reputation, therefore, due solely to the ineradicable narcissism of the Japanese?

If so, why is there recently a revival of interest in Lafcadio Hearn the writer not only within Japan but also in the West? We see books such as Robert Rosenstone's *Mirror in the Shrine* (Harvard, 1988), Jonathan Cott's *Wandering Ghost* (Knopf, 1991), Louis Allen's new anthology: *Lafcadio Hearn, Japan's Great Interpreter* (Japan Library, 1991), Carl Dawson's *Lafcadio Hearn and the Vision of Japan* (Johns Hopkins University Press, 1992) and Paul Murray's *A Fantastic Journey: the life and literature of Lafcadio Hearn* (Japan Library, 1993) appearing successively on the Asian bookshelf. To our satisfaction, Hearn's newly translated books are selling well in Japan – I myself have translated Hearn's *Kwaidan* and other ghostly stories into Japanese – and Hearn seems to eclipse again other eminent Japan interpreters of the mid-twentieth century, whose opinions were once so highly appreciated by both Westerners and Japanese alike in the years following Japan's defeat in 1945. What has happened to Lafcadio Hearn or more exactly what has happened to Hearn studies to make this change in appreciation possible?

Professor George Hughes, who is currently teaching at the English Department of Tokyo University, where Hearn himself taught for seven years a century ago, recently writes about this unexpected change in his review article on Murray's book:

> There was a time when Lafcadio Hearn scholarship seemed to be taking place on a branch line leading in the opposite direction from the main line of literary and cultural studies. Hearn scholars agonized over minor points of biographical and bibliographical detail, but their concerns bore almost no relation to topics of general interest. The writings of Hearn, and the writings *on* Hearn, came to seem to most people examples of wrong-headed, self-indulgent, faded exoticism.
>
> In the past ten years, however, all that has changed. Critical interest has shifted dramatically in its focus; the branch line of Hearn studies now looks much nearer the centre than anyone had thought, and is suddenly busy with traffic. Newspapers now carry stories about Hearn discoveries – or at least newspapers in Japan do.[1]

Let me explain this remarkable shift in interest from racial, social, literary, religious and biographical points of view, by taking up three examples of his retold stories. How has Lafcadio Hearn been rediscovered in Japan? And the main topic of my article is how to look at this remarkable change in an international perspective, or more precisely, how to redefine the meanings of Hearn's interpretations of Japan in today's intercultural context.

WHO WAS THE GREATER JAPAN INTERPRETER,
CHAMBERLAIN OR HEARN?

In order to rehabilitate Lafcadio Hearn, who was for a time almost forgotten in the West, the first question I would like to raise is who was the greatest Western interpreter of Japan in pre-World War II years. Two prominent names inevitably cross our minds: one of them is the British Japan scholar, Basil Hall Chamberlain (1850–1935), and the other is the American writer of Irish-Greek origin, Lafcadio Hearn (1850–1904) who went from New York to Vancouver via Montreal by the then recently completed Canadian Pacific Railway and from Vancouver to Yokohama on board the Canadian Pacific steamer, *Abyssinia*, in the twenty-third year of the reign of the Meiji Emperor, that is, in 1890.

I am going to make a comparison of these two great Japan interpreters because I find the contrast of the two personalities very interesting: Chamberlain is considered by many scholars as a very orthodox Japanologist, while Hearn is not; and the respective reputations of Chamberlain and Hearn differ considerably in Japan and the West. Until the early 1930s, Hearn's works were very popular in the West, while he was little known among the Japanese, as there were no Japanese translations of his writings available at that time. Japanese travellers abroad were often accosted by those who had read and loved Hearn's writings. It was because of this Western appreciation of Hearn, that the scholar Ichikawa Sanki, who had succeeded Hearn at the department of English Literature at Tokyo University, began somewhat belatedly to collect materials concerning Hearn for its library. In the West, however, views changed dramatically. According to the American scholar Arthur Kunst:

The great Pacific War with Japan in the 1940s seemed for a time to have obliterated Hearn from the American consciousness, a kind of guilt over a youthful infatuation. The misleading notion of Hearn as a spokesman for Japan left him without literary defences when Japan and things Japanese became enemy.[2]

Since then, Hearn's reputation has not recovered in North America, where after the war a whole new generation of competent interpreters of Japan replaced him. Hearn finally became an example not to be imitated by serious students of Japan. The present-day American Japanologists are proud of their academic achievements. They are conscious of being successors to the great British Japanologists of pre-war days. They hold, therefore, in high regard the opinions voiced by Basil Hall Chamberlain, the British dean of Western scholars of Japan. For example, the first of the well-known five-volume series on Japan's modernization, published by Princeton University Press, opens with a quotation from Chamberlain's *Things Japanese*: 'To have lived through the transition stage of modern Japan makes a man feel preternaturally old; for here he is in modern times. . . and yet he can himself distinctly remember the Middle Ages.' Although experiences of the same kind were shared by Hearn, the American academic did not see fit to quote Hearn's observations. Why? I do not think it was simply because Hearn had romanticized old Japan. I rather think because it was the authoritative Chamberlain who discredited Lafcadio Hearn by publishing a debunking article on him in the last edition of *Things Japanese*.

HEARN ACCORDING TO CHAMBERLAIN

Chamberlain's article, published posthumously in the 1939 edition of *Things Japanese*, contains this passage:

During the first few years (of Hearn's stay in Japan) his enthusiasm was at fever pitch; he had found the Land of the Gods, and his *Glimpses of the Unfamiliar Japan* glorified the Japan which he imagined he saw.

Pity only that Lafcadio lacked the sense of reality, or rather he saw details very distinctly while incapable of understanding them as a whole. Not only was this the case mentally but also physically. Blind of one eye he was extremely short-sighted of the other. . . He had never properly seen either the horizon or the stars. His life was a succession of dreams which ended in nightmares. In his ardour he became a naturalized Japanese, taking the name of Koizumi Yakumo. But awaking from his dream he realized that he had taken a false step. The Japan he cared for could not be the Europeanized, vulgarized Japan of today, but rather some ancient Japan, pure of Occidental defilement, a Japan so perfect that, in fact, it could never have existed except in his own fancy. The Japanese Government was equally disappointed; for it had engaged him convinced that he would bring European public opinion to favour all the modern changes which, on the contrary, he never ceased to curse. Matters stood thus when he died suddenly (in 1904).[3]

Chamberlain and Hearn were both born in 1850. Chamberlain came to Japan as early as 1873. Born of an upper-class English family, given a very good education, linguistically gifted, Chamberlain quickly distinguished himself as a Japan scholar. He translated into English the *Kojiki* or *Records of Ancient Matters* in 1882. The translation was published as a supplement to volume 10 of the *Transactions* of the Asiatic Society of Japan, of which Chamberlain was the leading figure for many decades.

Lafcadio Hearn came to Japan in 1890 at the age of thirty-nine, seventeen years later than Chamberlain. Hearn's early years are described by Chamberlain in the above-mentioned article as follows:

> Lafcadio Hearn (1850–1904) was born at Leucadia, one of the Ionian Islands. His father was an Irish doctor, his mother a Greek; but the couple soon separated, abandoning their children. Lafcadio's education was undertaken by a great-aunt, a strict Roman Catholic, with whom he quarrelled while yet a lad. He found his way first to London, then to the United States, where being penniless and timid he suffered many hardships. . . At length he found employment in the newspaper office (in Cincinnati). . . where he might have settled down in tolerable comfort.

However, according to Chamberlain, the romantic Hearn soon grew tired of Cincinnati and moved to New Orleans, to the French West Indies, and finally to Japan 'as always, with an empty purse'. Hearn's knowledge of the Japanese language was of course much inferior to Chamberlain's masterful knowledge. When Chamberlain's article on Lafcadio Hearn was published in the last edition of his *Things Japanese* in 1939, Hearn's credibility as a Japan interpreter was fatally impaired. Hearn, in short, was branded as a romantic nomad. This negative evaluation on Hearn by the authoritative Chamberlain immediately found acceptance in the English-speaking world. It was the time when the reputation of Japan was at its lowest in Anglo-Saxon countries. For the general reading public, a militaristic Japan could not be the wonderful country depicted in so many of Hearn's writings. So, it was quite natural for the Americans and the British to accept Chamberlain's depreciation of Hearn. Moreover, Chamberlain, according to Sir George Sansom[4] was known for his constant search for truth, and his knowledge of things Japanese seemed incomparable. What was more, Chamberlain knew Lafcadio Hearn personally quite well. It is natural for readers to believe what Chamberlain said about Hearn's romanticizing of old Japan: '. . . Japan so perfect that it could never have existed except in Hearn's own fancy'. Appearing in 1939, Chamberlain's posthumous article on Hearn was like a delayed-action bomb. For the war-time British, it was almost self-evident that a Britisher who had gone native and who had become a naturalized Japanese should end his life in nightmares.

Throughout the war years, so far as I know, there was only one widely read history of English Literature which reveals a high regard for Lafcadio Hearn. This exceptional book had, in fact, been written neither by an Englishman nor by an American, but by the French Anglicists Émile Legouis and Louis Cazamian. Cazamian writes as follows in their *l'Histoire de la Littérature Anglaise*:

> Au moment même où le Japon va se transformer, Lafcadio Hearn découvre avec passion l'âme héroïque, la chevalerie exquise dissimulée dans la tradition de sa courtoisie souriante. Lui-même a rapporté de l'Occident le dernier mot de l'intellectualisme scientifique, la philosophie de Spencer; il croit rester fidèle à l'évolution souveraine, alors que son être

est séduit, conquis par le charme d'une terre et d'une race aux horizons inchangés. Artiste et psychologue, écrivain délicat, il boit à longs traits ce philtre qui apaise la soif inconsciente de son être profond. Ses livres sont une révélation; et le monde anglo-saxon, enorgueilli des principes de vie qui ont fait jusqulà sa force, y apprend à respecter une morale, une religion, un art entièrement indépendants.

This highly favourable appreciation of Hearn was unique and the article made a sharp contrast with other histories of English Literature. Among others the *Cambridge History of English Literature*, published during World War II went so far as to qualify Hearn's lectures on English literature at Tokyo Imperial University as 'completely valueless', while the same lectures by Hearn had been extolled by the British critic Edmund Gosse[5] in the 1920s; the poet Edmund Blunden who himself taught at Tokyo University before and after WWII was shocked by the unfair treatment of Hearn by the narrow-minded writer of the *Cambridge History of English Literature*, which was fortunately slightly amended in its later editions. It is clear that the reputation of a writer, of a scholar, or of a Japan specialist fluctuates with the passage of time. In Japan, too, Chamberlain's negative evaluation of Hearn was accepted literally after Japan's defeat. Many of Hearn's books reprinted in Japan and elsewhere have even today on their book covers such phrases as 'Hearn's last years were filled with the bitterness of disillusionment', a phrase derived from Chamberlain's statement.

CHAMBERLAIN'S PREVIOUS APPRECIATIONS OF HEARN

We may, however, ask here if Chamberlain's article on Hearn is exact or not. Was Chamberlain really fair when he depicted Hearn in that manner, denigrating his one-time friend? First, let us have a look at what Chamberlain himself had said when he and Hearn were on good terms. The previous editions of *Things Japanese* contained no article entitled 'Lafcadio Hearn'. Still, Hearn's name appears quite often in Chamberlain's book. For example, in the fifth edition, published in 1905, Hearn's name appeared among others in the article 'Books on Japan'. The first book recommended in that article is *The Mikado's*

Empire by the Rev. W.E.Griffis. Lafcadio Hearn's name comes second. The following is a quote from that edition – note the warmth with which he is described:

> Lafcadio Hearn's *Glimpses of Unfamiliar Japan*, together with the succeeding volumes entitled *Out of the East* and *Kokoro*. Never perhaps was scientific accuracy of detail married to such tender and exquisite brilliancy of style. In reading these profoundly original essays, we feel the truth of Richard Wagner's saying, that 'Alles Verständniss kommt uns nur durch die Liebe.' Lafcadio Hearn understands contemporary Japan better, and makes *us* understand it better, than any other writer, because he loves it better.

Every year from 1894 onwards Hearn published a book on Japan. During his fourteen years in Japan, Hearn wrote more than thirteen books on Japan. It was an amazing feat, and Chamberlain himself admired this author ungrudgingly. *Glimpses* was dedicated in token of affection and gratitude 'To the Friends, Paymaster Mitchell McDonald, U.S.N. and Basil Hall Chamberlain, Esq., Emeritus Professor of Philology and Japanese in the Imperial University of Tokyo', the title Chamberlain was so proud of for the rest of his life. For him who had not been accepted at Oxford and who had missed a university education, it was a sort of vindication. McDonald was the man who practically edited *The Writings of Lafcadio Hearn* in sixteen volumes published by Houghton Mifflin Company in 1922, eighteen years after his friend's death. In the early 1890s, Chamberlain and Hearn were very good friends. In a letter to Hearn dated 19 January 1893, Chamberlain wrote to Hearn, felicitating himself on having such a good friend. He used a French expression: 'Les beaux esprits se recontrent'. Both of them were among the chosen few who could understand Japan and the Japanese.

When we study what Chamberlain had said before, it is clear that it was Chamberlain who changed his opinion on Lafcadio Hearn. In the 1939 edition of *Things Japanese*, Chamberlain had deleted many of his former laudatory phrases. When, and why, did that reversal of opinion take place? It is true that even before Hearn's death in 1904 they had become a little estranged, but their relationship was not that bad. After his death, Hearn's Japanese wife and son visited Chamberlain quite often. Moreover, in December 1910 Chamberlain, just before leaving Japan forever for Europe, wrote a heart-warming recollection of his friend, entitled 'Lafcadio Hearn', the existence of which was known for a long time only through its Japanese translation published in the November 1911 issue of the monthly *Kokoro no hana*. The English manuscript was recently found and was reproduced in the 1990 issue of *Hearn*. Let us read the complete text of Chamberlain's 'Lafcadio Hearn':

> The memory of Lafcadio Hearn remains with me as a dream – a dream all too short, as happy dreams are wont to be. His exterior was not specially prepossessing. His figure was squat with latterly a tendency to obesity, while a blind, salient eye quite spoilt one side of his face. But a few moments' intercourse made one forget these outward disadvantages. His gentle, yet eager, almost pleading manner went straight to the heart, disarming criticism. His talk never descended to trivialities; philosophy and literature, poetry above all, were his favourite themes. He lacked no great quality except humour, which seems unaccountable in one of Irish descent. But then his childhood had been sad, his youth and early manhood a sore struggle, single-handed, against hunger and neglect. The iron had eaten into his soul, and he *could* not be gay. His published works and his now celebrated letters display the same characteristics; but in my opinion his books are superior to his talk, and his letters superior to his books. He will live on in these charming unstudied compositions, and be remembered and reprinted as one of the best letter-writers in the English language, along with Horace Walpole, Edward Fitzgerald, and Mrs Carlyle. As a stylist, he is indeed superior to all of these. His style expresses his whole manner of thinking, which was at once poetical and scientifically exact. He always has matter for a treatise, his numerous facts have been carefully observed at first hand, he loves to accumulate details. But the working out is that of the perfect artist of the musician in words. What he managed to see, despite one worthless eye and another eye good for little, is surprising. He used to walk round a room with his face almost touching the wall, so as to know and be able to tell to others all that was in it. In composition, he was as conscientious as in private life. Allied to the sadness already mentioned, were a certain

shyness and an aptness to take offence. In his latter years he broke with almost all his old friends, some word, some look, some airy nothing having hurt his over-sensitive feelings. Also it would seem that he had a presentiment of his early and sudden end. He had much work to do, and little time left in which to do it. So he remained alone, preferring to give to a few personal friends the impression of coldness or ingratitude, in order the better to serve the large and enduring public. To this circumstance we doubtless owe his last two works.

Hearn's was a lovable personality, and to literature he gave the very best that was in him. He did harm to none, his books have given pleasure to thousands, and have helped to raise the name of Japan high among the nations. Those who had the privilege of knowing him do more than honour his memory: they love it.

                                        Basil Hall Chamberlain.
                                        December, 1910.

Although Chamberlain was a man of two faces – one for the Westerners and the other for the Japanese – I still believe that Chamberlain's warm feelings towards his deceased friend, which are expressed in this article written for his Japanese readers, are genuine and true. From these writings I deduce that something must have happened later, after Chamberlain's return to Europe in 1911; something that changed radically Chamberlain's opinion concerning Lafcadio Hearn.

HERR HOUSTON STEWART CHAMBERLAIN

We know that an unhappy incident shattered the aging Chamberlain immediately after the outbreak of World War I, in the summer of 1914. On his return to Europe, Chamberlain chose to retreat to Geneva, Switzerland, where he seemed to spend quietly the rest of his life. However, three years after his retirement, the tranquillity of his mind was broken by the unexpected behaviour of his younger brother, Houston Stewart Chamberlain. Houston, who had married Eva, the daughter of Richard Wagner, was then living in Bayreuth. After the outbreak of the war, he became a naturalized German citizen and was extremely vocal in his anti-British propaganda – he became more German than ordinary Germans. Basil Hall Chamberlain was extremely annoyed by

his all too notorious renegade brother, who was known as
'Herr Chamberlain' in the British press. The elder brother's
complaints were reiterated in almost every letter sent to his
former secretary Sugiura Tōshirō. These letters, which always
began with the phrase 'My Dear Boy', are all kept in Aichi
Kyōiku University. In a letter dated 22 January 1915,
Chamberlain writes:

> And to add to the public horrors, there is this scandal about
> brother Houston. What have we done as a family, I wonder,
> to merit such disgrace? Our father and his brothers – five
> valiant men, if ever such existed – all served their country with
> might and main, while now. . .

From this kind of letter we may be allowed to make the
following conjecture. Shaken by his bitter experience with his
brother, Basil Hall Chamberlain began to detest any Britisher
who renounced their British nationality to become a
naturalized citizen of an enemy country. I suppose that the
aged Chamberlain could well have developed an animosity
towards Lafcadio Hearn, who had deserted Great Britain,
when Japan in the 1930s began to be more and more
aggressive towards the British Empire, the land of Chamberlain's many glorious ancestors: his father was a vice admiral;
among his uncles one was a marshal, another was an admiral;
his maternal grandfather, Basil Hall, was a captain of the British
navy who went as far as Korea at the beginning of the
nineteenth century.

Moreover, the aging Chamberlain must have been jealous
of his deceased friend. While Chamberlain was living in
Switzerland in the 1920s, Hearn's reputation was rapidly
increasing in francophone Geneva. As a Japan interpreter,
Chamberlain's name was completely eclipsed by the fame of
Hearn, whose books were successively translated into French.
The favourable appreciation of Hearn was written by Louis
Cazamian in the above-mentioned *Histoire de la Littérature
Anglaise* published by Hachette in 1924. But for Chamberlain,
it was not just a simple personal matter. As a Japan scholar, he
must have been afraid that Hearn's writings would give
misleading impressions, that is, too-favourable images of Japan
to Western readers. Anyway, the octogenarian Chamberlain

added acrimonious remarks on Hearn, first, in the French
translation of *Things Japanese* (*Moeurs et Coutumes du Japon*,
1931) and then, in a more detailed article, for his sixth and last
edition of *Things Japanese* (1939). In this way, Chamberlain
succeeded in discrediting Hearn's reliability as a Japan
interpreter. I am afraid, however, that, in the long run,
Chamberlain's defamatory article on Hearn has had a
boomerang effect on Chamberlain himself. It is true that
some British Japanologists, such as Richard Bowring (see his
recent article[6]), reappraised Chamberlain's overall status in the
pantheon of Western writers on Japan. Surely it is possible to
admire Chamberlain and Hearn for different reasons.
However, they will not be amused if they know the true
nature of Chamberlain's article on Hearn.

HEARN, A PROPAGANDA AGENT?

Let us first examine what Chamberlain writes about Hearn.
First point: did the Japanese government engage Hearn as a
propaganda agent? If so, why should the government send him
to such a far away provincial city as Matsue, where there were
very few changes in the 1890s? Did Hearn become a
naturalized Japanese in his romantic ardour? In August 1891,
when asked by Hearn about the possibility of marriage with a
Japanese girl, Chamberlain frankly advised him not to marry a
Japanese woman legally. Instead, he urged Hearn to just live
with a Japanese girl, as was common practice for foreigners of
the day. We know from a picture taken by Percival Lowell
that Chamberlain himself had his Japanese 'girl' and we know
that Chamberlain had very good taste in women. However,
Hearn, who had detested his British father because of his
maltreatment of Lafcadio's Greek mother, did not want to
repeat a misconduct of the same nature towards an Oriental
woman, especially when she became the mother of his son.
Hearn, therefore, married Koizumi Setsuko legally. I think this
point is the greatest difference between writers of Japonisme,
such as Pierre Loti and Hearn.

I should add one more explanation for Hearn's assuming
the Japanese name of Koizumi Yakumo. At that time – the
time of the unequal treaties – to become a naturalized Japanese

was the only means by which a Westerner could leave his inheritance to his Japanese family without any legal troubles with his Western relatives. Hearn, who always thought, rightly or wrongly, that he had been robbed of an immense inheritance from his great-aunt, Sarah Brenane, by relatives, was extremely careful about the matter of inheritance. It was mainly Hearn's financial consideration for his Japanese wife and children that led him to take Japanese citizenship in 1896. At that time Hearn was perfectly conscious that he would not be treated as a genuine Japanese because of his Caucasian face and especially because of his limited ability in the Japanese language.

★ ★ ★

PART II: *OSHIDORI*, EMBLEM OF CONJUGAL AFFECTION

DID HEARN'S LIFE END IN NIGHTMARES?

Let us continue our examination. The second point is: did Hearn's life 'end in nightmares', as Chamberlain had written? It is interesting to note that even though Hearn's last years were far from nightmares and that fact was attested by many recollections – among them Setsuko's *Reminiscences*, which were translated into English by Yone Noguchi in his book *Lafcadio Hearn in Japan* as early as 1910 – some Westerners still prefer to believe in the aged Chamberlain's acrimonious comment.

To those who believe in the superiority of their own civilization, no example fits better than the story that a Westerner who took Japanese citizenship ended his life miserably in Tokyo. It has become a custom for Western biographers of Hearn to talk of his disillusionment with Japan towards the end of their books. It is unfortunate that none among them is capable of reading letters written in Japanese by Lafcadio and Setsuko towards the end of his life. Almost a century later, in December 1994, their collected letters, written in the so-called Herun-san Japanese, were published for the first time in *Reikon no tankyūsha Koizumi Yakumo*, a small but touching book edited by Muramatsu Shinichi.[7] Hearn spent summer vacations together with his children in a village called Yaizu, near Shizuoka. Lafcadio's and Setsuko's letters written and received there in their last years are as idyllic as a fairy tale. They are untranslatable; you had better read them as they are in their unforgettable pidgin Japanese.

Apart from such external evidence, let us also examine some internal evidence. In order to prove how Lafcadio and Setsuko worked closely towards the end of his writing career, let us analyze how the short ghost story called '*Oshidori*' came into existence. As is little known abroad, practically all of Hearn's retold stories were works accomplished through the collaboration of Lafcadio and Setsuko. Setsuko read aloud Japanese stories for her husband, explaining in Japanese difficult passages that were beyond his understanding. Lafcadio wrote down in English what he heard from her in Japanese, adding many artistic modifications. He was extremely careful about the change of tone in Setsuko's voice. Lafcadio could seize the nuance of feeling thanks to that method.

Among Hearn's thirteen books on Japan, the book most read by the Japanese is *Kwaidan*, published in 1904, the year of Hearn's death; and among the seventeen stories gathered in the volume, 'Oshidori' is one of the three most popular ghostly tales, the other two being 'The Story of Miminashi-Hōichi' and 'Yuki-Onna'. One of the reasons why 'Oshidori' is well known among the Japanese derives from the simple fact that it is quite often chosen in Japanese English textbooks for high school students. As the story is very short, I quote it here before making some comparisons with its Japanese original:

Oshidori

There was a falconer and hunter, named Sonjō, who lived in the district called Tamura-no-Gō, of the province of Mutsu. One day he went out hunting, and could not find any game. But on his way home, at a place called Akanuma, he perceived a pair of *oshidori* (mandarin-ducks), swimming together in a river that he was about to cross. To kill *oshidori* is not good; but Sonjō happened to be very hungry, and he shot at the pair. His arrow pierced the male: the female escaped into the rushes of the farther shore, and disappeared. Sonjō took the dead bird home and cooked it. That night he dreamed a dreary dream. It seemed to him that a beautiful woman came into his room and stood by his pillow, and began to weep. So bitterly did she weep that Sonjō felt as if his heart were being torn out while he listened. And the woman cried to him: 'Why – oh! why did you kill him? – of what wrong was he guilty?. . . At Akanuma we were so happy together – and you killed him!. . . What harm did he ever do you? Do you even know what you have done? – oh! do you know what a cruel, what a wicked thing you have done?. . . Me too you have killed – for I will not live without my husband!. . . Only to tell you this I came.'. . . Then again she wept aloud – so bitterly that the voice of her crying pierced into the marrow of the listener's bones; – and she sobbed out the words of this poem:

Hi kururéba
Sasoëshi mono wo –
Akanuma no
Makomo no kuré no
Hitori-né zo uki!

[At the coming of twilight I invited him to return with me –! Now to sleep alone in the shadow of the rushes of Akanuma – ah! what misery unspeakable!]

And after having uttered these verses she exclaimed: 'Ah, you do not know – you cannot know what you have done! But tomorrow, when you go to Akanuma, you will see – you will see. . . ' So saying, and weeping very piteously, she went away.

When Sonjō awoke in the morning, this dream remained so vivid in his mind that he was greatly troubled. He remembered the words: 'But tomorrow, when you go to Akanuma, you will see – you will see.' And he resolved to go there at once, that he might learn whether his dream was anything more than a dream.

So he went to Akanuma; and there, when he came to the river-bank, he saw the female *oshidori* swimming alone. In the same moment the bird perceived Sonjō; but, instead of trying to escape she swam straight towards him, looking at him the while in a strange fixed way. Then, with her beak, she suddenly tore open her own body, and died before the hunter's eyes. . .

Sonjō shaved his head, and became a priest.

The original story[8] is found in *Kokonchomonjū*, compiled by Tachibana no Narisue in 1254. Hearn – or more precisely, his Japanese wife Koizumi Setsuko – used a Tokugawa edition of the book published in the seventh year of Meiwa (1770) by Kashiwaya Seiyemon, an Osaka publisher. The first line of the Japanese text reads: 'Michi no kuni Tamura-no-gō no jūnin Uma-no-jō nanigashitokaya yū onoko. . . ' The correct name of the falconer and hunter is Uma-no-jō, but since the Japanese text Hearn's poorly educated wife used was a woodblock edition printed in a running style, it was difficult for her to read it. She mistook the Chinese character Uma for Son; but fortunately, the two-syllable name Sonjō sounds better than the four syllable Uma-no-jō. I do not want, however, to dwell on minor matters of this kind, since there are many more interesting intentional modifications by Lafcadio Hearn.

Both the original Japanese story and Hearn's English adaption have the same cause of tragedy: the falconer had killed the male of a pair of *oshidori*, or mandarin ducks, and that night, a beautiful woman, appearing in the falconer's dream, complained of the death of her beloved and after sadly reciting an *uta*-poem, disappeared. Afterwards, to his great surprise, the falconer found that the female of the pair had committed suicide. Impressed by the bird's singular act, the hunter shaved his head and became a priest. This is the gist of the original story as well as of the English adaptation by Hearn.

Let me now explain Hearn's modifications. The original Japanese story is much shorter than Hearn's English version; it is generally the case with Hearn's retold stories that they are longer and more amplified than the original stories. In the case of 'Oshidori', too, we can discern two types of modification: one concerns the structure of the story, and the other concerns the character of the heroine. Both the original and adapted stories are composed of three time segments. One evening, the falconer on his way home killed an *oshidori*; this first part is a factual exposition, and there is not much difference between the *Kokonchomonjū* story and Hearn's. The second part takes place the same night: the falconer sees a beautiful woman in a dream. Until this point, Hearn follows exactly the original pattern. But in the third part, both the place and the time differ considerably from the original story. The hunter Uma-no-jō of *Kokonchomonjū* found the dead *oshidori* duck together with the dead body of the drake in his gamebag two days later ('naka ichinichi arite nochi, egara o mikereba e-bukuro no oshi no metori no hara o onoga hashi nite tsuki-tsuranukite shinite arikeri'). The female bird had committed suicide by disembowelling her own body in the hunter's bag in which her husband's dead body had been put. This manner of voluntary death must have reminded Hearn of *harakiri*, the Japanese samurai manner of committing suicide.

Hearn dramatizes this final part in the following way. First, he sets the scene at the same Akanuma river where the hunter Sonjō had killed the male. Troubled by the dream, Sonjō went to Akanuma at once when he awoke the next morning. It is more direct than the two days later of the original story. Moreover, the scene of the suicide takes place right before Sonjō's eyes; the impression the hunter, and consequently we readers, get is incomparably stronger. The dramatic final scene is shocking. This sense of immediacy is the most conspicuous change invented by Hearn, and there are many who are of the opinion that Hearn's finale is much better than the ending of the *Kokonchomonjū* story.

The next question concerns the transformation of the heroine's character. The Japanese woman of the medieval story is modest and charming. Asked by the hunter Uma-no-jō why she was weeping so sadly, the small beautiful woman answered: 'Kinō Akanuma nite, saseru ayamari mo haberanuni toshigoro no otoko o koroshi tamaeru kanashibi ni taezushite, mairite uree mōsunari. Kono omoi ni yorite wagami mo nagarae haberumajiki nari.' The woman uses the polite form of expression even to her husband's killer. She complains of the death of the man with whom she had spent many years (toshigoro no otoko). She complains sadly, but she does not accuse the hunter Uma-no-jō of having killed her husband, and she only says: 'Because of this I don't think I'll live any longer.'

While the woman of *Kokonchomonjū* remains passive in her complaints, the heroine of Hearn's story is active, and she accuses the hunter with a passionate cry. In her accusation, the

word 'kill' is used three times, and the exclamatory words
'what' and 'why' are used seven times. The cry of Hearn's
woman is not only more intense but also much longer than
the complaint of the original story, which I have quoted in
full. The difference is that while the medieval Japanese woman
of *Kokonchomonjū* does not cite the injustice of the hunter's
deeds, the heroine of Hearn's story is angry and resentful. Not
only her words but also her attitude have considerably
changed. The woman of the original story wept sadly
(samezame to naki itari), but her voice becomes more
piercing and more shrill in Hearn's version. The verbs Hearn
uses for his heroine are various, from weak 'weep' and 'sob' to
strong 'utter' and 'exclaim'. The adverbs also indicate her
passionate attitude: 'bitterly' is used twice, and there are also
other adverbs, such as 'aloud' and 'piteously'. There is,
moreover, a sort of confrontation between the suffering victim
and the hunter; she protests: 'Me too you have killed.'

The character of the woman thus depicted by Lafcadio
Hearn is considerably different from the original Japanese
woman. In *Kokonchomonjū*, the small pretty woman was so
modest in her complaints that the hunter took pity on her,
while in Hearn's story the woman was so vocal and aggressive
that the hunter Sonjō was disturbed, and this distress
remained when he awoke the next morning. This is
precisely the reason why Sonjō went at once to Akanuma.
In order to end the story there with that dramatic final scene
reminiscent of *harakiri*, the accusation of the woman in the
hunter's dream had to be a passionate and ominous one, and
from the point of view of artistic composition, it is
understandable why Hearn modified the character of the
heroine. This modification, too, is considered by many critics
to be an improvement. Japanese students of Western literature
generally approve of Hearn's changes. In a sense, Hearn
humanizes the heroine, because she freely and heartily vents
her spite on the hunter. In the *Kokonchomonjū* story, which
was a Buddhist fable, the hunter was moved by *mono no aware*,
pity for all living things, and became a priest, while in Hearn's
story, we get the impression that the hunter became a priest
not because he had been moved by religious piety but
because he had been scared. The female bird's suicide in

Hearn's story is considered to be her vengeance. The original Buddhist fable is in this way transformed into a weird tale, or a *Kwaidan*.

There are, however, some Japanese criticisms against Hearn's heroine. Japanese students of Japanese literature do not always approve of Hearn's modifications: she has become Western in her attitude. She has a stronger ego than the original feminine figure. Hearn translates the *uta*-poem in the following way: 'At the coming of twilight *I* invited *him* to return with me –!' In the context of the retold English story, this interpretation may be natural, since Hearn's heroine has a strong character and acts on her own initiative. But is it really natural for a Japanese woman of the Buddhist fable to invite her man to sleep with her? Is not the correct subject of the *uta*-poem, 'Hi kururéba sasoëshi mono wo', not the male of the pair? In Hearn's story, the heroine uses 'I' too many times. Is this self-assertive attitude of hers not too egocentric? Hearn's heroine is less sympathetic and less likeable than the original Japanese woman. The revenge suicide in front of the hunter Sonjō is indeed very different from the original story. Such are the critical comments made by some of the Japanese students of Hearn.

'THE WONDERFUL "TROIS CONTES"'

Lafcadio Hearn is said to have idealized Japanese womanhood in many of his stories and essays. Why, then, is Hearn's heroine in 'Oshidori' so Westernized? Is this modification not contrary to Hearn's general attitude? Is it true that the literary artist Hearn wished to dramatize the final scene of 'Oshidori' and that need for dramatization made the heroine more aggressive and more resentful than the original female character? But are there any other causes and motives? After having checked the modifications and the inventions by Hearn within the text of the story, let us ponder some other possibilities.

In some previous stories retold from Oriental literatures, Hearn has already added elements taken from Occidental authors. For example, in 'The Story of Ming-Y' in *Some Chinese Ghosts* (1887), Hearn mixes the Eastern Paradise of

Peach Blossom Spring with the Western ideal world depicted
by Edgar Allan Poe in some of his tales of natural beauty. So
while reading 'Oshidori', I began to wonder if it might have
some other sources besides the Japanese *Kokonchomonjū*. My
tentative conjecture is as follows: As is well known, Hearn
was throughout his life a great admirer of French literature.
In the United States, where he lived from 1869 to 1890,
Hearn was known as the best English translator of Flaubert,
Gautier and Maupassant. Hearn was a self-educated man in
matters of literature; if he had any master, it was Gustave
Flaubert. In America, Hearn had read Flaubert and translated
his *La Tentation de St Antoine*. He brought only a limited
number of books from the United States to Japan in 1890,
since he had no idea that he would remain there for more
than fourteen years. One of the very few French books he
brought with him was Flaubert's *Trois Contes*. In a letter
Hearn sent from Kumamoto to Basil Hall Chamberlain dated
14 July 1893, Hearn mentioned the book as 'the wonderful
Trois Contes'. In the Toyama University Library where
Hearn's books are preserved, there is a copy of the *Trois
Contes* formerly owned by Hearn (edition Charpentier,
published 1877). A book so fondly read by Hearn might have
influenced him when he retold the *Kokonchomonjū* story.
There are remarkable parallels between 'Oshidori' and the
following passage from 'Saint Julien l'Hospitalier', the second
story in Flaubert's book:

> Le cerf, qui était noir et monstrueux de taille, portait seize
> andouillers avec une barbe blanche. La biche, blonde comme
> les feuilles mortes, broutait le gazon; et le faon tacheté, sans
> l'interrompre dans sa marche, lui tétait la mamelle.
>
> L'arbalète encore une fois ronfla. Le faon, tout de suite, fut
> tué. Alors sa mère, en regardant le ciel, brama d'une voix
> profonde, déchirante, humaine. Julien exaspéré, d'un coup en
> plein portail, l'étendit par terre.
>
> Le grand cerf l'avait vu, fit un bond. Julien lui envoya sa
> dernière flèche. Elle l'atteignit au front, et y resta plantée.
>
> Le grand cerf n'eut pas l'air de la sentir; en enjambant par-
> dessus les morts, il avançait toujours, allait fondre sur lui,
> l'éventrer; et Julien reculait dans une épouvante indicible. Le
> prodigieux animal s'arrêta; et les yeux flamboyants, solennel

comme un patriarche et comme un justicier, pendant qu'une
cloche au loin tintait, il répéta trois fois.
'Maudit! maudit! maudit! Un jour, coeur féroce, tu
assassineras ton père et ta mère!'
Il plia les genoux, ferma doucement ses paupières, et
mourut.

There was a happy family of deer. But their domestic
happiness was suddenly destroyed when the hunter Julien
killed the child and the mother. Let us make a comparison.
In Hearn's 'Oshidori', a newly added element is that the
female bird, instead of trying to escape, swam straight towards
the hunter, looking at him in a strange fixed way. It is the
same with Flaubert's great deer; he came straight towards the
hunter Julien, looking at him in a strange fixed way. 'Il
avançait toujours' with his burning eyes (les yeux flamboy-
ants). The female of 'Oshidori' cried out with a human voice;
it is the same with the female of the *Trois Contes*: She looked
up at the sky and cried out with a deep voice: 'Alors sa mère,
en regardant le ciel, brama d'une voix profonde, déchirante,
humaine.' The male of the *Trois Contes* repeats three times:
'Maudit! maudit! maudit!' This repeated curse of his may find
its parallel in the female *oshidori*'s repeated words: 'You will
see, – you will see. . . ' The deer dies before the eyes of the
frightened hunter Julien, while the female bird kills herself
before the eyes of the frightened hunter Sonjō. Both Julien
and Sonjō become priests, and the cause of their conversion
is, in both cases, the impressive eyes, the impressive voice,
and the death of the animals, although the degree of
impression may differ. In any case, the human voices of the
animals whose loved ones had been killed touch the hearts of
the hunters.

Here, I would like to add some biographical explanantions.
Hearn disliked hunting. He loved insects and animals. He
wrote many essays on insects during his fourteen-year stay in
Japan. While listening to the *Kokonchomonjū* story read aloud
by his wife, Hearn must have felt anger, and that was translated
into his heroine's character. Under the external influence of
Flaubert and under the internal influence of his own
temperament, Hearn transformed the original story. Most of
his retold stories are works of his own taste and art.

Consciously or unconsciously, he recreated the original stories. Since Koizumi Setsuko stood between the original Japanese stories and the writer Hearn, he could be much freer than ordinary translators. The secret of his success lies in this method. The dramatic final scene of 'Oshidori' makes a stronger appeal than the Japanese story even to Japanese readers. We do not know if Hearn might be called a Japan scholar, since he was rather free in his art of retelling. It should be added, however, that it is almost the same with the great Orientalist Arthur Waley, since Waley was extremely imaginative in his art of rendering the *Tale of Genji* and other Oriental works into English.

As I have said, the Japanese like Hearn's tales very much, and in the case of 'Oshidori', I think I could add one more half-hidden reason for its popularity. The story tells of a strong conjugal affection, stronger even than death. 'L'amour plus fort que la mort' is a favourite theme of Lafcadio Hearn, who was an admirer of Théophile Gautier. But in the case of 'Oshidori', published shortly before Hearn's death, I feel the conjugal affection described in the story is that shared by Lafcadio and Setsuko. If the husband and wife did not love each other, they could not have produced such works.

Basil Hall Chamberlain was a Japan scholar known for the accuracy of his information; but the proud scholar was misled by his own pride. His pride, tinged with racism, derived of course from his belief in the superiority of Western Christian civilization. Nowhere was this supremacist conviction so apparent as in his view of inter-racial sexual relationships. Chamberlain did not like the idea of the Britisher going native, and he added to the last edition of *Things Japanese* the article 'Lafcadio Hearn', saying: 'His life was a succession of dreams which ended in nightmares. In his ardour he became a naturalized Japanese,... But awaking from his dream he realized he had taken a false step.'

If Chamberlain means by nightmares Hearn's domestic unhappiness or disillusionment as a Japan interpreter, Chamberlain is mistaken. As Hearn adds a footnote to the story, a pair of *oshidori* have been regarded as emblems of conjugal affection in the Far East; as a work of close collaboration between a British husband and a Japanese wife, the retold story of 'Oshidori' will be remembered as the emblem of the conjugal affection of Lafcadio and Setsuko.

CHAMBERLAIN AND HEARN ON JAPANESE MUSIC

The issues raised by the two contrasting personalities, Chamberlain and Hearn, are very much relevant even today, as it has something to do with the difference in recognition of the position of Japan and its culture in the global community. Between the two interpreters, there was a difference in their basic assumptions, deriving probably from their respective backgrounds. Chamberlain, who was a son of an English upper-class family, naturally believed in the superiority of Western civilization. Not only to Chamberlain but also to leading Japanese intellectuals of the time, the superiority of Western industrial civilization seemed self-evident, and the modernization of Japan was of course synonymous with its Westernization. To Chamberlain, in particular, everything Western was superior to Japanese. The following is just an example.

Chamberlain, whose brother – as already noted – was married to Wagner's daughter, was a great admirer of Wagnerian music; his contempt for Japanese musical instruments was such that he began his article on Japanese music as follows:

> Music, if that beautiful word must be allowed to fall so low as to denote strummings and squealings of Orientals, is supposed to have existed in Japan ever since mythological times. . .
> May this (performance of Western music by Japanese artists) happen here before another century elapses, and then may all the *samisen*, *kotos*, and other native instruments of music be turned into firewood to warm the poor, when – if at no other previous period of their existence – they will subserve a purpose indisputably useful!
> (*Things Japanese*, 1905 edition).

In contrast, Hearn, who had already been interested in folklore music of the East even before coming to Japan, had a different attitude. Indeed, one of Hearn's friends in his American days was the folklore musicologist Henry Krehbiel, to whom he dedicated his book *Some Chinese Ghosts* in 1877.

Like Paul Claudel some thirty years later, Hearn was attracted
by the shrill sound of the Japanese bamboo flute. Hearn writes
in 'The Diary of an English Teacher': 'Music which at first no
Western ear can feel pleasure in, but which, when often heard,
becomes comprehensible, and is found to possess a weird
charm of its own.' 'Weird' may not be a complimentary word,
but that sensation is the beginning of an aesthetic appreciation.
In this way, Chamberlain's supremacist conviction vitiates
many of his judgements. However, precisely as Chamberlain
was so confident in the superiority of Western civilization, his
authoritative *Things Japanese* was for a long time immensely
popular among Western residents in Japan. For those
Europeans who came to Japan and who found the Japanese
language extremely difficult, Chamberlain's book was the
most useful encyclopaedia. The longer they lived in Japan,
separated from the Japanese within their closed community,
the more they relied upon it. There was a kind of vicious
circle, and even half-Westernized intelligent Japanese joined
it. Some Japanese diplomats and scholars, too, depended
heavily on Chamberlain's *Things Japanese*, when they were
obliged to explain their own country in English to foreigners.
     Then, why was it possible for Hearn to be free from many
of Chamberlain's Euro-centric convictions? Interestingly, both
Chamberlain and Hearn were educated for a considerable
length of time in France. However, Hearn did not share
Chamberlain's Euro-centric viewpoints. Was Hearn's stance
really healthy or just reactionary? Let us have a look at Hearn's
upbringing. As is written in Chamberlain's article, Hearn, who
was the son of an Irish surgeon of Protestant stock and of a
Greek mother, was brought up by a wealthy great-aunt of
Catholic belief after his parents' divorce. The boy was,
however, driven out into a penniless state, when she went
bankrupt. Through his late teens and twenties Lafcadio was
obliged to lead a wretched life. He detested his British father,
regarding him as the cause of so many of his miseries. Turning
his back against what his father represented, he first emigrated
from Britain to America and then came to Japan.

HEARN, THAT *RARA AVIS*

Hearn, in fact, was that *rara avis*, a Western observer of Japan who, coming to the Far East in the 1890s, did not take as an act of faith the superiority of Western Christian civilization. For example, far from adhering to the opinions of the mainstream of Western Orientalists, Hearn was adamant in his conviction that for ordinary citizens of the lower strata of society, that fundamental human right, freedom from horror, was safeguarded better in Japanese slums than in European capitals or America's great cities. In this respect, one should never forget that Hearn, besides having been far from the bottom in Dublin, lived near the bottom of society both in English and American great cities, and that he was a shrewd newspaperman in Cincinnati and in New Orleans. He was a skilful reporter and very interested in crime.

Here, let me explain what sort of Japanologist Hearn was. His great difference from other Japan scholars is that he was a literary artist, although Hearn did not write plays, poetry or novels during his Japanese years. It is, indeed, difficult to accommodate many of his writings within the context of literary history, as many of Hearn's essays should be considered 'Japanese studies'. Hearn did not seek knowledge for the sake of information. He tried to use Japanese materials for the sake of his artistic aspirations. He could not stay quietly within the limits tacitly prescribed by the rules of a discipline. By the way, his having obtained Japanese citizenship does not necessarily mean that Lafcadio Hearn, alias Koizumi Yakumo, is a Japanese writer. He wrote in English. His stories and essays were written for English-speaking readers. Hearn's best contributions appeared in magazines such as the *Atlantic Monthly*. When he wrote 'we', he meant 'we Westerners'. Through his publications he belonged to the American literary world. His English spellings were American. In this sense Hearn was an American writer.

We can recognize in this writer's works two dominant strains: that of stylistic artistry and that of cultural interpretation. I fear that Hearn sometimes sacrifices the accuracy of the latter for the sake of his aesthetic need. This tendency of Hearn's must be particularly repugnant to the Japan specialists of the later generations. But Hearn at his best is superb: his mastery of illustration serves remarkably well as a tool of cultural interpretation. Hearn should not be judged separately as a literary artist without inventive capacity or as a Japan interpreter without scientific discipline. Lafcadio Hearn should be evaluated on his own terms. As an example of a blending of the two dominant strains, I have already explained truth and fiction in 'At a Railway Station' in a commentary attached to a new anthology of Hearn's writings published from Japan Library.[9]

★ ★ ★

PART III: THE ANIMISTIC WORLD OF *KWASHIN KOJI*

GENERATION VERSUS CREATION

Here, let us have a look at another story, which is based on Hearn's subtle understanding of Japanese animism. 'The Story of Kwashin Koji' is not only well perfected as a small piece of fantastic literature but it is extremely interesting as it reveals the cardinal point of East Asian aesthetics, and by extension, the relationship between nature and selfhood in traditional Japanese literature.

In novels as well as in dramas, endings are crucially important. For some authors, the final scene of a work is almost tantamount to a display of their utmost ability as literary artists. Indeed, many literary works practically end when the main character ceases to be active: in tragic works heroes and heroines die or disappear towards the end and there must be a good reasonable cause for their final disappearance. The interest of a piece of literature often consists in the rationalization of that seemingly irrational process, and that unexpected, still logically explainable ending or dénouement is a feat of dramatic art.

By way of comparison, I am going to look at two forms of disappearance of heroes at the end of a novel. In all four cases, the heroes disappear into a surface: two heroes into a picture and the other two heroes into a wall. The problem dealt with here lies, however, not in technicalities of dramatization but in the manner in which the phenomena of disappearance are explained. It deals, therefore, with philosophical presumptions or prerequisites which are taken for granted by authors as well as by readers. I have chosen two sets of examples each; one group comes from the East Asian literary tradition, and the other from the West European literary tradition. As Hearn makes a fine use of Oriental tradition, I am going to dwell at more length on the first set; anyway, by juxtaposing the supernatural manner of disappearance of the heroes, East Asian as well as Western, and by elucidating the underlying theoretical presuppositions, I hope I will make suggestions concerning the characteristic relationship of self with nature in East Asian literature which seems to be rather different from that in Western European literature.

In my opinion, the difference most probably arises from the difference in underlying conceptions concerning the origin of mankind. The East Asian notion of 'generation of mankind' or autogenesis has had a deep influence on Japanese literature: the pervasive animistic view has produced literary theories and practices considerably different from Western theories and practices, upon which the conception of 'creation of mankind' seems to have left indelible characteristics. It is no wonder that the Western nomenclature of literary science is rich in vocabulary such as 'author' and 'creation', while East Asian vocabulary of poetics is rich in animistic terms such as 'the spirit of language' (*kotodama*) and *kiin-seidō* or *qiyun shengdong*. However, before discussing abstract terms, let us take a close look at concrete examples.

THE FINAL DISAPPEARANCE OF 'KWASHIN KOJI'

The Japanese author I am going to look at is Ishikawa Kōsai (1833–1918). He was a well-known man of letters in his day, because of his deep knowledge of classical Chinese. These days, however, no Japanese literary historian pays attention to Ishikawa's stories written in *kanbun* or classical Chinese. They are as forgotten as some Western literary works written in Latin by Neo-Latin poets. Ishikawa's ghostly stories, *Yasōkidan* (volume I published in 1889 and volume II in 1893) written in *kanbun*, however, had fortunately caught Koizumi Setsuko's attention because of their weirdness, and Setsuko read them aloud to her husband, Lafcadio Hearn, who made three adaptations from *Yasōkidan*, writing them down in English. 'The Story of Kwashin Koji', included in *A Japanese Miscellany*, Hearn's eighth book in Japan published in 1901, is considered one of his best retold stories. By the way Hearn himself mistook his contemporary Ishikawa Kōsai for a man of the past, and described his *Yasōkidan* as a 'curious *old* book' in the footnote.

The gist of the story is as follows:

During the period of Tenshō (1573–1592) there lived in Kyoto an old man called Kwashin Koji. Dressed like a Shinto priest, he made his living by exhibiting Buddhist pictures and preaching Buddhist doctrine. The old man had a *kakemono* or hanging scroll on which were depicted the punishments of the various hells, and he would discourse to the people crowding to see it, and explain to them the Law of Cause and Effect – the law of *contrappasso*, if I may use Dante's expression. At that time, Oda Nobunaga was ruler of Kyoto, and one of his retainers happened to see the picture being displayed. He had Kwashin Koji come to Nobunaga's palace. Nobunaga was surprised at the vividness of the picture:

> . . . the demons and the tortured spirits actually appeared to move before his eyes; and he heard voices crying out of the picture; and the blood there represented seemed to be really flowing – so that he could not help putting out his fingers to see if the painting was wet.

Observing Nobunaga's evident desire to possess the *kakemono*, the retainer Arakawa asked Kwashin Koji whether he would 'offer it up' as a gift to the great lord. Kwashin Koji refused and asked a hundred ryō of gold for that picture. Arakawa later that day killed the old man and took the picture. The next day, Arakawa presented the *kakemono*, still wrapped, to Nobunaga. However, when it was unrolled, there was no picture at all – nothing but a blank surface. It was decided that Arakawa, being guilty of deceiving his master, should be punished.

Scarcely had Arakawa completed his term of imprisonment, when news was brought to him that Kwashin Koji was exhibiting the famous picture. Arakawa could hardly believe his ears; but the information inspired him with a vague hope that he might be able to secure the *kakemono*. Finally, Arakawa caught the old man. However, in the court Kwashin Koji defended himself. He said that the picture was only a copy, and that Arakawa, after having stolen the picture, had changed his mind about giving it to Lord Nobunaga. Kwashin Koji said that Arakawa had devised a plan to keep it for himself, and that was the reason why he had given a blank *kakemono* to Nobunaga. Arakawa was ordered by the chief officer to be beaten with a bamboo until he told the truth.

After punishment was wrought on Arakawa, Kwashin Koji laughed, saying that he purposely brought the punishment upon the rascal and told the officer that Arakawa must have been ignorant of the truth and that Kwashin Koji should now explain the whole matter satisfactorily. Here is what Kwashin Koji said to the chief officer, translated faithfully into English by Hearn from Ishikawa Kōsai's original. The argument deals with Oriental aesthetics.

In any picture of real excellence there must be a ghost; and such a picture, having a will of its own, may refuse to be separated from the person who gave it life, or even from its rightful owner. There are many stories to prove that really great pictures have souls.

Here Kwashin Koji cites an example of sparrows painted by Hogen Genshin that flew away, leaving blank the spaces which they had occupied upon the surface of a sliding-screen, and another of a horse that used to go out at night to eat grass. Kwashin Koji then proceeds to the explanation of the present case. He believes the truth to be that inasmuch as Lord Nobunaga never became the rightful owner of his *kakemono*, the picture voluntarily vanished from the paper when it was unrolled. Kwashin Koji further makes a new proposal:

But if you will give me the price that I first asked – one hundred ryō of gold – I think that the painting will then reappear, of its own accord, upon the now blank paper.

Nobunaga ordered the hundred ryō to be paid, and to the amazement of all present, the painting reappeared. The colours, however, seemed to have faded a little; and the figures of the souls and demons did not look really alive, as before. Perceiving this difference, Nobunaga asked Kwashi Koji to explain the reason of it. Here is his answer:

> The value of the painting, as you first saw it, was the value of a painting beyond all price. But the value of the painting as you see it, represents exactly what you paid for it – one hundred ryō of gold. . . How could it be otherwise?

All these explanations, although very mystifying, are founded upon a presumption that a picture of real excellence has a spirit and has its own will. This animistic philosophy has something to do with the ending of the story. After some incidents, Kwashin Koji finally was thrown into prison because of his insolent acts. Just at that time Lord Nobunaga came to his death through the treachery of Mitsuhide, who was told of the case of Kwashin Koji. Accordingly, Koji was summoned into the presence of the new lord, who treated the old man as a guest, and commanded that a good dinner should be served. Towards the end of the banquet, in return for the new lord's kindness, Kwashin Koji was going to display a little of his art. He pointed to a large eight-panel screen upon which were painted the *Eight Beautiful Views of the Lake of Ōmi* known as *Ōmi-Hakkei*. In one of the views a boat was represented, occupying upon the surface of the screen, a space of less than an inch in length. Here is the final part of the story:

> . . . Kwashin Koji then waved his hand in the direction of the boat; and all saw the boat suddenly turn, and begin to move towards the foreground of the picture. It grew larger and larger as it approached, and presently the features of the boatman became clearly distinguishable.
> Still the boat drew nearer, – always becoming larger, – until it appeared to be only a short distance away. And, all of a sudden, the water of the lake seemed to overflow, – out of the picture into the room; – and the room was flooded; and the spectators girded up their knees. In the same moment the boat appeared to glide out of the screen, – a real fishing-boat; – and the creaking of the single oar could be heard. Still the flood in

the room continued to rise, until the spectators were standing up to their girdles in water. Then the boat came close up to Kwashin Koji; and Kwashin Koji climbed into it; and the boatman turned about, and began to row away very swiftly. And, as the boat receded, the water in the room began to lower rapidly, – seeming to ebb back into the screen. No sooner had the boat passed the apparent foreground of the picture than the room was dry again! But still the painted vessel appeared to glide over the painted water, – retreating further into the distance, and ever growing smaller, – till at last it dwindled to a dot in the offing. And then it disappeared altogether; and Kwashin Koji disappeared with it. He was never again seen in Japan.

In the original *kanbun* text by Ishikawa Kōsai the description is much more brief, as is generally the case with many classical Chinese works, whose stylistic characteristic is concision. I have tentatively made the following literal translation.

There was a screen upon which were painted the *Eight Beautiful Views of the Lake of Ōmi*. A boat there was about an inch in length. Kwashin Koji then waved his hand, inviting it to come. The boat, wavering, drew nearer and glided out of the screen, and it grew as large as several feet long. At the same time, the water of the lake flooded the room, and all spectators were surprised, girding up their *hakama* skirts in haste. They were standing up to their girdles in water. Kwashin Koji was now in the boat, and the fisherman calmly rowed the boat and they went away we know not where.

Compared to this original, we are struck by Hearn's amply creative retelling, putting in so many evocative details. Following the passing of time, Hearn marvelously describes the final scene. Especially impressive is Hearn's invention that Kwashin Koji went back into the picture together with the painted vessel.

HOW WANG-FO WAS SAVED

In my opinion, the French author Marguerite Yourcenar practically copied this final scene in her story 'How Wang-Fo Was Saved'. This piece, considered the best among her *Oriental Tales*,[10] might be summarized as follows. The old painter Wang-Fo and his devoted disciple Ling were wandering along the roads of the Kingdom of Han. They were caught by soldiers, and Ling, who had tried to defend his master, was first beheaded. Wang-Fo himself was condemned by the Emperor to have his eyes burned out. However, the painter was given a last chance. The Emperor said: 'To offer you brushes, paints, and inks to occupy your last hours is like offering the favours of a harlot to a man condemned to death.' Wang-Fo then began to finish a sketch he had left undone, by adding a touch of pink to the tip of the wing of a cloud, and,

> . . . he painted onto the surface of the sea a few small lines that deepened the perfect feeling of calm. The jade floor became increasingly damp, but Wang-Fo, absorbed as he was in his painting, did not seem to notice that he was working with his feet in water.
>
> The fragile rowboat grew under the strokes of the painter's brush and now occupied the entire foreground of the silken scroll. The rhythmic sound of the oars rose suddenly in the distance, quick and eager like the beating of wings. The sound came nearer, gently filling the whole room, then ceased, and a few trembling drops appeared on the boatman's oars. . . The courtiers, motionless as etiquette required, stood in water up to their shoulders, trying to lift themselves onto the tips of their toes. The water finally reached the level of the imperial heart. The silence was so deep one could have heard a tear drop.[11]

It was Ling who rowed the boat, and around his neck was tied a strange red scarf.[12] Wang-Fo said to him softly, while he continued painting: 'I thought you were dead.' 'You being alive,' said Ling respectfully, 'how could I have died?' And he helped his master into the boat.

'Let us leave,' said the old painter.

Wang-Fo took hold of the helm, and Ling bent over the oars. The sound of rowing filled the room again, strong and steady like the beating of a heart. The level of the water dropped unnoticed. . . The courtiers' robes were dry, but a few wisps of foam still clung to the hem of the Emperor's cloak.

The painting finished by Wang-Fo was leaning against a tapestry. A rowboat occupied the entire foreground. It drifted away little by little, leaving behind it a thin wake that smoothed out into the quiet sea. One could no longer make out the faces of the two men sitting in the boat, but one could still see Ling's red scarf and Wang-Fo's beard waving in the breeze.

Yourcenar was a French author exceptionally interested in East Asian literature. In the same *Oriental Tales* there is 'The Last Love of Prince Genji', which is a kind of *kumogakure-no-maki* chapter, imagined by Yourcenar, as Lady Murasaki herself did not dare to write the passing away of the Shining Prince. Yourcenar, moreover, was very fond of Mishima for whom she wrote a book of critical essays, *Mishima ou la vision du vide*; even in 'How Wang-Fo Was Saved' one may easily detect some common tastes such as homosexuality shared by the two authors. As for the source of this story of Wang-Fo, she pretends in her postscript that 'the story is based on a Taoist fable of ancient China'. Although this statement is intentionally misleading – as I believe its source to be 'The Story of Kwashin Koji' – it is not entirely false, as Ishikawa Kōsai's story itself was based on the Taoist fairy tale tradition of *shenxian* or *shinsen*, which is a kind of wizardry. The legendary Kwashin Koji must have been considered as a kind of *sennin* or hermit gifted with magic power in popular fantasy throughout the Tokugawa period.

DISAPPEARANCES OF HONORÉ SUBRAC AND DUTILLEUL

Let us examine the special charm of this type of ending, peculiar to *shenxian* stories, by juxtaposing some other endings or disappearings, and by so doing let us try to elucidate the special relationship between self and nature in East Asian literary traditions, which Hearn understood so remarkably well.

'La Disparition d'Honoré Subrac' (1910) is a well-known fantastic story written by the French surrealistic poet Guillaume Apollonaire (1880–1918). Honoré Subrac, who had committed adultery with a woman, was so afraid of her vengeful husband that he finally succeeded in disappearing into a wall by his instinctive apatetic faculties. His explanation is as follows:

> C'est bien simple. Il ne faut voir là qu'un phénomène de mimétisme. . . La nature est une bonne mère. Elle a départi à ceux de ses enfants que des dangers menacent, et qui sont trop faibles pour se défendre, le don de se confondre avec ce qui les entoure. . .

This disappearance of Honoré, which takes place just before the amazed husband's eyes, is so unexpected that the ending is extraordinarily effective. However, what makes the French hero's final disappearance different from Kwashin Koji's disappearance is the rational explanation given to it: *mimétisme* or mimetic process, which is in accordance with the general notions of physical science.

The realm of the fantastic is thus made one with the domain of the real, by means of this scientific explanation. It is the same with the ending of Marcel Aymé's 'Le Passe-Muraille' (1943), a work apparently inspired by 'La Disparition d'Honoré Subrac'. The hero of this fantastic story, Monsieur Dutilleul, is capable of passing through walls. However, early one morning he is unable to get out through the thick wall of a Montmartre residence where he has passed delicious hours with a lady, because that night, before coming, he took, instead of an aspirin, the wrong pill! All these final disappearances are extremely interesting and well-written. However, the space in which these modern French heroes are acting is still three-dimensional, and rationalizing explanations given to their seemingly supernatural disappearances are very much scientific, at least in their vocabulary: mimétisme, apatetic faculties, misuse of drugs. Definitely Honoré Subrac and Dutilleul are seen as conditioned by the laws of physics, while Kwashin Koji and Wang-Fo transcend them.

Of the two Oriental stories, the ending of Kwashin Koji is more natural and smooth than that of Wang-Fo, and there is a good reason for this. In that well-constructed story of Kwashin Koji, readers are gradually accustomed by many preceding episodes to the notion that a picture may have a soul. Although the hero is apparently Kwashin Koji, the real latent issue in this story is the aesthetic conception that a work of art may have a will of its own. Theoretically speaking, various preceding events concerning the *kakemono* or the hell scroll are explained by that animistic philosophy. As pictures have their own souls, it is possible that they can react to those who have given them life. Between this Oriental idea of art and the Greek idea of Pygmalion (and its modern Western variations such as Wilde's 'The Picture of Dorian Gray') there are many resemblances; still, we should recognize an important difference.

THE EASTERN TRADITIONAL AESTHETICS OF CALLIGRAPHY

Here let me give you a general observation. Categories of arts generally correspond in every part of the world: as there is literature in the West, so there is literature in the East. It is the same with sculpture, architecture, music and painting. However, one category of art is curiously lacking in the West, while it is conspicuously flourishing in the East: that is the traditional art of calligraphy. In this art, whose history is as old as Chinese characters, what counts is not the objective meaning of that which is written, expressed or painted, but the manner of writing itself. In this art, which is very akin to the art of painting by their common use of brush and ink, what counts is not the theory of mimesis or the representation of reality, but the animation of brush strokes. Photographic realism is something most alien to this art. Let me tell you my personal experience. I am very fond of Italian Renaissance painters and their followers; one of them came to Qing China in 1715. This Italian Jesuit painter, Castiglione, known as Lang Shining in China, interests me very much; however, when I saw his paintings among the masterpieces of Chinese painting in the Palace Museum in Taipei, I must confess I was most unfavourably impressed by the absence of *kiin-seidō* in his horses so accurately painted like illustrations in scientific textbooks of zoology.

Kiin-seidō or *qiyun shengdong* means liveliness of spirituality. It is the most important key concept of aesthetics, not only in the art of calligraphy, but also in the East Asian art of ink painting. This view, I believe, derives from the prevailing belief shared by many Oriental connoisseurs that what is worthy of admiration is something beautifully animated. So much so that this spirit is appreciated not only in works of calligraphy or ink painting but also in works of poetry and prose as well. In Japan from the time of the most ancient anthology, the *Manyōshū*, edited in the middle of the eighth century, *uta*-poetry that has a spirit of its own and that survives the mortal poet is said to have *kotodama* or the spirit of the language. This notion of the spirit of the Japanese language is very popular among the Japanese, although it has often been denigrated by linguistic scientists such as Roy Andrew Miller as a conception familiar to primitive tribes.[13] However, thanks to that belief, which considers a language as something more than a simple tool of communication, there opens up a certain magical dimension intrinsic to the metaphysical continuum bridging a work of art and those who appreciate it. Is it not an undeniable fact that, while reading classical works of literature, we sometimes feel a revival of something remote, and that they give us the impression as if the works had their own souls? So long as there is such a strong appeal on the part of works of art, it is quite natural to say that they have their own spirits. It is further felt that the shapes of the creatures or the persons therein depicted would separate themselves from the paper or the silken roll upon which they were depicted and would perform various acts, so that they become by their own will really alive.

GHOSTLY JAPAN

This type of thinking and feeling may not be popular in countries with Judaeo-Christian traditions.[14] However, in the monsoonal regions of Asia the notion of creation by a single transcendental author is rather foreign, not only in religious matters but also in literary matters. In the West the vertical relationship between the commanding author and the created work has been much clearer than in the East: the writer has been the almighty creator who engineered every detail. In Japan, according to the opening chapter of the Japanese mythology, *Kojiki* or *Records of Ancient Matters*, as human beings or their ancestors 'were born from a thing that sprouted up like unto a reedshoot when the earth, young and like unto floating oil, drifted about',[15] so works of art, too, have more often been generated than created. Think of the spontaneous growth of mold or earthworms in a warm rainy season, and think of the spontaneous spread of *haiku* poetry in Japan: they are more generated than created, and each small part of a work grows independently. Think of the origin of *haiku* or *hokku*. Even if the first unit of seventeen syllables is cut off from the main body of the whole series of *renga* (linked poetry), it is still independently alive. Haiku, the most popular literary form in Japan, in this sense is like an earthworm: if its head or its end is cut off, that separated part alone becomes a new life by itself. Moreover, in gatherings of amateurs, in composing linked poetry you do not need to have an almighty director who orchestrates every part. Parts generate by themselves.

If the relationship between an author and his work is like this, and autogenesis is the fundamental idea not only of religion but also of poetry in many parts of East Asia, the author's self-conscious mind, which used to count so much in the construction of Western-style novel, as he was considered the master architect of the world, begins to lose its dominant importance in this part of the world. Here he is not a supreme commander any more. The writer interacts more spontaneously with his own work. The philosophy of interaction thus conceived is beautifully illustrated through the mouth of Kwashin Koji, when he explained the changing physiognomy of the hell scroll. Probably as there is that explanatory episode in the first half of the story, the final disappearance of Kwashin Koji becomes not only more natural and smooth, but also leaves a finer after-taste than the slightly heavy disappearance of Wang-Fo and Ling.

Again, if the relationship between an author and his work is reciprocal and interdependent, it also suggests that the relationship between one's self and its environment is less antagonistic. The animated nature receives amically those who care for it. Nature to the Japanese of former times was not something to be conquered, and this animistic correspondence seems to be well caught by Hearn in his retold story when the *sennin*-like Kwashin Koji returns in it forever.[16]

I have used so far the adjective 'animistic' which sounds more scientific than literary. The animated nature is to its inhabitants a world full of ghosts. Japan, a country of the so-called eight million divinities, has many ghosts, too. Hearn entitled, therefore, one of his books *In Ghostly Japan*. 'Ghostly' was an adjective which Hearn was extremely fond of. Hearn was very much attracted by ghostly aspects of Japanese culture. Japan, according to Hearn, is a world animated and even ruled by the spirits of the dead. This tendency of his fondness for animistic interpretation is not only apparent in his travel sketches such as *Glimpses of Unfamiliar Japan*, but also in his academic treatise *Japan, an Attempt at Interpretation*. However, nowhere is his interest in spectral matters so conspicuous as in his retold stories. One of the literary expressions of the animistic world of Japan is the genre called *kwaidan* or ghostly tales. Lafcadio Hearn was exceptional among Western interpreters of Japan in that he not only showed a keen interest in the ghost psychology of the Japanese but also succeeded in catching subtle nuances within it. To our surprise, he was able to recreate in English that weird world of goblins and spirits.

As I have mentioned earlier, among Hearn's thirteen books on Japan, the book most read by the Japanese, either in English or in Japanese translation, is *Kwaidan* or ghost stories. This, indeed, is no small feat for a writer whose mother tongue is not Japanese. No foreign writer or scholar has surpassed him in this field, though there have been many Japan specialists who are much more linguistically talented than Lafcadio Hearn. I believe that the principal reason for Hearn's appeal to the Japanese derives from Hearn's sympathetic understanding of Japanese animism, which Western missionaries and arm-chair professors did not always try to understand in that age of 'civilization and enlightenment'. Compared with Hearn's contribution as the author of *Kwaidan*, his contribution as Japan's apologist seems very small in the Japanese general reader's mind today.

As to why the Japanese world of the dead began to be so familiar to Hearn's mind's eye, I will not deal with it here, as I have already extensively discussed it in connection with his Irish dimension elsewhere.[17]

★　★　★

PART IV: 'THE RECONCILIATION' RECONSIDERED

GHOST WIFE STORIES

As the rediscovery of Lafcadio Hearn has had something to do with the worldwide success of Kobayashi Masaki's celebrated film *Kwaidan* (1964) based on Hearn's ghost stories, let us discuss the first episode of the omnibus film. It is a film version of Hearn's ghost wife story 'The Reconciliation', which is included in a volume entitled *Shadowings* published in 1900.

'The Reconciliation' by Hearn, too, has a Japanese original and Hearn himself specifies it in a footnote. He says 'the original story is to be found in the curious volume entitled *Konseki Monogatari*'. The more commonly accepted pronunciation of the title is *Konjaku Monogatari*, which was written towards the beginning of the twelfth century. The original story is the 24th tale of Chapter Twenty-Seven, one of the non-religious tales of Japan. As it is very short and since it is not included by Marian Ury in her translation of *Tales of Times Now Past* I will provide a rough translation of the tale, using the 1897 edition published by Tsujimoto Shōkodō, which Koizumi Setsuko read aloud for her husband.

At a time now past, there lived in Kyoto a samurai who was very poor and who had no job. When a nobleman who was his acquaintance was appointed Governor of a distant province, the samurai asked the favour of accompanying him to the province as his retainer. The new Governor granted the request to the samurai, who, upon departure, divorced his wife – a good-natured, beautiful young woman, who had endured the years of poverty with him. It was hard for him to separate himself from her, but in order to go to a distant land the samurai thought he had better marry another woman who was rich and resourceful. The samurai went to the province with this new wife.

However, after several years the samurai found that he still very much loved his former wife, whom he had abandoned in Kyoto. He began to wish to see her again, and this desire became so strong that he suffered from it even physically. When the Governor's term expired, the samurai returned to the capital with him. The samurai felt that he had divorced his former wife without any good reason. He wished to go back to live with her again.

As soon as he arrived in Kyoto, the samurai sent his second wife back to her family. Not allowing himself even the time to change his travelling garb, he went to the house where his former wife used to live. As the gate was not closed, he entered. The house had a deserted look, and was seemingly unoccupied. He felt extremely sad. It was September the twentieth, the moon shone brightly and the air was chilly. The samurai was chilled to the heart. But on entering the house, he found his wife at her usual seat. No one else was there. Her eyes met his, and without any air of resentment she greeted him with a happy smile:

'What's happened to you? when did you come back?'

Then the samurai told her how he had missed her, how he had thought of her for many years, and said:

'Now let us live together. Tomorrow my goods shall be brought here, and my servants shall come to wait upon you. Tonight I have come here only to tell you this.'

She seemed to be greatly pleased on hearing these words, and in her turn she told him about all that had happened during the years of his absence. As it became late in the night, they lay down in a room facing south to sleep together.

'Have you no one in the house to help you?'

'No, I could not afford a servant.'

They still had much to tell each other. As dawn approached, they slept. When daylight came streaming brightly into the room, the samurai awoke and was surprised to find beside him the corpse of his wife, a corpse dried up to skins and bones.

'What is this?'

The horror was unspeakable. He ran away and jumped into the garden. 'This must be a hallucination'. He looked back again at her, but there lay the corpse of the dead woman.

Hurriedly, he put on his clothes and went into a neighbouring house and asked as if he were a newcomer. 'Is there no one in that house?' The neighbour answered:

'As the husband had gone away to a distant province, the wife fretted a great deal and fell sick. No one cared for her. Last summer she died. No one took care of the dead body. As her corpse remains there, no one dares approach the house. It remains deserted.'

Hearing this he again was horror-struck; without saying a word, he went away.

What horror! It must be the soul of the woman that remained there. She lingered there to see him. She had longed so much to see him again that she came back to their bridal chamber. How pitiful! So the tale's been told.

Those who are familiar with the *Tales of Moonlight and Rain* by the eighteenth-century writer Ueda Akinari[18] or with their film version by Mizoguchi Kenji will recognize in the above *Konjaku* tale the prototype of Akinari's *Asaji-ga-yado* (the House amid the Thickets), as Akinari's tale, too, is based on it.

HEARN, A WRITER OF RETOLD STORIES

Before analyzing the modern adaptation made from the same *Konjaku* tale by Hearn, let me again refer to Hearn's linguistic ability in Japanese. He could not read classical Japanese, but he had a very good understanding of spoken Japanese. Lafcadio and his Japanese wife Setsuko always communicated in Japanese, as Setsuko did not speak English at all. Hearn's method of rewriting Japanese weird tales was as follows: Hearn would ask his wife to read aloud Japanese *kwaidan* which he wrote down in English. While writing them down, the artist Hearn modified details and enlarged the contents. The English story 'Oshidori', which we have already read, is three times longer than the Japanese original, and it is almost the same with the English story 'The Reconciliation'. There are two reasons for the modifications: first, Hearn had his own literary taste, and second, Hearn took into consideration his American and Victorian readers' sensibilities. Hearn's ghost stories, which are today more popular in Japan than in the United States, were written for American and British readers. His best stories appeared often in the *Atlantic Monthly* towards the turn of the century. Hearn at that time was highly appreciated in Boston literary circles. As more than half of his American readers were educated women, Hearn was obliged to pay attention to their feminine sensitivities.

At this point we had better look at some passages of Hearn's retold story before moving on to examine the final transformation. As the samurai of the original *Konjaku* tale is too egocentric in his behaviour towards his first wife, Hearn describes in detail the samurai's state of repentance. This is a

new element introduced by the American author. Hearn
explains:

> But it was in the time of the thoughtlessness of youth, and
> the sharp experience of want, that the Samurai could not
> understand the worth of the affection so lightly cast away. His
> second marriage did not prove a happy one; the character of
> his new wife was hard and selfish; and he soon found every
> cause to think with regret of Kyoto days. Then he discovered
> that he still loved his first wife. . .

Though the hard and selfish character of the second wife is
vividly visualized in Kobayashi's film, Hearn does not mention
it in detail; he rather tells us the good characteristics of the first
wife:

> . . . her gentle speech, her smiles, her dainty, pretty ways,
> her faultless patience. . . Sometimes in dreams he saw her at
> her loom, weaving as when she toiled night and day to help
> him during the years of their distress.

As the samurai had repented and as the first wife was
gentle and patient, there was, in fact, the possibility of a
happy reunion. The title of the story itself is well chosen:
'The Reconciliation'. Readers have, therefore, a premoni-
tion of a reconciliation. The part played by the title is
important, as it suggests a happy ending. We may wonder if
American women today would pardon such a selfish man.
We imagine, however, that even in the United States around
the year 1900 there were women who would forgive a
thoughtless husband if he tried to make atonement. I admit,
however, that there is selfishness even in the atonement of
the samurai: if he goes back to his first wife, he has to divorce
his second wife. This act may constitute a new cruelty. Hearn
adds extenuating circumstances in parenthesis: the second
wife had given him no children, and he sent her back to her
own people.

The homecoming scene is impressive and Hearn describes
in detail the romantic air of the deserted house. Hearn
elaborates on the important scene of the meeting as follows:

> He pushed the screen aside, and uttered a cry of joy; for he
> saw her there, – sewing by the light of the paper-lamp. Her

eyes at the same instant met his own; and with a happy smile she greeted him, – asking only: – 'When did you come back to Kyoto?'

Then the samurai explains and apologizes to his former wife for his past bad behaviour. I am wondering if it is a real improvement for the story to have this rather long passage of apology. I find some of Hearn's expressions such as 'self-reproach' to be too modern a word for a medieval tale. At any rate, Hearn had to conform to the ethical standards of the American readers of his day. After having talked far into the night, they lay down. The Japanese version which Hearn used is an Edo version of the original *Konjaku* tale. It is not as blunt as the original text which says: 'futari kaki-idakite fushinu'. It is still clear in both Japanese versions that the two had sexual intercourse, while Hearn, a writer of the Victorian period, was less explicit in his description. The husband and wife's lengthy talking about servants and other daily affairs at this point seems to be a bit dull. Their conversation might be interpreted, at best, as a literary trick on the part of Hearn, since it gives us the impression that the reconciliation between the two was almost complete, and that they slept afterwards.

I very much admire the awakening scene in Ueda Akinari's version. The hero of *Ugetsu Monogatari* vaguely knew that he was cold, and groping with his hands, he tried to pull up the covers. But to his surprise, leaves rustled under his touch, and as he opened his eyes a cold drop of something fell on his face. In Ueda's tale, the pale shining moon of dawn still remains in the sky, while in Hearn's story the awakening of the husband is not as slow. Here is Hearn's passage, which constitutes the climax:

> When he awoke, the daylight was streaming through the chinks of the sliding-shutters; and he found himself, to his utter amazement, lying upon the naked boards of a mouldering floor. . . . Had he only dreamed a dream? No: she was there; – she slept. . . He bent above her, and looked, – and shrieked; – for the sleeper had no face!. . . Before him, wrapped in its gravesheet only, lay the corpse of a woman, – a corpse so wasted that little remained save the bones, and the long black tangled hair.

One of the most salient characteristics of Japanese *kwaidan*
is, as ghost stories everywhere, that they give readers a shock at
the culminating point of the story. The shock is already strong
in the original *Konjaku* tale: 'otoko uchi-odorokite mireba,
kaki-idakite netaru hito wa karekareto karete hone to kawa to
bakari naru shinishi hito narikeri.' (He awoke and was shocked
through to find beside him the corpse of the woman he had
embraced the night before, a dried-up corpse of skin and
bones.) In Hearn's version the shock is also visually impressive,
as Hearn adds a new element, the black hair: 'Before
him. . . lay the corpse of a woman, – a corpse so wasted that
little remained save the bones, and the long black hair.'
    The long black hair is very symbolic. When 'The
Reconciliation' was turned into a movie by the director
Kobayashi Masaki, this first of the four episodes of the film
Kwaidan was entitled 'Kurokami' (The Black Hair). In the
final scene we see not only the long black hair together with
white bones but also we see the long black hair pursuing the
horrified husband when he tries to run away, screaming. Thus,
in the film we are given the impression that the ghost of the
former wife returns to this world to avenge herself on the
disloyal husband. I do not think, however, that the ghost is
that vindictive either in the original *Konjaku* tale or in Hearn's
story.

A NEW FEMINIST INTERPRETATION

However, a transformation of Japanese womanhood begins
when some American feminists and Japanese returning from
abroad begin to interpret 'The Reconciliation' in their own
way. The new interpretation is as follows: the samurai hero of
the Hearn story is too self-centred to be really forgiven. A
normal self-respecting woman cannot accept such an egoistic
fellow again. The abandoned wife must have fretted and
resented her fate terribly before she died. Consequently, the
ghost of the dead wife must have tried to take revenge.
According to some returnees from the United States, 'The
Reconciliation' by Hearn is a story of revenge. The title 'The
Reconciliation' is a trick on the part of the American writer. It
is true that the first wife is depicted as very gentle and sweet

throughout the story. This, too, is probably a trick. The samurai as well as the readers are tricked by her gentle appearance. The sweeter she looks, the more effective will be the final shock, and this final fatal shock is her calculated revenge. The samurai as well as naïve readers have been induced to believe that the husband and the wife have been reconciled. This is not true, however. It is a reconciliation feigned by the abandoned wife who hopes that this deception will make the final shock even more horrible for the unfaithful samurai.

I wonder if readers generally will accept this new interpretation, which partly derives from the film *Kwaidan*: the director Kobayashi chose vindication instead of reconciliation. That is the reason why in the final scene the black hair of the dead woman pursues her horrified ex-husband. If this interpretation is correct, we have to say that there is a tremendous transformation of Japanese womanhood in Hearn's story. I do not believe, however, that was the intention of the *Konjaku* author or of Lafcadio Hearn. In fact, towards the end of the original tale it is clearly stated that the ghost of the dead woman appeared to the samurai because of her longing of many years. The theme of the *Konjaku* tale is, therefore, what the French romantic author Théophile Gautier calls 'l'amour plus fort que la mort'. (Love that is stronger than death.) And this is precisely the theme Hearn likes most. Moreover, Hearn generally idealizes Japanese womanhood, and in this story Hearn also emphasizes the following qualities of the first wife: her gentle speech, her dainty, pretty ways, her faultless patience. All these are probably the qualities Hearn found in his Japanese wife Setsuko. Indeed, Setsuko had toiled very hard to help the impoverished Koizumi family of samurai origin. She wove night and day, and even on the eve of her marriage to Lafcadio Hearn, she was seen at her loom. Hearn knew this and often commended her for it before their children. In the Lafcadio Hearn museum in Matsue there are samples or swatches of cloth woven by Setsuko. I cannot imagine that Hearn, who wrote the story while listening to the voice of his Japanese wife, could change the heroine into a vindictive woman. It is known that while reading old Japanese tales for her husband, Setsuko always identified herself with the heroine. Not only that, if we read the text carefully, we see the husband clutch at the vain hope that his wife might still be living. This is not the act nor the sentiment of a man on whom his former wife takes vengeance.

Of the three versions, one from Japanese literature of the early twelfth century, one in a Japanese film awarded a Grand Prix at Cannes (1964), and one from American literature at the turn of the century, the original *Konjaku* tale is probably the most impressive because of its grotesqueness in a compact form. Kobayashi Masaki's film version 'The Black Hair' is excellent as a visual representation, and in visual terms a revenge is generally more telling than a reconciliation, as a revenge scene makes a direct appeal to our senses. Hearn's retold story contains probably too much explanation and apology to be really forceful. However, precisely because Hearn was not a feminist, his story 'The Reconciliation' represents very humanely the feminine qualities of Japanese womanhood. Not only Japanese men but also Japanese women love Hearn's retold stories, because they feel in them a genuine conjugal affection, which outlives Lafcadio and Setsuko: love is stronger than death.

By contrast, we understand why we do not like some excessive forms of feminism, both Western and Eastern. It has now become clear that their underlying unconscious belief is: hate is stronger than death. That is the reason why some feminists interpret Hearn's 'Reconciliation' as a story of revenge. Their interpretations suggest that the driving force of some feminists is resentment. We know that the resentment of alienated women is very strong, but I personally cannot accept any liberation movement, either political, social or sexual, so long as it is based on hate rather than love. How is it possible for us to like a piece of literary work whose dominant theme is that hate is stronger than death, although there are countless stories worldwide which tell of such hate?

GHOST WIFE STORIES IN EAST ASIAN TRADITION

In order to better understand Hearn's 'The Reconciliation', let us consider the identical theme of ghost wife story in a historical perspective.[19] Apart from Ueda Akinari's 'The House Amid the Thickets', there are three stories of the same theme in China (*New Tales of the Trimmed Lamp* by Qú Yòu or Ch'ü Yu [1341–1427]), in Korea (*New Tales of the Golden Carp* or *Kumo Sinhwa* by Kim Si-sup [1435–1493]) and in Vietnam (*Tales Romanesque*).

The Chinese 'Story of Ai Qing' is about a charming prostitute named Luó Ai-ai who is later married to a wealthy man, Zhào. She was a good and dutiful wife. Zhào soon was summoned to serve at an office away from home, and was detained for some years before he could finally return. Meanwhile, Ai Qing (Luó Ai-ai) was forced to marry a local millionaire during a civil strife, but she resisted by hanging herself. After Zhào returned and learned of what had happened, he exhumed her corpse, weeping copiously, and reburied her. A month later, his ghost wife appeared and spent the night with him. Next morning, she told Zhào she had to leave and be re-incarnated.

The Korean tale 'Yi-saeng Looked over the Fence' has a 'happier' ending compared to the Chinese story, although it was written under the direct influence of the Chinese original. By the way, the Korean tale as well as the Vietnamese tale were written in classical Chinese. Ch'oe was a maiden from a rich family who fell in love with scholar Yi. They were later married after some difficulties with their families. When the red turban bandits seized the capital, scholar Yi fled and his wife was captured. She resisted the molestations of the bandits and was killed. When peace was finally restored, Yi came back to his house. Late at night, his ghost wife appeared before him. Although the scholar knew she was a ghost, he nevertheless loved her as a living person. They lived together for three years. One night, Ch'oe told her husband that their union in this world was coming to an end, and it was time for her to return to the Great Divide. Soon after, scholar Yi, too, passed away.

Although Korean culture has a strongly self-assertive identity of its own, in this case, the story closely follows in style and form the tradition of classical Chinese romance. In the case of 'The House Amid the Thickets', as it is based more on the *Konjaku* tale than on the Chinese 'Story of Ai Qing', there is less pedantry, and no deliberate display of the author's poetical talents. In this Japanese tale Katsushiro is a good-for-

nothing scoundrel who wanted to leave for Kyoto to make
some money as a merchant. His wife Miyagi told him not to
go, but he did not listen to her. After he finished his business
and was on his way home, Katsushiro was robbed. He
returned to Kyoto again and fell ill. Fortunately, he was saved
by his friend's father-in-law and he stayed in the old man's
house for seven years. Meanwhile, Katsushiro's home village
was ransacked by soldiers, as it was a time of civil war. When
he finally returned to his native place, he could barely
recognize his house. His wife answered the door, and they
both wept. Next day, Katsushiro awoke and found himself
sleeping amidst the thickets. The site was actually not far away
from the grave of his wife.

There is a decisive difference between the Japanese group of
tales (the *Konjaku* tale, 'The House Amid the Thickets', 'The
Reconciliation' and 'The Black Hair') and the Chinese group
of tales. In the Japanese group of tales an unexpected twist
occurs when the husband awakes: he finds that the wife he
slept with was a ghost, while in the Chinese group of tales the
protagonists as well as the readers know beforehand that the
wife, who is appearing before the returning husband, is a
ghost. This difference is critically important, as the final shock
at the culminating point is a *sine qua non* of a good short story.
Literary artists should build up suspense in narrative; otherwise
stories, although didactic from the viewpoint of Confucian
ethics, tend to be pointless.

The ghost wife story is a projection of the human
subconscious struggling against the finitude of human life.
Writers as well as readers wish that she may continue to live
even after she dies. Whether she is the Chinese Ai, the Korean
Ch'oe, the Japanese wife in the *Konjaku* tale or the woman in
Hearn's story, she appears to respond to the longing of her
dear husband. Ai Qing said most appropriately in the Chinese
story: 'I am touched by your longing for me. Even though I
am far away in the nether world, I am sad and mournful. This
is why I want to appear before you tonight.' Though not that
explicit, the wife in Hearn's story '. . . seemed as fair and
young as in *his fondest memory of her*', and '. . . she answered
him with loving gentleness, *according to his heart's desire*'. All
these expressions suggest that the ghost wife appears to

respond to the wish of the husband. They also suggest the force which makes the impossible possible, the incredible credible, the force that breaks the limits of the finite span of human life.

Biographically speaking, Lafcadio Hearn was separated from his beloved Greek mother at the age of four, when his Anglo-Irish father abandoned her. Hearn's longing for the Eternal Feminine starts from that traumatic separation. In many cases, Hearn's writing is an unconscious effort to turn the separation into a reunion. Although an agnostic, Hearn is a man of religious temperament and aspires to something beyond the finitude of life. That is the reason why his ghost stories have such an enduring charm: Hearn is a man who likes dreams so much.

Interpretations of works of literature inevitably reflect the trends of the times. The feminist interpretation of the ghost wife story is very indicative of a new trend. However, most people in East Asia still accept the word 'reconciliation' at its face value, when they read Hearn's story. If a ghost wife story is an expression of the author's heart's desire, contrary to the vocal assertion of feminist reading, Hearn's story could be considered a secret hymn in praise of his Japanese wife and of a sweet home that the American author Hearn had finally found in the Far East of pre-modern times.

* * *

PART V: FROM HEARN'S *KWAIDAN* TO SŌSEKI'S GHOST STORIES

HEARN VERSUS SŌSEKI

The person whom I am going to discuss in this last section is a Japanese who suffered terribly because of some justifiable comparisons with Lafcadio Hearn. The Japanese in question is no other than Natsume Sōseki (1867–1916), one of the greatest of modern Japanese writers.

Hearn, as is well known, was practically ousted from Tokyo University in March 1903 after nearly seven years' service. Hearn was so popular and respected by his Japanese students that they went on strike at the English Literature Department. After that unhappy incident a young unknown Japanese lecturer appeared on Monday 20 April. It was Natsume Sōseki, aged thirty-six, who until the end of the previous year had been studying in London on a government scholarship. Although Japan had been sending students abroad since the 1860s, they were selected from students specializing in practical fields such as science, engineering, medicine and law. It was only from the year 1900 that the Japanese government began to send abroad specialists in foreign literature, and Sōseki was the first Japanese English Literature scholar sent to England. At that time the education policy was to replace Western professors with newly returned Japanese scholars. It was an inevitable process of nationalization of higher education in an independent country.

Although Hearn already had Japanese citizenship and the Japanese name of Koizumi Yakumo, he had still been exceptionally well treated as a Westerner, and the financial burden was considerable. With Hearn's pay Tokyo University could hire not only Sōseki, but also Ueda Bin and a Western part-time lecturer as well. However, no Japanese professor could have been well received by Imperial University students, if he replaced such a highly esteemed professor as Hearn. There followed inevitably a sharp antagonism between Professor Natsume Sōseki and the students. Sōseki was the typical Japanese male who never talked about public matters with his wife. However, at that time, after two months of lecturing, Sōseki confessed to his wife Kyōko that he would submit his resignation, being unable to give satisfactory lectures to his students. The fact is that Sōseki or any other person who sat in Hearn's chair was unlucky.

Dissatisfied with his academic job because of this first bitter experience, Sōseki four years later quit the University to become a professional writer. He quickly rose to fame and in his novel *Sanshiro* written in 1908 we see the name of Koizumi Sensei appear quite often, as the novel deals with the life of a university student in Tokyo. However, what seems most strange is the following fictional 'newspaper article' inserted in chapter XI. It says:

Heretofore, the University's programs in Foreign Literature had been in the charge of foreign professors, upon whom had devolved all teaching duties. But now, at long last, in response to the march of time and the demands of many students, the lectures of a Japanese were to be recognized among the compulsory courses. A search for an appropriate individual had been under way for some time, and the announcement of a decision in favor of one Mr So-and-so was to be made shortly. This particular man was an outstanding scholar who, until recently, had been studying abroad under orders from the government, and his appointment was no doubt most fitting.[20]

Though this is fiction, it is fairly evident that the Mr So-and-so in question is Natsume Sōseki himself, and though this newspaper article is set in a fictional story, it goes too far to say that the appointment of a new Japanese lecturer is going to be made 'in response to the demands of many students'. Historically speaking, it was against the demands of many students that Sōseki was appointed. How was it possible for Sōseki to write such a glaring lie even if it was in a novel? Was the writer Sōseki so self-conceited?

SŌSEKI'S 'TEN NIGHTS OF DREAM'

The question is puzzling, and the answer seems to lie in Sōseki's having written *Ten Nights of Dream* in the summer of 1908, just before serializing his novel *Sanshiro* in the *Asahi* newspaper. *Ten Nights of Dream* contains ghost stories in a modernized form. Sōseki was a man of Edo culture by birth and was familiar with ghost story narration. It is conceivable that, when asked to write ten short stories for ten consecutive issues of the *Osaka Asahi* newspaper from 25 July to 5 August – the best season for ghost story-telling in Japan – Sōseki wrote *Ten Nights of Dream*, partly to compete with Hearn's *Kwaidan*. Indeed, the similarity of the theme of Sōseki's 'Third Night' with Hearn's Izumo legend of Mochida-no-ura retold in his travel essay 'By the Japanese Sea' – theme of an abandoned child's relationship with his father – has already been noticed.[21] Let us compare, this time, Sōseki's 'First Night' with 'The Story of O-Tei' collected in Hearn's *Kwaidan*. 'The First Night' begins this way:[22]

I dreamt.

I was sitting by the bedside, with my arms folded, when the woman lying there on her back quietly remarked that she would die now. She lay with her soft-profiled oval face framed by her long hair spread out upon the pillow. The depth of her white cheeks was moderately tinged with the warm hue of blood; and the lips, of course, were red. No sign whatever of a dying person. Yet, in so calm a voice, the woman had distinctly said that she was dying. I, too, felt that perhaps she might indeed die. So, bending over and looking directly into her face, I asked 'Really? You're dying?' The woman opened her eyes wide as she answered that of course she was dying. They were large moistened eyes and their centres, surrounded by long eyelashes, were an entire jet-black. Vividly, at the bottom of those jet-black pupils, an image of myself appeared.

Noting the utter luster of those black eyes, eyes so deep as to be almost transparent, I wondered how she could possibly be dying. So, carefully lowering my mouth beside the pillow, I said again 'You aren't dying, surely are you?' To this the woman, with her voice still quiet and her black eyes held half-sleepily wide open, told me again that she was dying; that it couldn't be helped. . .

After a little while the woman spoke again.

'When I am dead, please bury me. Dig a hole with a large shell. . . Then, by the graveside, wait for me. I'll come to you again.'

The man asks her when she will come and see him. The woman says with resolution: 'Wait for me a hundred years. . . For, without fail, I'll come again to see you.' Her eyes began to flow, tears fall down her cheeks and she is already dead.

COMPARISON WITH HEARN'S STORY OF O-TEI

In 'The Story of O-Tei' Hearn's story begins also with the heroine's death-bed scene. O-Tei in her fifteenth year was stricken by a fatal consumption. When she became aware that she must die, she sent for Nagao, her betrothed, to bid him farewell. As he knelt at her bedside, she said to him:—

'Nagao-sama, my betrothed, we were promised to each other from the time of our childhood; and we were to have been married at the end of this year. But now I am going to die; – the gods know what is best for us. If I were able to live for some years longer, I could only continue to be a cause of trouble and grief to others. . . I am quite resigned to die; and I want you to promise that you will not grieve. . . Besides, I want to tell you that I think we shall meet again.'. . .

When Nagao says that they'll meet again in the Pure Land, she responds softly:

'Nay, nay! . . . I meant not the Pure Land. I believe that we are destined to meet again in this world, – although I shall be buried tomorrow.'

She then asks him to wait for her to be born a girl again and to grow up to womanhood. Eager to soothe her dying moments, Nagao promises to wait for her. She says: 'If you be not unwilling to receive me, I shall be able to come back to you.' She then ceases to speak. O-Tei is dead.

Both stories have common structural patterns: a man is sent for by a woman in her dying hour. She is conscious of her imminent death and tells him that she is going to die. She is quite resigned. When he seeks to console her by tender words, she asks him to wait for her in this world. The man answers in the affirmative; then, closing her eyes, the woman dies. The man then waits; the image of the woman becomes dim, and the years go by. When all hope seems vain, quite unexpectedly he recognizes her in her new form. The moment of the reunion is of course the happy end of both stories. The moment of that meeting is told by Ishikawa Kōsai in his *Yasōkidan*, which is Hearn's original story. Nagao finds in a village-inn at Ikao a young girl who strangely resembles O-Tei. When he speaks to her, she responds in the unforgotten voice of the dead girl; and when he questions her, she makes the following answer:

My name is O-Tei; and you are Nagao, my promised husband. Seventeen years ago, I died: then you made in writing a promise to marry me if ever I could come back to this world in the body of a woman. . . And therefore I came back.'
As she uttered these last words, she fell unconscious.

And here follows Hearn's succinct ending which is much finer than Ishikawa Kōsai's lengthy ending, which explains all the domestic complications.

> Nagao married her; and the marriage was a happy one. But at no time afterwards could she remember what she had told him in answer to his question at Ikao: neither could she remember anything of her previous existence. The recollection of the former birth, – mysteriously kindled in the moment of that meeting, – had again become obscured, and so thereafter remained.

'The Story of O-Tei' was published in 1904, the year of Hearn's death. *Ten Nights of Dream* were written four years later in 1908. At least three of Sōseki's 'dreams' have some resemblance to Hearn's ghost stories. Although the plot is quite similar, 'The First Night' gives us, however, an impression very different from 'The Story of O-Tei'. Let us check the differences: Hearn's story is told objectively in the third person, while Sōseki's story is told more subjectively by the first person 'I'. The relationship between the man and the woman is very clear in 'The Story of O-Tei', as Nagao and O-Tei are betrothed and there is a tender affection between them, while we do not know what sort of relationship exists between the man and the dying woman in Sōseki's 'Dream'. Hearn's Nagao listens gently to what O-Tei says in the last moment of her life, while Sōseki's 'I' was sitting by the bedside, with his arms folded. I am wondering if there is any sensible person who, bending over and looking directly into a sick person's face, could ask 'Really? You're dying?' Moreover, Sōseki's woman here is so beautiful that we are unable to imagine that she is dying and, we should add, there is no truly sad feeling. The anonymous woman in Sōseki's story is more like a pre-Raphaelite woman posing as dying in a colourful oil-painting. In fact, the impression we get from Sōseki's 'Dream' is the picturesque quality of the scene. When we look at a dying woman in a painting, we do not feel any particular sadness; that is the case with Sōseki's beautiful woman.

In Hearn's story, apart from the miracle of O-Tei's rebirth in another woman's body, everything is realistic; while there is a strong element of the surreal in Sōseki's story. Let us consider the time sequence. In Hearn's story, except for the miraculous re-birth, all events are biologically possible: a young man of nineteen can wait seventeen years to marry a young girl of sixteen. On the contrary, it is unrealistic and biologically impossible for a human being to wait a hundred years or, as is the case with Sōseki's 'Third Night of Dream', to be responsible for a crime committed a hundred years ago. Sōseki's man and woman are not only beyond ordinary human nature in their expectations but also beyond ordinary human feelings. Contrary to the tender affection existing between Nagao and O-Tei, there is no human warmth between Sōseki's man and woman. Professor Denise Brahimi explains in her introduction to the new French translation of *Kwaidan*[23] that one of Hearn's motivations in retelling Japanese legends such as 'The Story of O-Tei' is the problem of the relationship with the former Self (le problème du rapport au Moi antérieur). This is most plausible, and I would say this problem has something to do with Hearn's inner wish to meet again his separated mother. In this kind of evocation of a dear dead woman Hearn shares common tastes with Edgar Allan Poe whose works he appreciates very much.

SŌSEKI'S LONGING FOR A WORLD OF LIGHT WITHOUT HUMAN PASSION

In Sōseki's case what the author, who was a child abandoned by his father just like Lafcadio, longs for, is going into a world of light without human passion (goyoku-shichijō o shari-shita betsutenchi), another world exempt from all human vexations whatsoever. Let us examine how the man waits for this blissful state of salvation.

> I sat down. . . Thinking that I would be waiting thus for a hundred years, I sat there watching the round stone on the grave; . . . with my arms folded. By and by the sun came up from the east as the woman had foretold. It was a big red sun. And, eventually, . . . that big red sun went down into the west. . . I counted 'One'.[24]

It is almost Samuel Becket, waiting not for Godot, but for

the dead woman to come back. However, what is presupposed in Sōseki's 'Dream' does not belong to the real earthly world of common sense. As her coming back is settled as almost self-evident for the man, he is waiting. The man comes near to the world of common sense only once when he begins to have doubts: 'In the end, watching the mosses crawling over the grave stone, I came to think the woman must have fooled me.' It is human to have doubts. However, he is mistaken. Just at that moment she reappears. Let us read Sōseki's ending, which is very different from Hearn's:

> Then, from under the stone a blue stem. . . grew toward me. . . till it reached my sitting chest-height. The next moment a slender bud, whose head bent lightly from the tip of that gracefully swaying stalk, opened its petals soft and full. Right in front of my nose the pure white lily poured its scent to drench my very bones. Then, as dew dropped from far high distances, the flower gentled to and fro, swayed by its own white weight. I thrust my neck forward and kissed those pallid petals from which a cold dew dripped. As I drew my face back from the lily, I happened to glance up at the far-off sky; where a single star was twinkling.
>
> And only then, then for the first time, did I realize that the hundredth year had come.[25]

Sōseki's ideal world is, as symbolized by the white lily, vegetative. His world in 'The First Night of Dream' is beautiful; it is even charged with sexuality, but it still is without warm passion. In his philosophy Sōseki is very Oriental and wishes to be cut loose from the ties of the earthly life. Although this piece is highly appreciated by many critics, I am not able to understand it sympathetically. However, what is interesting technically is that Sōseki has become a word painter using many colours, while Hearn, the former word painter of the impressionistic school, has become very sober towards the end of his life. The Japanese writer Sōseki, under Western influence, has become a colourist, using many Chinese characters with *me-hen* (whose left-hand radical means 'eye'), while the American writer Hearn, under Oriental influence, has become very monochromatic like *sumie* painters in black and white.

It is up to readers to decide which of these two stories they prefer. However, one thing is certain. Sōseki, by the production of these ghost stories in modernized form and by that of long novels such as Hearn had never achieved, regained confidence as a creative artist. In the summer of 1908, Sōseki himself must have judged his *Ten Nights of Dream* better written than his predecessor's *Kwaidan*. Until the year before, even while writing novels, Sōseki continually attacked academics for their intellectual vanity, as is conspicuously the case with *Gubijin-sō*. From the Autumn of 1908 Sōseki all of a sudden felt free to write about the Tokyo University he had once abhorred. In *Sanshiro*, which he began to serialize from September 1908, Sōseki not only described student life but also referred to Hearn by his Japanese name Koizumi Yakumo Sensei, and Sōseki's tone is very favourable towards him. Sōseki was so secure in himself as to insert the fictionalized newspaper article which we have quoted at the beginning of Part V. Indeed, Sōseki in the 41st year of Meiji was the most in demand and the most popular writer among the Japanese, especially among university students. In that year Sōseki was offered a lectureship at Kyoto University which he declined. Sōseki was approached by the Tokyo University authorities to come back to the Literature Department. He of course declined the offer. If we take into consideration all these aftermaths, the appointment in the year 1903 of the then little known Natsume So-and-so as successor to Lafcadio Hearn seems to have been not a bad choice; and although Dean Inoue Tetsujirō's handling of the matter was not very tactful with regard to Hearn, in the long run the replacement of Koizumi Sensei by Natsume Sōseki seems to be justifiable.

2

HEARN AND JAPAN: AN ATTEMPT AT INTERPRETATION

Earl Miner

SOME PROBLEMS IN UNDERSTANDING HEARN

The importance of Japan to Hearn and of Hearn to Japan may be so evident that there seems little finally to interpret. What he has written[1] or, indeed, what has been written about him show that 'Hearn and Japan' are inseparable topics. Yet it seems generally agreed that a century after his arrival to teach in Matsue fresh assessments seem desirable.

There are some problems. The chief one involves the essential issue, which I shall be raising in various guises: just who is this author about Japan? The Japan that Hearn knew and the Hearn who knew Japan have been set into contexts by various scholars. Some examples. About a quarter of a century ago, Beongcheon Yu presented a full and serious study, *An Ape of Gods: The Art and Thought of Lafcadio Hearn.*[2] More recently, Hearn has been discussed as a thinker and writer by Hirakawa Sukehiro.[3] From time to time there appear English selections of Hearn's works. In 1977 there appeared *The Buddhist Writings of Lafcadio Hearn.*[4] More recently, Francis King has chosen and edited just over thirty pieces by Hearn.[5] Japanese scholars have also been productive in examining the wider context of Hearn and what he represents. Murakata Akiko has recovered large portions of the papers of Ernest Fenellosa, and Kodama Sanehide has examined relations between Japan and American poets.[6] In spite of, or perhaps because of our perplexities, Hearn seems to have an importance that requires recognition.

HEARN'S ROLE

To define his importance with any confidence, we should alter our question: What role did Hearn play? This raises simple but fundamental questions that comparatists have largely ignored. We tend to assume that there is Country A and Country B, there are Poet 1 and Poet 2, and there is influence. This logic implies a syntax consisting of proper nouns but lacking verbs other than an implied 'happens'. Nothing just happens. I am a subscriber to the fallacy of a single explanation: in human affairs more than one cause always operates, and more than one reason must therefore be given. But by the same token, the individual causes should be identified as far as possible instead of labelling multidimensional events with a single term like 'influence'. Especially if we take influence to mean the pattern of Freudian anxiety posited by Harold Bloom's model. The idea that Hearn dreaded the influence of Japanese predecessors is not worth rational opposition.[7] Moreover, circumstances a century ago were different from circumstances today, and therefore any satisfactory account must include historical considerations.

There seem to be three basic roles necessary to intercultural relations. One is the dual authorial connection, including both the transmitting author or authors and the receiving author or authors. In 1890, so little was known by Western readers about individual Japanese authors that the connection could not exist. It is significant that at that time the dominant authorial connection – if indeed it can be called so – was between Japanese woodblock print-makers and the ceramic artists and Western painters or writers who included references to those arts as subject matter in poems and novels. As is well known, Zola, Van Gogh, and particularly Whistler were greatly taken by the woodblock prints.[8] Only later did

Westerners gain a sense of individual literary artists – Bashō or Akutagawa, for example. During Hearn's earlier years in Japan, there might be Western receiving authors or artists, but there were no known transmitting Japanese authors or artists. A second important role is that of the describer and explainer. Contrary to what many people think today, *nihonjinron* is not a modern invention. In full-blown form it was invented – if not by the *Kojiki* – by *kokugakusha* like Norinaga, but even before *kokugaku* appeared, Jesuits and Dutch traders sought to describe, to explain Japan to Europe. In Hearn's time, by far the most learned of such people was Basil Hall Chamberlain, author of *Things Japanese*, and, as the title page for the second edition in 1891 puts it, 'Emeritus Professor of Japanese and Philology in the Imperial University of Japan'. Chamberlain had an excellent command of Japanese at a time when there were none of today's many aids to a foreigner seeking to learn Japanese and study Japan. It is little wonder that Western historians esteem Chamberlain more than any other foreigner of the time precisely for his knowledge and his ability to use it to describe and explain.

The third role is that of intermediary or go-between. The familiar and conspicuous example of this role is Fenellosa. His papers were passed on to Pound about a quarter of a century after Hearn arrived in Matsue and had the greatest specifiable literary impact of any intermediary. Of course to be accurate, we must say the 'Fenellosa' here means the Japanese he consulted as well as the man himself.

Clearly, these three roles are not necessarily distinct ones. Years ago when I was doing the investigations for my little book on *The Japanese Tradition*, I was baffled to understand how Pound had come to know the story of the play *Hagoromo*. Only years later did I discover that Chamberlain had offered a translation in the 'Theatre' section of *Things Japanese*.[9] Only recently have I learned that Pound also had in his possession a still unpublished Fenellosa version of *Hagoromo*.[10] Why he did not adapt it for publication remains unclear. Could it be that he was forestalled by Chamberlain?

This discussion of three roles relates to Hearn, because (in my opinion at least) he played his own versions of all three. To substantiate the claim, we may consider the roles in reverse order. Without question, Hearn was an intermediary of a high order. So high, in fact, that he was almost more a tutelary spirit than an actual intermediary. People who read Hearn knew that they had drunk from the pure spring of Japanese life, even if they were apt to be very hazy indeed as to just what they had gained from Hearn. Working on *The Japanese Tradition*, I wrote to a number of authors about the sources of their knowledge of Japanese literature, art, or other features of life. John Gould Fletcher's reply perfectly summarizes the sense of many of the time: 'I recall reading *haiku* in Lafcadio Hearn's translation (not very exact), also in Basil Hall Chamberlain's book on Japanese poetry.'[11] One really cannot learn about haiku, much less haikai, from Hearn. Fletcher seems to have had in mind the 'Poetry' entry in Chamberlain's *Things Japanese*, or perhaps even W.G. Aston's *History of Japanese Literature*. But Fletcher's point really holds in a special sense. When people thought of sources for their knowledge of Japan and its culture, the first name to come to mind was 'Lafcadio Hearn . . . (not very exact)', and the second was Chamberlain. Hearn was successful in imparting the assurance that his works offered very comprehensively what one needed to know about Japan. Perhaps the details were 'not very exact', but the spirit was present even if the letter was lacking.

In other words, as an intermediary, Hearn combines the functions of the explainer. In Fletcher's spirit one may say that if a Chamberlain or Aston were the source for one's specific knowledge of haiku, Hearn nonetheless made it possible for a Western reader to understand what the haiku mind was like. Although his readers seem to feel that Hearn was almost ethereal, he himself was quite down to earth about his writings. At the end of the preface to *Glimpses of Unfamiliar Japan*, he writes:

> Of the twenty-seven sketches composing these [two] volumes, four were originally purchased by various newspaper syndicates, and reappear in considerably altered form, and six were published in the *Atlantic Monthly* (1891–93). The remainder, forming the bulk of the work, are new.[12]

The different pieces average about twenty-five pages in length, and one can well believe that Hearn expanded on those he had written for newspapers. It is perhaps more to the point that in these first works published after arriving in Japan the recurrent topic is not so much *Japanese life* (as that phrase is usually understood) as Japanese religion, spirits, and death.

PLACING HEARN AS A WRITER

I wish to argue that in addition to his roles as explainer and intermediary, Hearn also played a role as a literary rather than scholarly or journalistic author. That is, although his role as an author included and was coloured by his functions as explainer and intermediary, we still read him today because he transcended those other roles and became a poet.

That proposition is probably easily accepted until one tries to describe the kind of poet Hearn was. He was not so much a retranslator as a transferer of Japanese stories.[13] As we have seen, Hearn speaks of his individual pieces as sketches.[14] It is a just if modest term, meaning 'A brief account, description, or narrative . . . ; a short or superficial essay or study' (*Oxford English Dictionary*, 2). Since in these early sketches the nature of Hearn's art is the more visible for being less elaborated, it is worth a look at the fifteenth sketch in *Glimpses of Unfamiliar Japan*. 'Kitsune' itself consists of fifteen parts of the lore of foxes in Japan. The first three sections give local and historical background. There follow sections treating stories Hearn picked up – no doubt by questioning – in Matsue as well as from written sources. There is for example a letter to a fox spirit attributed to Hideyoshi (*Writings*, 1, 368–69) and a recollection of Ikku's *Hizakurige* (387–88). Other sections (e.g., x, xi, xiii, xiv) are so mixed that they are difficult to characterize except as small versions of the mixture of the whole.

Hearn clearly sought to evoke by power of style what his titles proclaim: *Glimpses of Unfamiliar Japan*, *Gleanings in Buddha-Fields*, *Exotics and Retrospectives*, *In Ghostly Japan*, *Shadowings*, and others of similar name and nature. It was as important to him as to his readers that the mystery of Japan be manifested. Hearn tried his hand at explaining often enough, but the artist in him sought to *create* rather than explain the 'unfamiliar' and 'ghostly'. This side of Hearn is the rich, mysterious side, Victorian *yūgen*, so to speak. As Rexroth puts it, 'He was certainly one of the masters of the Stevensonian style' (p. xi). But perhaps Basil Hall Chamberlain – who had nothing of the unfamiliar or ghostly about him – was a bit more to the point than Rexroth. In praising one of Hearn's early works, he says:

> Of course the style is too ornamental for every day use; but then we do not spend every day playing at *dolce far niente* under tropical suns. The impression – the taste left in my mouth by your wonderful descriptions is like that of some luscious fruit or triumph of confectionery, which, –though one could not live on it altogether, –appropriately graces a royal or a wedding table.[15]

And he concludes: 'I would not have you lightly throw away that magic which you know so well how to wield' (ibid.).

Chamberlain seemed to feel that Hearn's style was at once far too 'ornamental' and yet part of what made Hearn's writings what they were. Hearn himself is reported writing to the Tokyo professor in 1893:

> After four years of studying poetical prose, I am forced now to study simplicity. After attempting the utmost at ornamentation, I am converted by my own mistakes. The great point is to touch with simple words.[16]

Hearn is simple in the complex Victorian sense of needing to believe what he wrote. He did his best not to pretend in his writings. His style is the same as his often repeated theme: the real, the true Japan is to be found in the common people, not in the rich and powerful. With this democratic or folk standard there went another, more conservative, nostalgic one caught by two further titles among his works. Value is to be found in the Japanese 'kokoro' (the mind or spirit); it is to be found not in the up-to-date materialism drawn from the West but in 'kottō': in the antique, in curios. Japanese have believed these things for centuries, precisely because the ideals are superior to the reality.

HEARN VS. CHAMBERLAIN

Sooner or later, Japanese show what they are by taking a

decision – in the cases of the *junshi* (suicide to accompany
one's master in death) of General Nogi and his wife, and of the
seppuku of Mishima Yukio. I suggest that foreigners show what
they are in a choice between Basil Hall Chamberlain and
Lafcadio Hearn. Anybody can recognize the claims for
Chamberlain. His knowledge of Japan was far superior to
Hearn's in many ways. The ways include the language, which
Chamberlain really spoke, read, and wrote well. He knew
Japanese history, too. Chamberlain was one of the few early
giants of Japanese study and, unlike Hearn, he would be hired
again today by the University of Tokyo.

Chamberlain does have the qualifications, ranging from the
scholarly achievement of his translation of the *Kojiki* to his still
fascinating compilation, *Things Japanese*, which went through
so many editions and some changes. Historians and those of us
in search of solid information will be well advised to turn to
Chamberlain rather than to Hearn. For that matter, there are
better sources to learn about Japanese folk-tales than Hearn. At
least, he seems scarcely aware of the widely variant accounts of
Urashima Tarō.[17]

Yet I confess to prefer Hearn. Chamberlain was smart and
had the facts at his fingertips, but by comparison with Hearn
he was a man of hands and fingertips rather than of heart. We
can judge the two men by their use of that crucial term of
difference, 'oriental'. Hearn uses the term at times to suggest a
barrier to a Westerner's understanding. When a Westerner
talks with Japanese, 'the Oriental auditors' do not understand
what is so important in what we say, and we are led 'by our
own Occidental experiences' to misjudge the Japanese.[18]
Again, in describing the reactions of his Kumamoto students
to Western stories, he reports that 'Some particularly Oriental
sentiments were occasionally drawn out through discussions'
(*Writings*, 7, 39). 'Oriental' clearly designates responses
different from what might be expected in England or America.

Chamberlain's more negative view of Japan emerges clearly
in his comments on the Japanese arts. Here he is speaking of *nō*:

> [The high-class] audience come, not merely to be amused, but
> to learn, and they follow the play, book in hand; for the
> language used, though beautiful, is ancient and hard of

comprehension, especially when chanted. The music is – well, it is Oriental. Nevertheless, when due allowance has been made for Orientalism and for antiquity, it possesses a certain weird charm.[19]

Looking for 'Sculpture', one is referred to 'Carving', in which '. . . the strength of the Japanese lies rather in decoration and small things than in presentation and in great things' (84). As for painting by the Sesshūs and others, '. . . the circle of ideas within which . . . [they] move is too narrow for their productions to be ever likely to gain much hold on the esteem of Europe' (49). And here is what we discover from the last paragraph on Japanese literature:

> Sum total: what Japanese literature most lacks is genius. It lacks thought, logical grasp, depth, breadth, and manysidedness. It is too timorous, too narrow to compass great things. . . If Japan has given us no music, so also has she given us no immortal verse, neither do her authors atone for lack of substance by any special beauties of form. (295–96)

For some things commentary is unnecessary, and it will be plain what is involved in the choice between what I shall term the Professor Chamberlain of Tokyo and the Mr Hearn of Matsue.

INTERPRETING *JAPAN: AN ATTEMPT AT INTERPRETATION*

Hearn's *Japan: An Attempt at Interpretation* is so dominantly an account and so little a collection of sketches that it is unique in his work.[20] It must have cost him a great effort to change habits of mind, especially given so ambitious an 'attempt' to present the nature of then contemporary Japan. That was of course the time of friction leading to the later Japanese triumph of the Russo-Japanese War. In some respects, Hearn's account is simple or at least clearly understandable. It is rather what motives and emphases direct that clarity which may cause debate among us.

Everyone can see that one matter stands out remarkably, differentiating Hearn's account of a modernizing Japan from every other one I know of, written then or since. That feature is the extraordinary emphasis on religion. There are twenty-

two unnumbered chapters, or twenty if one does not include
the initial three or four pages on 'Difficulties' and the lengthier
closing 'Reflections'. The titles of ten of the main chapters
plainly designates religion as the emphasis, but it can be agreed
by all readers that every chapter concerns religion to some
degree or other.[21]

Obviously, Hearn felt that religion was the key to
understanding Japan. Less obviously, but equally importantly, his assumptions about historical reality are intellectualist
in the sense of Geistesgeschichte or l'esprit du temps. That is,
thought or spirit determines reality. It is not materialism or
economic determinism that his historical account relies upon.
This emphasis is the more remarkable, because Hearn makes
no personal commitment to religion. This reluctance to affirm
religion personally is explicit only in the case of Christianity.
There is a chapter on 'The Jesuit Peril', and his closing
'Reflections' reject modern missionary activity.

> With the return of all Europe to militant conditions, there
> has set in a vast ecclesiastical revival of which the menace to
> human liberty is unmistakable; the spirit of the Middle Ages
> threatens to prevail again; and anti-semitism has actually
> become a factor in the politics of three Continental
> powers... Never will the East turn Christian while
> dogmatism requires the convert to deny his ancient
> obligation to the family, the community, and the govern-
> ment–and further insists that he prove his zeal for an alien
> creed by destroying the tablets of his ancestors, and outraging
> the memory of those who gave him life.[22]

The questions arise when we consider the nature of the
alternatives to Christianity that Hearn sought, the relations
between the alternatives, and in short Hearn's conception not
only of Japan but also of himself in relation to Japan and his
native Western traditions.

'The real religion of Japan,' Hearn wrote, 'is that cult which
has been the foundation of all civilized religion, and of all
civilized society–ancestor worship' (*Japan*, 22). Three questions arise. First, how does Hearn show that ancestor worship
dominates Japanese religion? Second, can Hearn mean that
ancestor worship is or should be the basis of European society?
Third, how can he justify this seemingly primitive belief by

modern thought? There is a final issue: placing Hearn in all this. Hearn has essentially two proofs that ancestor worship dominates Japanese religion. One may be termed historical. His history relates to two main stages, Shinto and Buddhist. The Shinto version takes three forms: 'Domestic' 'worship of family ancestors' , 'Communal' 'worship of clan or tribal ancestors', and 'State' 'worship of imperial ancestors' (*Japan*, 22). This outline is elaborated at considerable length. Buddhism is treated second, because its entry into Japan can be more or less dated, whereas the origins of Shinto are lost in prehistory. Buddhism is of two kinds, the popular (pp. 174–95) and 'The Higher Buddhism' (196–216).

In a sense, Hearn answers all three questions by recourse to the ideas of Herbert Spencer, 'the wisest man in the world' (444). Spencer held that ancestor worship is 'the root of all religions' (25), making Shinto a kind of pristine faith. 'The Higher Buddhism' in turn is wholly compatible, Hearn argues, with the Spencerian doctrine of evolution.[23]

There is no doubt that Hearn has deeply pondered his issues, but there is also genuine question whether his answers can necessarily be ours almost a century later. For one thing, given the importance attached to ancestor worship, it is extraordinary that his index contains only two references (175, 178) to Confucianism and none to *shushigaku*. Much of what he attributed to Buddhism and especially to Shinto simply has that other source. A second problem is evident in the gap between his attachment to the beliefs of ordinary people and the connection of Spencerianism only to the 'higher Buddhism'. There is a third matter of great delicacy today. The current revival of Shinto thought comes in many guises: interest in animism, return to the simple purity of Shinto, and the sense that Shinto assumptions are characteristic and exclusive definitions of the Japanese state. Not all Japanese, or for that matter all foreigners, think the same thing about visits by high government officials to Yasukuni Jinja.

It is appropriate to recall that in 1946 Kishimoto Hideo saved Shinto and new religions such as Tenrikyō based on it by convincing the Supreme Commander for the Allied Powers (SCAP) of the distinction between shrine Shinto and state

Shinto. He argued in essence that Hearn's 'domestic' and 'communal' cults of ancestor-worship differed from 'the State Cult;– . . . the worship of imperial ancestors' (*Japan*, 22). Even here, the worship is not of the present *tennō* but of ancestors. These several distinctions are of very great importance to Japanese self-understanding and to foreign understanding of Japan. Kinds of mischief may develop on more than one side if the distinctions are not made clearly.

Towards the end of his study, Hearn changes his brighter for darker colours; words like 'constraints', 'danger', and 'peril' enter with increasing frequency. Japanese 'Coercion to which the individual is subjected' (380) more or less corresponds to kinds of ancestor-worship in origins: from socially below, from the communal, and from 'official authority' (389). Many problems are temporary, Hearn thinks, as Japan modernizes: 'Later on, no doubt, great changes will have to be made; meanwhile, much must be bravely endured' (396). Japanese society has had rapid revolutions, beginning with the opening of Japan, and followed by 'the reconstruction of society in 1871' (423). A third revolution came with 'a new oligarchy of wealth' (ibid.).

> There is every indication that, in the present order of things, the third revolution will run its course rapidly; and then a fourth revolutionary period, fraught with serious danger, would be an immediate prospect. (424)

The dangers lie within as well as without. Within, 'the absence of individual freedom in modern Japan would certainly appear to be nothing less than a national danger' (428). Using 'the applied science of the Occident', Japan has done the Western work of centuries in three decades, while 'sociologically' remaining at a stage centuries before the European Christian era (435). Hearn shifts from dangers within to those without in a single paragraph:

> I cannot resist the conviction that, when Japan yields to foreign industry the right to purchase land, she is lost beyond hope. . . Japan has incomparably more to fear from Russian or American capital than from Russian battleships and bayonets. (444)

That was written before Japanese victory in the Russo-Japanese War (1904–5). Hearn draws near an end in raising the issue of Christianizing Japan. He would accept the attempt if it were truly Christian, instead of being 'utilized by Christian nations for ends essentially opposed to the spirit of Christianity' (454). He also wrote some things that are painful to read:

> Needless to say that the aggressions of race upon race are fully in accord with the universal law of struggle–that perpetual struggle in which only the more capable survive. Inferior races must become subservient to higher races, or disappear before them. . . (454)

The implication is clear: Japan is, at least at present in 1904, an inferior race. Meanwhile, Europe and the United States are in danger of losing their superiority by virtue of 'Western religion, as hitherto conducted'.[24]

The closing vision is of Japan beset by internal dangers and outward perils. Perhaps her ability to alter so much so quickly will alleviate internal dangers. Perhaps her unity greater than that of China will preserve her from external peril. But neither hope is expressed with any degree of explicitness, and it would be equally reasonable to infer that Japan would crumble from internal danger or be destroyed by external perils. As promised, these are painful subjects to contemplate, and although there is not time to explore them, to ignore them entirely would be to falsify the man who became Koizumi Yakumo.

Who, finally, was that man? Where can we place him? It seems to me that there are two possible answers, and that it is even possible that although they seem contradictory that both may be true. One answer is that advanced by Hirakawa Sukehiro in his seventh chapter, 'Hearn's "Reversion to His Native Land"' ('Haan no "Sokoku e no Kaiki"'). In this very complex chapter, we discover a Hearn who was both Westerner and Japanese.[25] We are reminded that he was 'a literary figure solely in English' (274), and the expression '*kaiki*', strongly implies return to his Western heritage. It is worth recalling, after all, that Hearn spent only his last fourteen years in Japan, and that the circumstances of his life in

Japan subjected him to fluctuations in his attitude towards himself, Japan and the West.

Hirakawa also refers to Hearn's naturalization as a Japanese citizen (275), and a page later finds it possible to speak of Hearn's '"reversion to Japan"' ('Nihon e no kaiki') although soon thereafter he equates Hearn's native land ('sokoku') with the West (ibid.). On the next page, he speaks of the two elements in Hearn having a happy mutual influence on each other, adding the rhetorical question, 'Can we not speak of [Hearn] as a person who realized the dream of uniting East and West in his writing?' (276). On this view, there is a Western Hearn and a Japanese Koizumi who fortunately work together harmoniously, so that in the end Hearn may be said to have reverted to two native countries, Japan and the West.

I wish to present what may seem a darker portrait. Hearn's taking on a Japanese wife, name, and citizenship does not mean that any of the steps was easy. Moreover, not only were his writings in English and his Tokyo University lectures about Western literature. More than that, he had to instil in the audience of those who read him – in English – the belief that, however well he understood Japan, he described it from a position fundamentally the same as theirs. Hearn was read, and had to write to be read, as a Westerner, not as a Japanese.

At the same time, it is significant that we must speak of Hearn as a *Westerner*, not as Irish, Greek, English, or American. He has some claim to each but not a full claim to any. He was a person who had no native country to which to return. Hearn was a citizen of the world, which is to say a cosmopolitan fully at home in no country. So at least is my picture of Hearn before he went to Japan and indeed after he arrived. But there is also, I equally believe, another Hearn, the person prepared for by the man without a country, and the person who logically, if metaphorically, was ultimately reborn in Japan as Koizumi. And if in belonging to the West Hearn belonged to no single Western country, in being reborn in Japan, it was rebirth as an adult and as what may be described as only semi-Japanese.

The picture being drawn is of a man who could make full claim on no country, and that I believe was the source of Hearn's limits as well as his insights. His homelessness in the

West prepared him for Japan. The question then becomes one of what Japan meant to him. I think the best evidence is that reported from his wife, who once said to him in jest:

> 'You are not like [a] Westerner, except in regard to your nose.' Then he said. 'What shall I do with this nose? But I am a Japanese. I love Japan better than any born Japanese.'[26]
> Indeed, he loved Japan with his whole heart, but his sincere love for Japan was not very well understood by Japanese.[27]

That last clause is pregnant with meaning, 'but sincere love for Japan was not very well understood by Japanese'. By implication, Hearn is precisely not Japanese. For that matter, the same remark suggests that the speaker herself has ceased to be fully Japanese. She also became loosed from her cultural anchor, and like her husband became a ship between continents and islands. Surely there is something profoundly moving about the husband approaching Japan and the wife approaching the husband, each approaching and passing through the other like ghosts. Without questioning his love for her, the crucial thing is his love of Japan. Sympathetic readers also learn to love Japan, to weigh anchor, to fly no nation's flag, and to pass to and fro between Western continent and Japanese island. Those who succeed will often have painful thoughts about the West and Japan but retain steadfast loyalty, thinking of 'oriental' and 'occidental', if at all, in Hearn's rather than Chamberlain's terms. The would-be traveller between continent and island must pay, like Hearn, in the currency of respect for the West and love of Japan, and *vice versa*.

3

LAFCADIO HEARN: BETWEEN BRITAIN AND JAPAN

George Hughes

L afcadio Hearn has an account in one of his books of a
Japanese person who tries to take up Western ways. It is
called 'The Case of O-Dai', and was published in *A Japanese
Miscellany* in 1901. O-Dai is a young girl who goes to work
for foreign missionaries, is converted to Christianity and then
persuaded to throw the 'memorial tablets' of her ancestors
into the river. Her missionary employers, however, decide to
move on, to leave the town, and O-Dai finds that she is
ostracized by her fellow Japanese. Hearn puts what he calls
the 'universal feeling' against O-Dai into a kind of pseudo-
biblical speech:

> Against the Virtue Supreme of Filial Piety – against the religion
> of the Ancestors – against all faith and gratitude and reverence
> and duty – against the total moral experience of her race – O-
> Dai has sinned the sin that cannot be forgiven. Therefore shall
> the people account her a creature impure. . . (355–6).

She is stigmatized because of her disloyalty to her own
people. 'Like most converts of her class', Hearn tells us, 'O-
Dai was weak: the courage of her race had failed in her.' She
finally goes off to Osaka to sell herself as a prostitute. 'So
vanished forever O-Dai – flung into the furnace of a city's lust'
(385–9).

It is useful to bear this anecdote in mind, I think, when we try to assess Lafcadio Hearn's own place between Britain and Japan. Hearn tells the story of O-Dai as a warning to missionaries; but it is also the story of a person who tries to go between cultures. Hearn, like O-Dai, explored and took on the practices and thought patterns of another country. Why did he think *his case* was not the same as that of the young Japanese girl? Why did he think *he* could avoid being ostracized and stigmatized? How could he expect as a Westerner simply to enter the culture of Japan and throw off his past?

* * *

From the point of view of those of us who live in Japan it is easy to feel that Hearn was in fact successful in doing all these things; that he is quite simply the most important mediator between this country and the West. He has always had Japanese commentators and admirers: Yone Noguchi wrote soon after his death: 'We Japanese, have been regenerated by his sudden magic. . . He made us shake the old robe of bias which we wore without knowing it, and gave us a sharp sense of revival' (171). The tradition continues to this day: there are several excellent recent books on Hearn available in Japanese, particularly those by Hirakawa Sukehiro and Nishi Masahiko (and there is an interestingly controversial and more hostile account by a Japanese scholar who lives abroad, Ota Yuzo). If we go into the English language section of the Tokyo bookstores, we can also find a row of Hearn's own books still in print; the authoritative biography by Elizabeth Stevenson is still available, there is a new biography published in 1993 and at least two good recent anthologies of Hearn's work. We would get a different impression of Hearn's reputation, however, in Britain, where none of these books is likely to be available in bookshops. At an international conference in Europe in 1994, where I spoke about Hearn and some other writers, several people in the audience said they had never heard of Lafcadio Hearn (though it was a conference on literature); and even those who had heard of his work had not read it.

Well, one might say, these are people who are not interested in Japan. But again, among those who *are* interested in Japan – the famous Japanologist Donald Keene is a case in point – there is often a strong dislike and suspicion of Lafcadio Hearn. In particular we could make a substantial list of British writers who have been contemptuous and dismissive of Hearn. William Plomer, for example, says in the introduction to his book of short stories about Japan, *Paper Houses*, that he most definitely does not want to be considered a second Hearn. Hearn, he says, is 'unfortunate', 'myopic' in the fullest sense, and lacking in 'backbone' (x-xi). The novelist John Paris constructed the whole of his extremely popular 1921 novel, *Kimono*, around the idea that Hearn's version of Japan was 'narcotic smoke' (29). Wyndham Lewis quotes Hearn as an example of the worst kind of Western romantic (9), and D.J. Enright, too, dismisses Hearn in 1955, in *The World of Dew*, as 'incorrigibly romantic' (16) and 'a foreign enthusiast, attempting to deny his own blood' (65). Arthur Waley was so rude about Hearn that Kawabata Yasunari decided not to give him the manuscript Hearn notebook he had brought with him all the way from Japan (Keene 145). In some circles in Britain it must be said, Hearn represents exactly what a mediator and commentator on Japan should *not* be.

I wish to discuss Hearn between Britain and Japan, however, and the hostility of these British writers towards Hearn does not lessen my interest in him. Rather it is one of the things about Hearn that interests me very much – that makes him seem worth close analysis and study. It is odd perhaps to put Hearn between *Britain* and Japan, not just because of the hostility, but because Hearn was half Greek, half Anglo-Irish, spent his formative years in Ireland and first established himself as a writer in the United States. Some Americans discuss him as an American writer; some Irish (like his recent, fervently nationalist, biographer) hope to claim him as a true born Irishman.

There are good reasons for seeing his work in relation to French literature; and the novelist Jean Rhys writes in her autobiography that she heard of Hearn because he was the man who wrote about the West Indies (41). We might see Hearn as the archetypal déraciné; but it is also an important aspect of Hearn's reputation that so many countries feel they have a claim on him – and that such claims have limited validity. Britain is one possible starting point for a discussion of Hearn, since he was of course a British subject all his life until he changed his citizenship to that of Japan; he went to school in Britain; and Britain was the place where he wanted his books published. Hearn remains a representative figure for many British writers: when they think of writing about Japan they think somehow of Hearn.

But before we embark on a reading of Hearn between Britain and Japan we have, I think, to try to ask honestly what this means. Hearn is assumed to have moved 'between' cultures: is this really possible? One often hears it said, as in the introduction to the Tuttle editions of Hearn's work, that Hearn 'could. . . explain Japan as if he himself were Japanese'. But if that is true, whom was he explaining Japan to? Can we seriously suggest that he is between Japan and the West, if his largest audience is in Japan and his most important role is in explaining Japan to the Japanese?

★   ★   ★

We must start off I think by distinguishing between Hearn's role as mediator now, and his role as mediator between Japan and the West at the turn of the last century. There is a simple and fairly positive view that can be taken of Hearn's achievement as a writer in his own time. Hearn came to Japan in 1890, and in his first Japanese books, like *Glimpses of Unfamiliar Japan* (1894), or *Out of the East* (1897), Hearn was able to paint a picture of a rich culture in the life of rural and provincial Japan, much as his contemporaries, W.B. Yeats and J.M. Synge, were doing for Celtic culture in Ireland, or Pierre Loti was doing in Brittany for the Bretons. There was also a subtext, even in these early works, of the narrative of Hearn's own entry into the heart of Japanese culture. The same could be said for Synge and Loti, in Ireland and Brittany – but they were temporary visitors in the places they described; it was only Hearn who made the permanent gesture of really trying to enter, to stay and to become identified with a foreign culture. Hearn was interested in the ordinary life of Japanese people, in religious beliefs, superstitions and in folk culture. He thought very hard about how to introduce Japanese folk-stories to a wider audience, studying the style of writers like Rudyard Kipling and Hans Christian Andersen, in order to achieve their simplicity and popular appeal. The resulting later books, works like *Kotto* (1902) and *Kwaidan* (1904), which contained these re-told tales, seemed at the time to many Westerners to be products of an authentic journey into Japan. Hearn had become a Japanese citizen, taken the Japanese name of Koizumi Yakumo, was the father and breadwinner to a large extended Japanese family. He was to die in Japan without ever returning to the West. One of the members of the London Japan Society said at a meeting in 1902 that Hearn, though a British subject for most of his life, 'might be taken as a type of the Anglo-Japanese alliance' (VI, 123–4).

★   ★   ★

Hearn was not the first Western traveller in Japan, he was not a great linguist and not a great scholar. There are, in fact, many other authors who wrote on Japan in English in the late nineteenth century; why was Hearn so uniquely successful? Why did he draw admirers like Bernard Leach, or Edward Thomas, or J.M. Synge? I would suggest that, by the time he came to Japan, the groundwork of explanation of Japanese art had already been laid by writers such as Rutherford Alcock, Christopher Dresser, B.H. Chamberlain. But their books were all written from the outside, from the scholar/tourist's point of view. They did not have the mark of authentic inside experience about them. (Hearn's aim from the start was 'taking part in the daily existence of the common people, and *thinking with their thoughts*' [quoted in Tinker 330]). Much to his credit, he tried to accord depth to Japanese culture, to take Japanese ideas seriously. He did not, for example, see Japanese art as a matter of interesting oriental curios; he saw it shaped by an aesthetic which is important enough to challenge the Western one. Japan could, Hearn thought, if one were unprejudiced, modify almost every pre-existing sentiment.

We must not, however, suggest that Hearn was unique in what he said; it was rather that he struck a chord with many

Europeans at the time, particularly with those readers and writers of the fin de siècle who were questioning Western traditions. Moreover, although he was a Western writer, his books could function for Western readers as Japanese art objects in that great fashion for Japan that we call Japonisme. Perhaps this is most easily observed in Germany, where the Japoniste artist Emil Orlik illustrated translations of Hearn, and where Stefan Zweig, in his introduction to a translation says: 'One no longer perceives Hearn's books as written with the pen, but rather drawn with the paint-brush of the Japanese. . . While reading Hearn's novellas one has to think of the colourful wood-cuts, the greatest treasures of Japanese art. . .' (quoted in Webb 126).

There are several reasons, then, why these works by Hearn were so attractive when they were first published. Hearn's own view was: 'The difference between myself and other writers on Japan, is simply that I have become practically a Japanese' (Murray 186). No doubt he was right; but how do you become *practically* a Japanese, especially when you do not really speak or read the language? I have suggested elsewhere that the answer seems to be that becoming *practically* a Japanese for Hearn was in many ways a kind of performance. (See 'Lafcadio Hearn and the fin de siècle.') In *Glimpses of Unfamiliar Japan* he includes his diary as a teacher, describing how 'My favourite students often visit me of afternoons. They first send me their cards, to announce their presence. On being told to come in they leave their footgear on the doorstep. . .' (462). This is a fairly ordinary scene, perhaps, for a foreigner teaching in Meiji Japan. Ernest Fenollosa or Edward Morse or W.E. Griffis could have written in the same way. But Hearn draws us gradually into the scene, to introduce us to a select group from which most Europeans are excluded. The students sit on his tatami floor and talk with him: 'To sit as the Japanese do', he says, 'requires practice; and some Europeans can never acquire the habit. To acquire it, indeed, one must become accustomed to wearing Japanese costume. But once the habit of thus sitting has been formed, one finds it the most natural and easy of positions, and assumes it by preference for eating, reading, smoking, or chatting. It is not to be recommended perhaps for writing with a European

pe'n. . .' (462). Sitting on the floor, it seems, can be a 'natural'
position for Hearn, though strangely one must still 'acquire' it,
learn it. Partly one does this – or Hearn does this – by
becoming accustomed to wearing Japanese clothes. Developing new 'natural' habits in this way, wearing Japanese clothes,
is almost like experimenting with a new identity. On his
journey to Oki, Hearn says, 'Being small and dark, and dressed
like a Japanese, I excited little attention among the common
people: it seemed to them that I was only a curious-looking
Japanese from some remote part of the empire' (*Glimpses* 616).

For some contemporary readers all this seemed powerfully
authentic and convincing. Edward Thomas insisted that Hearn
had 'made himself a mirror in a manner unapproached by
other observers of foreign countries'. Indeed, he went on:

> To impute observation to his [Hearn's] maturest work is an
> insult; he had become the thing observed: he was a Japanese
> writer 'in perfect accord with the sweet glamour of Old Japan'
> (91).

We might object that even if Hearn's prose feels that way to
his readers, this is a literary effect, created in English. Has he
really been able to move between cultures? It might equally
well be claimed that he is involved in Japan in a kind of acting,
a make-believe or role playing – what a recent scholar of
Orientalism has called 'cultural transvestism' (Behdad 59). And
his performance raises again those questions with which I
started. Why was it only he who could move between
cultures. Was Hearn really able to do what O-Dai could not
do?

★   ★   ★

At one level – at the level of self-conscious role-playing –
Hearn obviously *was* able to change his cultural practices. But
we should note that like O-Dai he had also, whether he liked
it or not, become a stigmatized personality. I have mentioned
already how his work has inspired hostility among British
writers – but things go much further than that. Hearn stands
accused in many accounts of being not only misleading about
Japan but actually mad, or at least horribly decadent, or

perhaps both. Hearn's early biographer and his former friend
and doctor George M. Gould was one of the first to suggest
this. He said 'Hearn [was] atheistic, disloyal and unethical'
(192), obsessed with sexual licence and 'sensualistic porno-
graphy'. And he concluded that Hearn was a victim of a
'morbid psychology'. It is surprising how many biographers
have taken it upon themselves to suggest that Hearn was a
victim of mental disease. Nina Kennard's biography insists that
there was 'unhealthiness of mind' in Hearn, related to 'an
inherited predisposition to insanity' in his mother (16; 343).
Francis King's recent collection of Hearn's travel writing talks
of a 'mental and spiritual disintegration' and the 'worsening
mania' of Hearn's Tokyo years (14). It does not really make
much sense to say that Hearn was mad in Tokyo (though no
doubt he was unhappy and depressed at times, like most
writers). He was a hard-working teacher, a good father and
husband who managed to provide for a large family and did no
harm to himself or others. By most definitions, people who
behave in this way are not mad.

But what about the charge that Hearn was decadent? This
is more complicated to answer, since even though he
distanced himself from the decadent manifestoes, Hearn was
strongly interested in the European literary movement we
associate with the 'decadent imagination'. He believed that
Western industrial society was decadent, and was opposed to
the Victorian imperialist ethos. He felt that English Christian
moralists were against him, and he was certainly against them.
'I begin to realize', he says in a letter, borrowing Meredith's
words, 'that I "have challenged humankind"' (*Veiled Letters*
182).

And if we can say that Hearn dropped some of the tricks of
the decadent artist when he arrived in Japan, he carried others
with him. Even in his late tales he loves to recreate the kind of
gruesome effects he had so relished in his youth. There is a
wonderfully macabre story in his *Japanese Miscellany* about a
female ghost who is jealous of her husband's new wife. She
comes back from the dead and demands that her successor
leave the house and not tell her husband why. The new wife
tries to obey, but cannot. Next morning, when the husband
enters his second wife's room he finds only her corpse. 'The

head was nowhere to be seen,' Hearn says, 'and the hideous wound showed that it had not been cut off, but *torn off*.' A trail of blood leads him to the garden where he finds the head of the woman still gripped by the awful skeletal hand of the dead first wife: '. . . the fleshless right hand, though parted from the wrist still writhed;– and its fingers still gripped at the bleeding head – and tore, and mangled – as the claws of the yellow crab cling fast to a fallen fruit. . .' (206-7). The influence of the decadent 'French school of sensation' seems fairly strongly in evidence here.

Hearn could still write like this, but his everyday life was not at first sight particularly decadent in Japan. That was presumably because he had already taken a really major step in contravening the rules of Western society. He had no need of minor acts of rebellion any more, he had rejected the whole Western world in an important symbolic gesture. He had actually stepped into the world of the Orient. In the imperialist jargon of the age, he had 'gone native', abandoning the household gods of the West, attempting to be practically Japanese.

In this respect, Hearn's move to Japan has much in common with earlier moves. He follows a pattern throughout his career of fascination with the new, then panic, then the need to escape. He wishes to escape from his culture, from his language, from his former friends, from his Western clothes, from his own body. He wishes to escape into another world. One part of Hearn – the part that wrote 'The Case of O-Dai' – knows that such an escape is impossible, that you cannot give up on the culture in which you were raised and in which you communicate. But a part of him also constantly fantasizes that escape could be possible – escape into another personality, another nationality – escape into Japan.

I would suggest, then, that Hearn stands between Britain and Japan as representative of an important fin de siècle fantasy, the fantasy of entry into the Orient. Many people in Britain and Europe thought about this kind of exit into a new culture, but few people actually carried it out. Of those who did, fewer still had the skills Hearn had to defend their newfound world against the powerful and ever-present threat of Western imperialism. Hearn felt the weight of the British

Empire he had left and (unlike B.H. Chamberlain) felt the need to balance Japanese claims against the cultural hegemony and sense of superiority of the West.

Hearn, as he realized himself, has special authenticity in his writing because he has made a move between cultures; but to move in this way is also seen by many people as tantamount to being a traitor to one's own culture; it is to become a stigmatized person, not truly Japanese, not truly British, one of the marginal outsiders who inhabit cultural boundaries. I have mentioned the discussion of Hearn at the Japan Society in London in 1902: in 1917, 13 years after Hearn's death, his name came up for discussion a second time. The meeting was chaired by a Professor Longford, who had been a British consul in Tokyo when Hearn was there. Longford described how Hearn appeared to him: 'He had an awkward shambling gait, and it was sad to see him shuffling through the streets of Tokio, clinging to the shadow of the walls and steadfastly avoiding the eyes of any fellow European whom he might chance to meet' (XVI 35).

Another member also contributed to the discussion, saying that 'Hearn in later years had shown in his letters a discontent, amounting almost to persecution mania. The Japanese had probably gauged him by the small esteem in which he was held by his [own] countrymen whom he had despised, and. . . had treated him accordingly' (XVI 35). The grammar of this is complicated, but the meaning is clear enough. Hearn has done what imperialist society dreads. To use the title of a Rudyard Kipling story, he has gone 'Beyond the Pale'. These people see Hearn as Hearn saw O-Dai: *Against the Virtue Supreme of Filial Piety – against the religion of the Ancestors – against all faith and gratitude. . . [Hearn] has sinned the sin that cannot be forgiven. Therefore shall the [Japan Society of London] account [him] a creature impure.*

Hearn performs, I have been trying to suggest, an extraordinary balancing act between cultures. He symbolized in his own time, as he intended, an authentic voice speaking from Japan. But his balancing act between cultures was also always a dangerous one, difficult to perform and unstable in its results. We may admire Hearn between Britain and Japan, and may think him an important figure, but we cannot expect his reputation ever to be accepted without controversy. For some people he will always be the first great mediator; for others he will always be an inverted British (or Irish, or American) version of the case of poor O-Dai.

4

LAFCADIO HEARN AND THE FIN DE SIÈCLE

George Hughes

Given the popular accounts of Lafcadio Hearn in Japan, it would be extremely difficult to form a picture of him as a fin de siècle artist. Over the years his image has, perhaps understandably, become softened by antiquarian nostalgia; his innocence has been played up, his sophistication played down. Apart from the obvious attempts at stylish beauty in his descriptive writings, fin de siècle elements have not attracted much attention. Hearn's constant experiment, his ferocious and risky contempt for conventions, his need to transgress against widely accepted codes of behaviour – these have been marginally acknowledged or pushed out of sight; and these are what connect his work most deeply with the fin de siècle. Conservative readings have sadly neglected what is most alive about him: Hearn was a man who believed firmly that 'Morality is not shown by an unavoidable obedience to codes – indeed it's often shown in the breaking of them' (*Japanese Letters* 344). The fin de siècle is the context in which he lived, thought and wrote. And since we ourselves are living through another fin de siècle, it seems apposite to reassess him in such terms now.

Hearn has always had his admirers, but there has also always been (and to an extent remains) a sense of scandal, hostility and distrust towards him in some quarters. To place Hearn within the fin de siècle is to see how the tradition arose, and to understand some of the reasons why it continues. Hearn tried to be an artist at a time when Nordau's *Degeneration* (1895) was widely admired as an analysis of the moral sickness of the artists of the nineteenth century (though it was not admired by Hearn himself). And there is no doubt that in many minds Hearn was exactly a 'degenerate'. In his years in Japan he was also by all counts a devoted father, a faithful husband, a much loved teacher, and a thoroughly responsible citizen. Why then should he have prompted such hostile diagnoses? And why should his name still function for many commentators on Japan as a symbol of the worst kind of approach by the West to the East? One explanation – and it is the one I wish to explore further here – is that Hearn is a typical fin de siècle 'performer'. The picture of Japan his books give us is intimately bound up with his own performance within it, and his performance needs to be read, rather as commentators like Alison Hennegan have read that of Oscar Wilde in the same period. The role that Hearn performs is exactly that of the representative fin de siècle artist in Japan. He is the Occidental who self-consciously and symbolically makes the decision to cross over, or enter fully into, the Orient.

★   ★   ★

Hearn's career in Japan does not, however, start from nowhere. And his early life in America leaves us in little doubt about the fin de siècle origins of his thought. As with most English-speaking writers who are identified with the literature of this period, his intellectual influences were mainly French. This was a deliberate choice (later reinforced by Spencerian evolutionary theories which stressed the benefit of a mix of cultures.) Throughout his life Hearn maintained his enthusiasm for the renaissance of European literature that he identified with figures like Gautier, Baudelaire, Nerval, Flaubert, Loti and Maupassant. His translations of works by Gautier and Flaubert were indeed used as standard translations until fairly recently: as we might expect it was the Flaubert of *La Tentation de Saint Antoine* that interested him rather than the author of *Madame Bovary*.

In later years, Hearn liked to suggest that he had actually studied in France in his youth, though it is difficult to work out when he could have done so. If he was telling the truth it cannot have been a long stay. But mentally at least we can say that he had entered France, and he described himself as a young man who 'worshipped the French school of sensation' (*Giglampz*, quoted in Yu 299). The French suggested stylistic experiment to him, and, along with Yeats, Wilde, Swinburne and Henry James, he found a release in French thought from the heavy respectability of the English-speaking world.

As a young man, Hearn believed, he tells us, 'only in the Revoltingly Horrible or the Excruciatingly Beautiful'. In his journalistic career in Cincinnati he said of himself that he 'revelled in thrusting a reeking mixture of bones, blood and hair under other people's noses at breakfast time. To produce qualms in the stomachs of other people afford[ed] him special delight' (Yu 299). His most famous piece of journalism from this period concerns a gruesome murder in a tan-yard in Cincinnati. The body had been placed in a furnace and become 'a hideous adhesion of half-molten flesh' (Mordell 29–47). Hearn describes - in repellent and fascinating detail – the sensation of actually touching the corpse of the murder victim.

> The skull had burst like a shell in the fierce furnace heat, and the whole upper portion seemed as though it had been blown out by the steam from the boiling and bubbling brains. . . The brain had all boiled away, save a small waste lump at the base of the skull about the size of a lemon. It was crisped and still warm to the touch. On pushing the finger through the crisp, the interior felt about the consistency of banana fruit.

All the resources of Hearn's imagery are used here (as a 'decadent' style typically uses them) to make extraordinary sensations vivid and perversely attractive: conventional attention to the moral and social context is defiantly suppressed. Hearn's focus is not seriously on the implications of the crime that has been committed, but on a sensory world that seems more real than morality, on what it feels like to push his finger past the 'crisp' or 'crisped' skull into the brain reduced to 'the consistency of banana fruit'.

This sensationalist piece of American journalism, we may suggest, owes not a little to Hearn's enthusiastic reading in French. Hearn talks elsewhere of the 'fantastic cynicism and obscene truth' as well as the 'beauties of weird thought' with which Baudelaire could describe death and vice (*Essays* 59). He mentions in particular Baudelaire's poem 'Une Charogne', which describes a corpse seen by the wayside in grotesque detail:

> Les jambes en l'air, comme une femme lubrique,
> Brulante et suant les poisons. . .
>
> Le soleil rayonnait sur cette pourriture,
> Comme afin de la cuire à point. . .
>
> Les mouches bourdonnaient sur ce ventre putride,
> D'où sortaient de noirs bataillons
> De larves, qui coulaient comme un épais liquide. . .
>
> (legs in the air, like a whore – displayed,
> indifferent to the last. . .
>
> The sun lit up that rottenness
> as though to roast it through. . .
>
> Flies kept humming over the guts
> from which a gleaming clot
> of maggots poured. . . [Trans. Richard Howard])

Baudelaire's style, Hearn says, has 'a strange sensualism. . . something quite exotic and new' (*On Art* 428). Along with Baudelaire it might also be suggested that Hearn had been reading Edgar Allan Poe. (And, appropriately for a writer of the fin de siècle, he admired Baudelaire's translation of Poe.) W.B. Yeats talked in the 1890s of Edgar Allan Poe's wine cup and its mood which 'passed into France and took possession of Baudelaire, and from Baudelaire passed to England and the Pre-Raphaelites, and then again returned to France, and still wanders the world, enlarging its power as it goes' (*Secret Rose* 143–4 n). Through Hearn it seems to have reached Cincinnati.

To indicate in this way the sources of Hearn's style is not, however, to denigrate his work. He has transferred literary techniques to a different scene and in a different context; and he has done so quite deliberately, as a challenge to the limits of acceptable American journalism.

★ ★ ★

It was not the idea of the refined aesthete, of the artist who withdraws from the world in search for beauty, that attracted Hearn in the fin de siècle aesthetic. His version of the artist is a figure who despises what he called the 'ridiculous and *moral*' in modern society, and is committed to an experimental attitude towards life. He planned a book with his friend Krehbiel in which 'Everything should be perfectly monstrous.' The aim was 'to plot together to outrage the public' (qutd. in Murray 6). The search for beauty was part of a wider challenge to the priorities, leading away from convention and into unknown territory.

Much of Hearn's early work in the United States thus betrays a fascination with abnormal or extravagant experience. He leads his readers to places where, as middle-class respectable citizens, they dare not go by themselves. In the Cincinnati slaughterhouse he drinks the fresh blood of animals and tells his readers what it tastes like. He describes opium dens, pauper graveyards, the world of the prostitute, of the poor, of mediums and crooked spiritualists – fringe and outcast life in general. And behind what he describes is always the suggestion that we should enter the scene prepared to imagine what it feels like, restraining our tendency to moralise.

Transgression of conventional boundaries for Hearn is more than a simple literary exercise: in some degree he also lived what he wrote. His most significant gesture of this period was undoubtedly his marriage to Mattie Foley in 1874 – the Jeanne Duval to his Baudelaire. He chose to marry a person of colour, the daughter of a slave, although he knew quite well that Cincinnati had a law against miscegenation, and that his marriage (which could not be carried out in public) would be an offence against the law. It would also offend the racial prejudices of many people around him. In the event, he proved incapable of sustaining the relationship. But 'the lower she falls,' he said of Mattie, 'the fonder I feel of her' (*Veiled*

Letters 129). His letters of the period reflect a strong sense of
guilt and confusion over what has become of Mattie, but no
regret that he has contravened the law. He left Cincinnati for
the more French (and therefore for him more attractive)
atmosphere of New Orleans. Here he could certainly not
expect to escape from racism – but he could indulge a taste for
the hothouse atmosphere of dying Francophone communities
in the world of the post-bellum South.

★   ★   ★

Hearn's early career, then, conforms to at least one picture of
the fin de siècle artist. He is not addicted to drugs or excited
by homosexuality, but he treats his life as an experiment; he
pledges himself 'to the worship of the Odd, the Queer, the
Strange, the Exotic, the Monstrous, (*Letters* I 328). In his spare
time from journalism he produces works like *Stray Leaves From
Strange Literature* (1884), or *Some Chinese Ghosts* (1887). He
develops a new more impressionistic style to describe the
South in 'dreams of a tropical city' – pieces that were later to
be published as *Fantastics and Other Fancies* (1914).

The open sensationalism of his early work is gradually
dropped in his later career, and his stylistic models change
(Pierre Loti and finally Kipling become more important to
him than Baudelaire), but the fundamental attitudes remain
interestingly intact. He continued to admire the forerunners
of decadence rather than those later French writers who were
explicitly decadent and were concerned to establish a theory
of decadence. In the 1890s he was still, however, prepared to
spend considerable time and energy reading the decadent
theories of Paul Bourget and discussing them in his
correspondence with Chamberlain. In 1894 he says of the
décadents that '. . . their art seems to me a sort of alchemy in
verse,– totally false, with just enough glints of reality –
micaceous shimmerings – to suggest imaginations of ghostly
gold' (*Japanese Letters* 309). We should perhaps remember, as
Richard Gilman points out, that 'In 1885, before the term
[decadent] had even taken full hold, some of the younger
Decadents began to call themselves Symbolists, getting their
cue, of course, from Mallarmé' (99). Hearn had certainly

started to lecture on Symbolist poetry in Tokyo in the 1890s, had a copy of Symons' book on the subject in his library, and had struggled with Mallarmé's 'L'Après-Midi d'un Faune'. (Though he had to admit to Chamberlain: 'I can't understand that thing at all. It pains my head, and hurts my soul.' He suggested hopefully: 'The beauty is really in that psychic truth of the desire to melt into another being' *Japanese Letters* 308.)

Hearn was not an immoralist, but his attitude to morality was justified, as Walter Pater's was justified, by a relativistic ethic. 'Relations alone exist,' he insists. 'The writer's danger is that of describing his own, as if they were common or permanent' (*Japanese Letters* 313). This relativism stemmed in part from his interest in science, but he combined it with a kind of apocalyptic evolutionary optimism, a sense that when the horrors of modern industrialism had run their course there was some unknown and possibly better future in store. The highest value for him was thus above morality and beauty, it was to be identified with an ecstatic leap into a future that is unknown and as yet unknowable. As so often in the fin de siècle, his description of this future is related to the supreme art form of music. This highest value is, he says: '. . . aspirational,– like music,– aspirational with all its springs of utterance piercing into the Future' (*Japanese Letters* 198).

The desire to move on and away from respectability, to push into the unknown, takes Hearn in his subsequent career from the United States to the West Indies and then to Japan. His restless progress reflects the longings of one of Baudelaire's 'Etonnants voyageurs,' or of Rimbaud's poet who must 'arrive *à l'inconnu*'. But, out of ideas that form the basis of so much second-rate fin de siècle writing, Hearn was able to shape an important, influential and highly individual oeuvre. We can, I think, pick up three threads which run through much of what he writes and which connect the earlier to the later work – all of which are highly representative of the complex of fin de siècle ideas: his interest in the topic of women, in ghosts and his attempt at a new kind of performance in an exotic setting.

★　★　★

It was in Japan that Hearn actually spent the decade of the 1890s, isolated in some ways from the excitement and scandals of the aesthetic movement in Europe, but keenly following the works of fashionable writers through magazines and journals like *La Revue des deux mondes*. Reading such journals he must have been well aware that, although he was cut off from the axis of London and Paris, he had chosen the right place to be. He had, as it were, stepped into the woodblock print that delighted the fashionable European aesthete of the day. Fin de siècle thought, as Hearn makes plain, could connect Japanese art directly with the fascinations of a transgressive life-style:

> How frightful to have to live altogether according to the proprieties! I'd rather die. Everything charming in life, as in Japanese art, is Irregularity and Eccentricity. The Perfectly Regular, the Mathematically Correct, is barbarism and cruelty (quoted in Stevenson 262).

Hearn's early work in Japan thus converts the country into a world of exotic fantasy – and it is one in which women play a large role. In *Glimpses of Unfamiliar Japan* (1894) he concentrates on impressions and personal experience, using rhetorical effects that create an aura of unusual pleasures and sensuous delights. At night in Matsue he sees:

> . . . the paper lanterns flitting over the bridge, like a long shimmering of fireflies. . . I see the broad shōji of dwellings beyond the river suffused with the soft yellow radiance of invisible lamps; and upon those lighted spaces I can discern slender moving shadows, silhouettes of graceful women.

This is the dreamed-of world of Orientalism, heavily laden with suggestions of the erotic. The Japanese women are not only beautiful, by interesting conjunctions they can be used to produce an atmosphere that is bizarre:

> . . . all over the city there rises into the night a sound like the bubbling and booming of great frogs in a marsh, – the echoing of the tiny drums of the dancing girls, of the charming geisha (*Glimpses* 197–8).

In contrast with the heavy moral disapproval that writers like W.E.Griffis brought to their descriptions of Japanese eroticism, Hearn brings delight in unusual sensations.

★　★　★

Hearn's attitude to women is always complex and fascinating: here we can only touch on its relation to the fin de siècle context, noting that it reveals unexpected continuities throughout his career. As Elaine Showalter has pointed out, the late nineteenth century is a period in which male and female roles become (at least as far as literature is concerned) strongly distinguished from one another. As far as male writers are concerned, women become more strange and distant – versions of the Other. This does not mean that men lose interest in the topic of women, rather that women are accorded intellectual and emotional difference from men, and pushed into roles such as those Hearn gives them: ideal women, suffering women, women as eternal mothers and, since they are assumed to be essentially unknowable, women as threatening nightmare creatures of cruel and perverse sexuality. Hearn speaks in his essay on 'The Eternal Feminine' (*Out of the East* 1897) of the 'Western worship of Woman as the Unattainable, the Incomprehensible, the Divine, the ideal of [quoting Baudelaire] "la femme que tu ne connaîtras pas"' (104). Such unknowable creatures can also become sensual temptresses, or corrupted and hungry ghosts; they may be the carriers of sexual diseases which threaten and devour their client men.

In Japan, Hearn's imagination constantly runs through such ambivalences, from his picture of the perfect long-suffering woman of 'A Woman's Diary' ('a simple woman of the people' *Kotto* 85), to female ghosts like that in 'Of a Promise Broken' (*A Japanese Miscellany*) who can rip a young rival apart in the most bloodthirsty fashion. Hearn's middle years, before Japan, have been seen as ones in which women and sex provided a 'master motive' or an 'illassible sexual craving' (Tinker 306). Hearn himself said that the 'influence of sex and sexual ideas has moulded the history of nations' (*Letters I* 256). He approved of the 'mad excess of love' and thought 'all history is illuminated by the *Eternal Feminine* (*Letters I* 315).

Like most fin de siècle writers Hearn was fascinated by the idea of prostitution. After his relationship broke up with Mattie he said he did not think he could love women any more: '. . . after all, so long as all women have to be bought, one might as well buy 'em when he wants 'em' (*Veiled Letters* 141). While in Japan he wrote a glossary of sexual slang for Sentaro Nishida that makes plain how familiar he was with the underground world of bought sex in the United States. And it should be noted that one of his earliest references to Japan was in a letter in which he speculated on how much it might cost to buy a Japanese woman for pleasure.

> Have also wild theories regarding Japan. Splendid field in Japan. Cost only 6.50 per *month* to keep a girl. Girls very pretty (*Veiled Letters* 148).

We see the other side of the same coin in an episode at Mionoseki, related by his son, in which Hearn rushed angrily from his hotel to snatch the boy from the hands of some prostitutes with whom he was innocently playing. He was apparently terrified that his son might be contaminated by these 'unclean women' (*Koizumi* 21). Woman as ideal is thus shadowed by woman for sale, by the nightmare of the supposed carrier of venereal disease. Hearn praised a story by R.L. Stevenson in which a 'beautiful girl [is] born with an irresistible tendency to bite and devour human flesh', because he said it was a 'frightful fable' of the 'deepest and greatest of social problems' (*Interpretations* I 273).

Once Hearn had settled into his married life in Japan it seems safe to assume that his interests shifted: and his later published work concentrates on the idealized image of womanhood or motherhood, on the capacity for suffering and the devotion to duty of women in Japan. But seen from the vantage point of fin de siècle ideas it is obvious that all these writings are part of the same intellectual and emotional complex (as is his idealization in Japan of the Western woman he could no longer meet, Elizabeth Bisland.) When he discussed ideal mothers in Japan we should recall the interesting conjunction he had made in an earlier letter, asking for a scientific explanation of the fact that:

> A woman wicked enough to tempt a man to cut his mother's throat *may* have a peculiar physical magnetism. The touch of her hand in passing, the character of a look from her,– although she be ugly,– may be irresistible, damning. (*Letters* I 401)

It is typical of one side of Hearn that he should anticipate a possible scientific explanation here; but as Jean Pierrot points out '. . . the decadent period coincided with the first systematic investigation into sexual psychopathology' (133). It is most revealing of the fin de siècle basis of Hearn's thought that he should want to put the new science of the age to the task of explaining 'woman', in terms that include bloody cruelty, sexual fascination, mothers and perversely irresistible ugliness.

★ ★ ★

Strangely enough, the most famous female icon of the 1890s becomes transposed through Hearn's Japanese experience into a man. Hearn had obviously read Walter Pater's *Renaissance*, the 'golden book' which Oscar Wilde claimed to have learned almost by heart. Pater's description of the Mona Lisa was particularly attractive: these were the lines that W.B. Yeats was to cut up into free verse and place at the front of his edition of the *Oxford Book of Modern Verse*:

> She is older than the rocks among which she sits; like the vampire she has been dead many times, and learned the secrets of the grave; and has been a diver in deep seas, and keeps their fallen day about her; and trafficked for strange webs with Eastern merchants; and as Leda, was the mother of Helen of Troy, and, as Saint Anne, the mother of Mary. . . (80).

In *Out of the East* (1897) Hearn transmutes these lines into a description of '. . . a farmer and his ox plowing the black soil with a plow of the Period of the Gods'. The image of a Japanese farmer in real life is thus heavily aestheticised, until he becomes the subject of Japanese art:

> That man I have often seen before in the colored prints of another century. I have seen him in kakemono of much more ancient date. I have seen him on painted screens of still greater antiquity. Exactly the same! Other fashions beyond counting have passed: the peasant's straw hat, straw coat, and sandals of straw remain. He himself is old, incomparably older than his attire. The earth he tills has indeed swallowed him up a thousand times a thousand times; but each time it has given

back to him his life with force renewed. And with this perpetual renewal he is content: he asks no more. The mountains change their shapes; the rivers shift their courses; the stars change their places in the sky: he changes never (126).

Again, to point out the comparison with Pater here is not to depreciate Hearn's work, it is rather to note his stylistic experiment. By inscribing Japan in Paterian terms he has managed to suggest an intellectual relation of great complexity and subtlety. Without forcing overt confrontation, he gives the life of the Japanese peasant a kind of equality with high Renaissance culture, as represented by the Mona Lisa. By emphasizing the relation of the peasant himself to the tradition of Japanese art, the coloured prints, *kakemono* and painted screens, Hearn tactfully suggests an authoritative line of Japanese art objects that can match in its own way the significance of Leonardo and the Mona Lisa in the West.

★   ★   ★

Hearn's obsession with the topic of ghosts has been widely noted (See 'W.B. Yeats and Lafcadio Hearn: Negotiating with Ghosts'.) To relate the topic more specifically to the complex fin de siècle ideas is to be reminded at once how seriously questions of the supernatural were taken throughout the intellectual and artistic community of this period. As Alison Hennegan points out, ghost stories reached a pinnacle of popularity in the fin de siècle, and 'many of the century's finest and most energetic minds were to devote themselves to investigation of the relation between seen and unseen worlds' (198). There was a widespread view among academics that scientific enquiry must go beyond the limits of superficial observation (what Symons calls the 'revolt against exteriority' [10]) – though how exactly this was to be carried out was not so readily apparent.

Hearn was interested in ghosts while William James was President of the Society for Psychical Research (1894–6), and Henry James (whose stories Hearn admired) was writing *Turn of the Screw* (1898). Jean Pierrot reminds us that the fin de siècle is also the high point of the French Occultist Movement and the French fashion for spiritualism. Hearn had learnt from Herbert Spencer that all widespread beliefs about the supernatural must have some foundation in the human psyche, and need to be explained rather than dismissed out of hand. In the 1890s, in Japan, the tradition of Japanese ghost stories was especially useful to him, since it could be used to point up cultural difference and at the same time suggest deep similarities in human emotions.

Much of Hearn's most enduring work in Japan has in fact proved to be his re-telling of traditional ghost stories, in collections like *Kwaidan* (1904) or *Kottō* (1902). His versions of 'Yuki-Onna' and 'Mimi-nashi-Hōïchi' have indeed been given a canonical status in the Japanese literary world and elsewhere (as he hoped they would), not unlike that of H.C. Andersen's 'Snow Queen' or 'Little Mermaid'. He was keen to collect material from written and oral sources, and Yanigata Kunio, the founder of Japanese ethnography (as Hirakawa Sukehiro reminds us) saw Hearn as an important predecessor (Murray 4).

Hearn was, however, not just a collector of stories; indeed, he was vague about his sources and quite prepared to manipulate material to fit a new book. His chief aim – rather than providing an academic record of folk culture – was to allow the modern reader to feel again some of the frisson which the ghosts of supernatural tales had once produced in their audience. Thus he begins the story 'In a Cup of Tea':

> Have you ever attempted to mount some old stairway, spiring up through darkness, and in the heart of that darkness found yourself at the cobwebbed edge of nothing? Or have you followed some coast path, cut along the face of the cliff, only to discover yourself, at a turn, on the jagged verge of a break? The emotional worth of such experience – from a literary point of view – is proved by the force of the sensations aroused, and by the vividness with which they are remembered.
> Now there have been curiously preserved, in old Japanese story-books, certain fragments of fiction that produce an almost similar emotional experience. . . (*Kottō* 11).

He goes on to tell a Japanese ghost story. The technique here is typical of Irish Victorian Gothic fiction, with its towers and cliffs and its suggestions of the 'curious'; it is not unlike Sheridan Le Fanu's work. But Hearn's introduction is surprisingly sophisticated about itself as a literary work, about its 'literary point of view', and its evaluation of the emotions of the reader. What follows the introduction is a fragmentary Japanese ghost story about a man who swallows a cup of tea in which the face of a strange young samurai is reflected. If we abstract this narrative from Hearn's introduction it may well seem unsatisfactory, since it breaks off without any resolution, leaving the young hero attacking the servants of the man whose ghost (or ghostly image in the cup of tea) he has swallowed. There is no attempt to explain what kind of ghost this is or to make the story cohere. But Hearn cannot simply present the material as it is: he believes that ghost literature is 'serious'. It contains fundamental truths. Modern science has proved 'beyond all question', he says, 'that everything which we used to consider material and solid is essentially ghostly, as is any ghost. If we do not believe in old-fashioned stories and theories about ghosts, we are nonetheless obliged to recognize to-day that we are ghosts of ourselves – and utterly incomprehensible'. (*On Art* 116) He concludes the chapter:

> Here the old narrative breaks off; the rest of the story existed only in some brain that has been dust for a century.
>
> I am able to imagine several possible endings; but none of them would satisfy an Occidental imagination. I prefer to let the reader attempt to decide himself the probable consequence of swallowing a Soul (17).

The ending thus refuses final explanations – not out of concern for the integrity of the source material, rather because this gives Hearn the chance to direct us towards an experiment at sensation: 'swallowing a Soul'. (And 'soul', as Jean Pierrot points out, is one of the key words around which fin de siècle debate revolves.)

Hearn's obsession with ghosts can be read in several ways. The torn-off bleeding heads and voices that speak through strange mouths represent typical motifs of the literary decadence and no doubt also reflect some personal problems of his own psyche. But his literary sensationalism with ghosts is also an attempt at serious experiment, in which Hearn develops in his own way the intellectual enquiries of the age.

★   ★   ★

Hearn's books on Japan (with the exception of *Japan: An Attempt at Interpretation*) are also serious within the discourse of his age insofar as they are conceived as art objects. They are miscellanies whose construction was widely taken to represent in an authentic way the asymmetrical aesthetic of the culture they describe. The image of Japan they contain is, however, also almost always intimately bound up with Hearn's own self-conscious performance in Japanese society. They are art objects which present *him* in Japan. Hearn does not pretend to be a fully objective observer.

In order to produce authenticity in these works Hearn has undertaken a step into an exotic world. There are many ways in which his step can be interpreted, not all of them flattering (See 'Lafcadio Hearn: Between Britain and Japan'); within the context of the present discussion it seems germane to note first that such a move into the exotic is quite simply one of the basic fin de siècle narratives (Lève l'ancre,' as Mallarmé writes, 'pour une exotique nature!. . .') Behind such a move is the implication that there are two distinct and very different worlds: an occidental world and an oriental world; a mundane world and an exotic world; a materialist world and a world of fantasy. The artist is the person who can go between them.

Symbolic patterning of this kind is very common in late nineteenth-century fiction, often involving shifts into places with different time-scales or worlds of dream and fantasy. It is part of Hearn's own mental grammar, and we might take as representative of the pattern a story by Théophile Gautier that Hearn recommended obsessively to others and translated: 'La Morte amoureuse'.

Gautier's story describes how a young man about to enter the priesthood suddenly catches the eye of an extraordinarily beautiful woman in church. He falls in love with her, and begins to lead a double life. At night he enters a dream world with her, a realm of beauty and erotic sensation: in the day he comes back to the world of the seminary and his awful guilt.

The woman is in fact a vampire, and is sucking the blood of the young man each night; but her attractions are none the less real to him. Thus, we find here the motif of the irresistible and demonic woman so attractive to Hearn, *and* that of a hero torn between two quite incompatible worlds.

Divisions between two such worlds are something that confront characters in Hearn's writings again and again – from his earliest work in *Stray Leaves from Strange Literature* (1884), to his late re-tellings of Japanese ghost stories. The deep importance of the concept to Hearn can indeed be gauged from the fact that it is also reflected in his expository prose, and even forms part of the framework for *Japan: An Attempt at Interpretation*. Here he writes that Japan was a world of:

... the strange, the beautiful, the grotesque, the very mysterious. Fortunate indeed were those privileged to enter this astonishing fairyland thirty odd years ago [i.e. in the 1870s], before the period of superficial change, and to observe the unfamiliar aspects of its life... (363–5).

Hearn, of course, was not so fortunate himself; he did not arrive in Japan until 1890. But he affirms nonetheless that he *was* able to step into a dream world: 'Even yet, in those remoter districts [i.e. Matsue] where alien influence has wrought little change, the charm of the old existence lingers and amazes.'

The charm for Hearn of this society is not simply nostalgic: he rapidly makes the point of its radical difference. He found it in many respects totally opposite, in effect incomprehensible, to the modern mind: '... no kinship of thought, no community of sentiment, no sympathy whatever could exist...the psychological interval was as hopeless as the distance from planet to planet'.

Yet it was such a profoundly strange world, such a mirror version of modern Western society, that Hearn desired to enter. Not only did he visit the place, he worked there, he lived there, he married into a Japanese family, he became a Japanese citizen. It is easy to criticize him for the way in which he made such a binary division between worlds, and placed Japan in an Orient as the 'Other' to the modern industrialized West. But such criticism overlooks the intellectual context from which Hearn springs: his way of thought is typical of his age. Moreover, the division into two worlds is a necessary prelude to his actual step into the Oriental world. He needs to emphasize difference, so that once there he can proceed to act as the advocate for Japan against the world he has left.

The balance between actually making this step and writing about it with full sensitivity for the Western reader – for the reader whose own world Hearn has attempted to leave – is almost impossible to maintain. He is acting out, as he suggests in 'The Dream of a Summer Day' (*Out of the East*), the journey of Urashima Tarō, back and forward to the kingdom of the Dragon King: '. . . he knew himself the victim of some strange illusion' (10). It is hardly surprising that from time to time in Hearn's letters we read complaints by him that his whole enterprise is doomed: he is rejected by the people around him: he does not understand them: they do not feel any sympathy with him: he has woken from the dream. But then again he does always turn back to his extraordinary performance as the occidental in Japan.

One of the most intimate and domestic accounts of this performance comes in a letter, when he writes to his friend Chamberlain with a full description of his day as a Japanese 'danna-sama' (*Japanese Letters* 178–82). At 6 a.m. each day the alarm rings:

> Wife rises and wakes me,– with the salutation *de rigeur* of old Samurai days. I get myself into a squatting posture, draw the never-extinguished *hibachi* to the side of the *futons*, and begin to smoke. The servants enter, prostrate themselves, and say good morning to the danna-sama. . .

At seven he breakfasts:

> I begin to put on my *yofuku*. I did not at first like the Japanese custom,– that the wife should give each piece of clothing in regular order, see to the pockets, etc.;– I thought it encouraged laziness in a man. But when I tried to oppose it, I found I was giving offence and spoiling pleasure. So I submit to the ancient rule.

He describes his whole day: work, meals, bath, games, lighting of lamps and family prayers.

. . . each of the family in turn, except myself, say the prayers
and pay reverence. These prayers are said kneeling. Some of
the prayers are said for me. I was never asked to pray but once
– when there was grief in the house; and then I prayed to the
Gods, repeating the Japanese words one by one as they were
told to me.

Finally, he gives the signal for bed to the household.
Sometimes he writes in bed:

But always, according to ancient custom, the little wife asks
pardon for being the first to go to sleep. I once tried to stop the
habit – thinking it too humble. But after all it is pretty,– and is
so set into the soul that it could not be stopped.

Obviously, this is all highly self-conscious: Hearn is not
completely part of the Japanese picture (he has whisky for
breakfast, and he kisses his wife's hand good-bye in the
morning, 'the only imported custom'); but his image of
himself is of one who is being gradually drawn into a sweetly
exotic and different world of pretty gestures and ancient
rituals. He is watching himself doing it and interpreting it all
the while to his friend Chamberlain. The persona he has
created here is the one recreated constantly throughout his
later Japanese books. The publisher's foreword to the Tuttle
editions nicely indicates how successful the process has been:
'Lafcadio Hearn is almost as Japanese as Haiku,' it begins.
'Both are an art form' (*Out of the East* ix).

There are comparisons to be made between what Hearn
attempted and the succession of 'marriages' Pierre Loti
described himself as making in exotic and Oriental cultures.
(See 'Entering island cultures: Synge, Hearn and the Irish
exotic.') Hearn admired Loti's style deeply and considered him
important as a writer who could genuinely communicate his
sensations of life in new places. But Hearn has also moved
beyond Loti, and attempted a serious revaluation of his own
values. From one point of view the whole performance is
typical of the fin de siècle artist – dressing up in exotic outfits.
From another it must be seen that Hearn has pushed such
games to their limit. He is after all not Japanese – or not in the
ways that matter to most of the people he passes in the street.
He is a Westerner in a kimono. Even the scripts he writes of

his performance are in English. He has embarked on his voyage into the culture with a dedication and intensity that escape Loti, but is still caught self-consciously between two worlds, a figure likely to be accepted in the end by neither.

★ ★ ★

It is not surprising, then, that there should be something deeply problematic about Hearn and his writing, even as there is so much that is important and interesting. Mary Douglas reminds us in *Purity and Danger* (1966) how cultures are constantly making patterns, forming classifications of what is acceptable and unacceptable, clean and unclean. The anomaly, the person or event in a marginal position, is considered a dangerous figure and potentially polluting to the society. And yet in some circumstances, symbols of the anomalous may also become poetical and enriching to the culture. Mary Douglas takes her examples from anthropological field-work, but in the European culture of the fin de siècle we can see that a figure like Oscar Wilde, on the margins of sexual identity, was made into a scapegoat for reasons of this kind. Wilde presented an outrageous challenge to the Victorian concept of sexual normality and brought immediate, vicious punishment upon himself. But at the same time his anomalous position transfigured him into a cultural icon. He is 'Saint Oscar', *and* he is an archetype of social pollution.

Hearn's challenge to his society – albeit in different areas – is similarly profound and disturbing. In Japan he wanted to write, he said, 'not simply as an observer but as one taking part in the daily existence of the common people and *thinking with their thoughts*' (Tinker, 330. Italics in original). But that is an impossible aim: in fact he is culturally neither chalk nor cheese; neither a true Westerner nor a true Japanese. He is a dangerous affront to conventions of nationalism and national identity. Even in the modern academic discourse on Japan he is a disturbingly ambiguous figure who exposes the power-plays of nationalists through the instability of his own status. He enriches modern culture precisely because he also disturbs those centres of gravity we like to consider fixed. He can function both as a profound artist and as an unhealthy, possibly insane, social pariah. (See 'Lafcadio Hearn: Britain and Japan').

* * *

The turn of the century was a period in which ideas of cultural degeneration and decadence were co-opted into pseudo-scientific classifications, to produce a theory of the madness of art and artists. Nordau's *Degeneration* describes not only the general process of cultural degeneration, but the personality type of 'the degenerate' (analogous with the supposed 'criminal type') and insists that it is especially prominent among the artists of the age. Fin de siècle artists are hysterics and fanatics, Nordau says, and they corrupt and delude their own society. With what must seem special relevance for Hearn scholars, Nordau elaborates this thesis to a connection with faulty eyesight: 'there is hardly a hysterical subject whose retina is not partly insensitive'. This was a connection that Hearn's erstwhile friend and biographer George M. Gould was to develop in his *Biographic Clinics*.

Hearn himself was contemptuous of Nordau's fake science; and my purpose in placing Hearn within the context of the fin de siècle is not to accept Nordau, it is rather an attempt to push aside the tradition of pathologic biography. I suggest we need to understand his role in *cultural* history rather than give him a place in a gallery of morbid fin de siècle psychologies.

To do this we need to appreciate how Hearn's own performance, which can provoke such distrust, is integral to his oeuvre. It is a performance calculated to disturb us at the same time as it may inform us, delight us and expand our sensual apprehensions of the world. It is deliberately under-taken with the assumption that one cannot finally be detached and objective about a foreign culture. Hearn strikes a blow against those who 'seem to stand on a sort of philosophical Eiffel Tower, from where looking down, the land and its people seem. . . most absurdly small' (2 *Gleanings* 84).

We cannot go back to reading Hearn's work in the same way that his contemporaries did; but we can now appreciate better how that work functioned within the context of fin de siècle ideas. It relies, as we have seen, on topics and techniques that were familiar at the time. If we can say that its treatment of such topics is more experimental and challenging than we might have expected, that is because Hearn himself broaches cultural boundaries in a way most others were content to leave unattempted.

Hearn's work exists, and must continue to exist, in the margin between two cultures. In our own fin de siècle of the 1990s, however, the marginal has assumed new importance, and we have been forced to assess in new ways our sense of how cultures and national boundaries work. It is on the dangerous ground of competing nationalisms that we find Hearn's performance in the Victorian fin de siècle. Not the least of his achievements as a writer of the 1890s is to have created a symbolic and enriching role for himself on these margins between Japan and the West.

5

ENTERING ISLAND CULTURES: SYNGE, HEARN AND THE IRISH EXOTIC

George Hughes

A comparison between the travel writings of Synge and Hearn is not at first sight either obvious or necessary. Synge's volume *The Aran Islands*, based on visits to the islands between 1898 and 1902, and then published in 1907, is usually discussed in relation to his career as a dramatist. Volume II of the *Field Day Anthology* introduces it typically, with a note which tells us that the extract 'has an obvious bearing on *The Playboy of the Western World*' (III 405). Why put it beside exotic writings on the subject of Japan by the deracinated, cosmopolitan Lafcadio Hearn? Hearn's *Glimpses of Unfamiliar Japan*, published in 1894, is also based on travel in the 1890s, but is quite unrelated to Irish, or indeed to any other drama.

There are, however, ways in which a comparison between these works makes sense. The idea of putting Synge's *Aran Islands* and Japan together would not have been strange to W.B. Yeats, since he wrote in 1921 that Japanese literature is like 'something [Synge] has recorded in his book on the Aran Islands' (Bushrui 263). But the standpoint I wish to take here is rather different from Yeats, since I wish to argue about Synge and Hearn specifically as travel writers, to indicate a common rhetoric from which their writings spring. Of the two writers,

Synge is the one whose work has been more fully discussed in the Anglophone critical literature, but I shall argue that his relation to the exotic (and in particular the debt he shares with Hearn to Pierre Loti) has been widely misrepresented. I am proposing to read both writers' island voyages as versions of exoticism – an Irish exotic, perhaps. It is a reading which, in the contemporary critical forum, immediately raises political problems – and I hope briefly to suggest what I think the politics of such an exotic might be.

★   ★   ★

The gap between Hearn and Synge, which seems so obvious at first, can be filled in slightly unexpected ways by biography. Both came from a Protestant Irish background (in Hearn's case on his father's side). Both were brought up in Ireland, but went on to develop a deep interest in the literary world of Paris in the 1890s. According to Maurice Bourgeois, Synge also prided himself on being distantly related to Hearn. And he admired Hearn's 'fiery prose style', especially in *Exotics and Retrospectives* (Bourgeois 13). Both Hearn and Synge, we might say, chose to observe cultures outside the social and linguistic group in which they had been raised. Synge admired the perceptions of what he called 'wanderers', who were 'in search of humanity and the mysterious external world' (*Prose* 351).

Hearn's interest in islands, no less than Synge's, is obsessive and long standing; it stretches back to his early career as a writer in the United States. His novel *Chita* of 1889 is subtitled 'A Memory Of Last Island', and his first book of travel writing is *Two Years in the French West Indies* (1890). Hearn spent his last years in Japan, from 1890 up to his death in 1904, and it could be said that his later work is about Japan and its island mentality. I would like to focus here, however, on his first Japanese book, *Glimpses of Unfamiliar Japan*, because it portrays Hearn entering the Japanese islands, as Synge's volume portrays him entering the Aran islands.

A comparison of *Glimpses* and *The Aran Islands* immediately raises before us thematic similiarities. Perhaps the most striking is that, unusually for travel writers, both are significantly

concerned with the language spoken on their islands, and the
feel of this language is constantly foregrounded in their
narratives. Language is not just a transparent veil over the
culture; it is integral to the otherness of the other culture
which they try to describe. Synge says: 'In 1898 I went to the
Aran Islands to learn Gaelic and lived with the peasants' (*Plays*
1, xi). Throughout his book he hears the 'continual drone of
Gaelic coming from the kitchen' (57), or the 'faint murmur of
Gaelic' over the water (82). Hearn, on his part, also went to
Japan determined to learn Japanese. Soon after his arrival he
wrote: 'I think that until one can learn at least the spoken
language of a people, and something of their emotional nature,
one cannot write truthfully concerning them.' (*Japanese Letters*
3). He records in *Glimpses* how, on his first day, he was
fascinated by the sight of Japanese writing. He went to sleep
dreaming of an active Japanese script moving around him, as
though he had somehow already entered the inner mental
world of Japan.

Both writers, however, also faced frustrations over language
– Hearn far more than Synge. About Synge's efforts to learn
Gaelic I can only rely on Declan Kiberd, who suggests that
despite problems he did achieve a sophistication of spoken
Irish to which few learners can attain. Hearn, it turned out,
was not to be a great Japanologist: he came too late to Japan
(aged 40); and he was not able to devote much time or energy
to Japanese. But he was able to use a form of the language – a
pidgin Japanese – in communicating with his wife, and unlike
most people in his position, he did not simply give up. The
difficulty of the languages both these writers faced was not, in
any case, something they would necessarily have wished away,
since it allowed them to suggest what Victor Segalen calls 'La
trahison du langage, et de langues' – a sense of impenetrability
and otherness (27).

These writers are both involved in a quest, and if we
consider exoticism, as Jean-Marc Moura does, to be a form of
writing in which the object of the writer's quest becomes
identified with a sense of place, then we can readily see how
both Hearn's and Synge's quests lead them through the
difficulties of language to an island culture which is somehow
pure, to a place untouched by modernity. It is of course a

quest which is never quite capable of realization. Synge arrives first at Aranmoor, but is disappointed when it turns out to be like any other village in the West Coast, and when he hears that George Petrie and Sir William Wilde and many others have been there before him. He goes on to Inishmaan where there 'seemed a simpler and perhaps more interesting type than the people here' (53). It is there that he sees 'the life is perhaps the most primitive that is left in Europe', though he has also to note that even there the men are bilingual (53). He makes the difficult journey on to the third island, but that is less satisfying again, because the people are 'more advanced than their neighbours' (140).

Hearn similarly travels where other visitors do not go, not to Tokyo or Kyoto, but to Matsue – an isolated town on the Japan Sea coast that he calls 'Chief City of the Province of the Gods' (139). But Matsue is not enough: he also moves further in search of more island-like islands. 'I resolved', he says, 'to go to Oki. Not even a missionary had ever been to Oki, and its shores had never been seen by European eyes. . . ' (553). The irony of his journey emerges, however, when he asks for Japanese food. He is promptly offered beefsteak with fried potatoes and roast chicken. 'Having made my way into the most primitive region of all Japan', he tells us, 'I had imagined myself far beyond the range of all modernizing influences; and the suggestion of beefsteak with fried potatoes was a disillusion' (585). No doubt Oki nowadays boasts a McDonald's.

The writers' quests are serious, they lead them into the difficulties of language, to the sense of entering another culture, even to attempting to dress the part. Hearn travels, he says 'in Japanese costume, and wearing a very large Izumo hat, which partly concealed my face' (616). Synge was interested in the dress of the Aran islanders but less adventurous. He did, however, change his shoes for pampooties and writes lyrically about their superiority: 'after a few hours I learned', he says 'the natural walk of man' (65).

Exotic writing, as Segalen points out, is concerned not just with a voyage to another place, but with a dislocation of time. Both Hearn and Synge consider that they are entering a primitive culture, a section of human history frozen in the past. (Japan is like 'the oldest Egypt', Hearn says, or 'the earliest Babylonia' [Edwards 30]). But the fact that the writers have managed to enter these places at all, contradicts the notion that they were truly isolated, and shatters the illusion that they wished to hold. As Hearn says in one of his letters: 'Even now there is no more fleeing into strange countries,– because there are no strange countries: everything is being interbound and interspun with steel rails and lightning wires' (*Veiled Letters* 169). The reverie of entering the past can only be called up by observation of customs surviving from an ancient life-style. Watching an Aran funeral-wake provides the kind of experience Synge desires, as does the Japanese custom of calling the names of the dead immediately after death for Hearn: these are indeed hints of a world distant from modern industrial society, and yet ironically the distance, once found, is also a sign of estrangement from the writers themselves. 'In some ways these men and women seem strangely far away from me', Synge writes. 'There is hardly an hour I am with them that I do not feel the shock of some inconceivable idea.' (113) Hearn complains suddenly that 'the unspeakable absence of sympathy, as a result, perhaps of all absence of comprehension, is a veritable tragedy' (*Japanese Letters* 359).

Moving through the two accounts by these two writers, then, one sees more and more in common: the interest in superstitions, the re-telling of folk tales, the narration of dreams, the contempt for modern schools and education, even the impressionistic account of the police and the way they work on the island. Hearn does not describe that 'impulse to protect the criminal', which Synge found to be universal in the West of Ireland, and which he so famously incorporated in *The Playboy of the Western World* (95). But like Synge he finds the islanders essentially innocent and policemen an intrusion: 'there are no thieves, and practically no crime' (601).

★   ★   ★

Why should there be such thematic similarities between these two accounts? It will hardly do to say that the life on Aran and in Japan is similar. It is, after all, the point of view, the subjectivity of their exoticism, that organizes similarities.

These books represent a new style of travel writing that first emerged in the 1880s and 90s. Synge wrote in a manuscript note to *The Aran Islands*: 'The general plan of the book is, it will be seen at once, largely borrowed from Pierre Loti, who has, I think, treated this sort of subject more adequately than any other writer of the present day'. (48) Hearn also made no disguise of his deep and devoted admiration for Loti. He even corresponded with him and was proud to have a portrait photograph of the author. He translated selections from Loti for journals in the United States (enough for a full volume to be published in 1933) and he constantly recommended Loti's work to friends and students. As we might expect, he could not agree with much of Loti's *Madame Chrysanthème*, though even here he admired its descriptive prose. He insisted to his students in Tokyo that '[Loti's] reputation does not depend upon his Japanese work. . . but upon some twenty volumes of travel containing the finest prose that has ever been written' (*On Art* 326).

Synge's interest in Loti has I think been misrepresented in recent critical literature. This is partly because attention has focused more or less exclusively on his reading of *Pêcheur d'Islande*, Loti's novel about fishermen in Brittany. It is quite possible to read *Pêcheur d'Islande* and to feel that it only incidentally echoes Synge's grey and foggy landscapes, or the emphasis on the danger of the fisherman's life. But Synge had been reading Loti since at least 1895, read *Pêcheur d'Islande* for the first time in 1898, and was still interested enough to discuss Loti's work in *The Speaker* in 1903. Large sections of his *Speaker* article have been omitted from the Allan Price edition of the prose works, though they indicate that Synge knew well not just *Pêcheur d'Islande* but also, at the very least, *Le mariage de Loti* – his account of a trip to Tahiti, which Tim Robinson says Synge actually took with him to the Aran Islands – as well as *Mon frère Yves* and *Inde (sans les Anglais)*. Synge thought, according to Maurice Bourgeois, that Loti was 'the greatest living writer of prose' (56) though, like Hearn, he tempered his admiration with reservations. Looking at Loti's works now it is still possible to see how they might represent a new highly subjective literary form, hovering somewhere between travel literature, the feuilleton and the novel. The writing can be

called decadent, since it declines to moralize itself, but it
throws up apparently fresh impressions of a world elsewhere,
unshaped by literary models. (Loti himself claimed that he
never read anything but his own work.)

To place *Glimpses of Unfamiliar Japan* and *The Aran Islands*
beside works like *Le mariage de Loti*, or *Aziyadé*, or even
Madame Chrysanthème is to see at once their common emphasis
on subjectivity and otherness. (It is to understand why Synge
might begin *The Aran Islands* so strikingly: 'I am in Aranmoor,
sitting over a turf fire, listening to a murmur of Gaelic. . .'
(49). In the letter prefacing *Madame Chrysanthème* Loti
famously admits that the three principal characters are 'Moi',
'le Japon' and 'the effect the country had on me' ['l'Effet que
ce pays m'a produit'] (43). Synge's short paragraphs, his
flickering narrative with impressions and snatches of dialogue,
his sudden shifts of time and place, are all to be found in a
work like *Le mariage de Loti*. Recent commentators such as
Roland Barthes and Alain Buisine have pointed to the
bleached, pale landscape Loti constantly uses: sea fogs or
deserts or grey rock. No doubt Synge was actually describing
Aran when he wrote of 'the dreary rock . . . sloping up from
the sea into the fog' or a landscape that was 'desolate. Grey
floods of water. . .' (49). But Hearn also describes in Japan the
'naked rock' and the 'sombre wilderness of dwarf vegetation'
(573). We could point out, as Tim Robinson does in the case
of Synge, that he has only described part of the landscape; but
we can more simply say that observation in both cases is
filtered through the kind of intensely subjective description
made fashionable by Loti. According to Hearn, English
descriptive prose of the period represented 'mind and eye'; but
'Loti is all eye, ear, smell, taste. . . He can describe!' (*On Art*
377).

Dressing up also provides a theme in common. If Synge
simply changes into pampooties on Aran, and Hearn wears a
kimono and large hat, Loti is obsessed with elaborate schemes
to dress himself in exotic foreign finery. In *Aziyadé* he goes to
secret rooms where three old ladies adorn him in deliciously
interesting oriental garments and swords. Typically, he looks at
himelf in the mirror, smiles and slides off into the sinister
Oriental crowds.

Stylistic and thematic similarities abound, then, but perhaps the most significant link between these three writers is quite simply the topic we began with – language. Loti too insists, in the most unlikely way, that he *will* learn the languages of the cultures he enters. In *Aziyadé* he performs the tour de force of learning Turkish in two months. He learns Japanese (he claims) in *Madame Chrysanthème* and in the *Mariage de Loti* he can talk to Rarahu in 'la langue maorie' (24).

Moreover, all three writers share an attempt to create a sense of the interlinguistic, a sliding between languages or a mixture of languages, that can represent the feel of another culture to the reader. *Le mariage de Loti* gives us word lists of Maori; *Aziyadé* and *Fantôme d'Orient* incorporate enough foreign words in the text for a six-page glossary at the end of the Folio edition. Hearn, in the same way, fills his English text with Japanese. He transcribes Japanese songs into Romanised script as though his readers could follow them. At other times he produces descriptions like that of a procession in Oki: 'spearmen wearing queues; and retainers in kamishimo; and bearers of hasami-bako. Yet ghosts these were not, but aged samurai of Matsue. . .' (623). The effect was deliberate; Hearn insisted that words have: 'faces, ports, manners. . . moods, humours, eccentricities. . . That they are unintelligible makes no difference at all' (*Japanese Letters* 105). His friend B.H. Chamberlain complained to him that mixing Japanese and English is like a 'mouthful of consommé in the middle of a plate of strawberries'. Hearn justified himself by quoting Loti's *Roman d'un Spahi*, which uses the words '*Anabilis Fobil;– faramata hi*' as a refrain. 'What do they mean?' he asks. 'I don't know;–. . . Loti says he cannot tell; the words "would burn the paper". Yet read that marvellous chapter; and then I will defy you to say those words have no effect upon you'. (*Japanese Letters* 115)

Hearn, like Loti, sometimes puts in a word-for-word translation. When two Japanese politely offer each other rice cakes or *mochi*, Hearn records one saying: 'I-your-servant mochi–for this-world-in no-use-have, Saké-alone this-life-in if-there-be, nothing-beside-desirable-is.' (560)

The Loti-esque use of foreign words is of course also found in Synge, though to a lesser extent. He puts in Gaelic, sometimes translates, sometimes does not. His use of Gaelic and his establishment of an Anglo-Irish literary dialect with a substratum of Gaelic has been fully discussed by Declan Kiberd and I think there is no need to go over that ground again here. But perhaps the most interesting question is why it works so well for Synge in sentences like: 'If you didn't know us so well.... you'd think it was a lie we were telling, but the sorrow a lie is in it.' (127) Why is this interesting, poetic, and appropriate, while Hearn's literal translations remain unhelpful and more than a little ridiculous? Perhaps it is simply that Hearn overdoes it: the sense of otherness is just too strong. Presumably, it is also the case that Synge's Anglo-Irish with Gaelic effects does correspond in some ways to spoken English, even if it is not an exact record. Nobody, however, speaks in Hearn's 'I-your-servant-mochi' style of English; and it certainly does not communicate (to me at least) what it is like to speak in Japanese.

What is to be gained then from the comparison I have attempted here, of Synge and Hearn in the light of Loti? In the first place, I think we understand better that Synge was not unique in his attempts to experiment with the role of language in the mediation between cultures – though we can say that the solution he arrived at was uniquely successful, and retains an interest that Hearn's and Loti's attempts do not. Second, we can see more clearly that complex feelings surrounding the sanctity of island culture are not unique to any of these writers. They all feel that modernization or social evolution is inevitable, but that islands represent a possible safe place, a kind of purity through otherness, and of course a place where one may find oneself. Hearn says he felt in Oki 'as nowhere else in Japan, the full joy of escape from the far-reaching influences of high-pressure civilization,– the delight of knowing one's self. . . well beyond the range of everything artificial in human existence' (625).

Through the comparison of these writers I think we come better to understand the politics of this writing, to realize that though it undoubtedly reflects in some part their experiences, it is also placed within the thematics and rhetoric of a fin de siècle exotic. It is easy to find passages in all three writers that are objectionable and patronizing about what Hearn calls the 'great common people' (xiii). But the politics of the fin de siècle exotic is not fully explained by pointing to its mistakes, by pointing to the shadow of social evolution or scientific racism that hangs over the intellectual world of the time. The reverie of exoticism is, as Victor Segalen says in his *Essai sur l'Exotisme*, 'le pouvoir de concevoir autre' (23). It is – particularly in writers like Hearn and Synge (and in Loti sometimes) – a way of allowing for the integrity of other cultures. I do not mean by this to defend all forms of exoticism, some indeed are loaded with prejudice and hostility (often unconscious). But neither in the case of Synge nor Hearn would a full reading of the works sustain such a complaint. They describe and then make a claim for a way of life that is outside the circle of experience of their readers. They feel a difference, but the difference is necessary to show their sense that there *are* other ways to run a society or organize ideas and social life. I would suggest that they learnt how to describe this otherness – how to break down the hegemony of the ethnocentric travel narrative – in considerable part from Loti. But I think it can be argued in all three cases that this exotic writing is a powerful gesture towards a more open-minded and heterogeneous conception of the world. Islands are different, are exotic, but for Synge and Hearn they are necessary places.

6

W.B. YEATS AND LAFCADIO HEARN: NEGOTIATING WITH GHOSTS

George Hughes

In early January 1874, at 16 Barr Street, Cincinnati, in the home of a certain Mr and Mrs Smith, the young Lafcadio Hearn encountered his father's ghost. Or, to put it more precisely, he *spoke* to his father's ghost: the ghostly voice came, rather indistinctly, he says, out of a trumpet. Ghosts speaking out of trumpets may seem a little improbable to us now, but Hearn's experience was not uncommon at the time. W.B. Yeats also spoke to ghosts through trumpets, in his case to the ghost of Leo Africanus, probably in 1912, at a séance arranged by Mrs Wriedt of Detroit on her visit to London (Cott 73–80: Goldman 108–29).

The question of whether one can actually speak to ghosts was of interest, indeed of very strong interest, to both these writers. But they were also concerned in a wider way to establish their standpoint in relation to ghosts – or, in other words, to negotiate a position in relation to them. If I cannot pretend to know how much they succeeded in their negotiations, I hope I can indicate how such negotiations could prove important and productive in their writings. There are significant differences as well as convergences in their attitudes, which emerge particularly when they turn towards Japan.

* * *

Before I try to show in more detail what I mean, it would perhaps be as well to provide some justification for putting Hearn and Yeats together – other than their experiences with speaking trumpets. There are some obvious points in common: both had Anglo-Irish parents, both were important members of the fin de siècle literary scene, both were interested in Japan and both were interested in ghosts. There are also some delicate, but nonetheless direct links between the two. Yeats is said to have particularly liked, as a definition of poetry, Hearn's phrase 'There is something ghostly in all great art' (*Collected Letters* III, 101 n. 1). He seems to have been familiar with some of Hearn's work, as he refers to Hearn in the introduction to his play *The Resurrection* (1931) (*Explorations* 396). The reference concerns 'the re-birth of the soul', for which Yeats says Hearn had found 'empirical evidence' among the Japanese. Yeats does not say what work of Hearn's he has in mind, and the comment is rather misleading in relation to Hearn. It usefully points up a difference in fundamental ideas between the two writers, though they do share an interest in the idea of rebirth.

Hearn undoubtedly admired the work of Yeats. He gave what must be some of the first university lectures anywhere on Yeats, certainly the first in Japan, sometime between 1896 and 1903. (One of the student transcripts of these lectures, from which the published versions have been taken, has some difficulty with the name, and settles finally on 'Samuel Batler Yeats'. [Kobinata ms.]) Hearn also wrote a letter to Yeats, about the poem 'The Host of the Air' from *The Wind Among the Reeds*, which he goes through in one of these lectures. He objected, in strong terms, to changes that Yeats had made from an earlier printed version. (The complaints are quite understandable from a teacher's point of view, since Yeats had left out some of the lines and phrases he focused on in his lecture.) Yeats replied promising a partial restoration, though he did not in fact change later versions (*Collected Letters* III, 101–2).

Hearn's letter to Yeats suggests that he has been attracted by their common Irish background and interest in Irish folklore;

but the lectures indicate that he has also (as we might perhaps expect from a fin de siècle figure like Hearn) been particularly impressed to read of Yeats's reputation in France. Hearn talks about Yeats in three lectures: 'Some Fairy Literature', 'Some Symbolic Poetry' and 'Two Mystical Rose Poems'. (*Life and Literature* 324–39: *On Poetry* 141–70, 729). In the lecture on fairy literature he discusses *The Land of Heart's Desire* (1894), which he says shows supernatural events, although 'the play of emotions is purely and intensely human'. He likes this because 'an impossible situation is made to become intensely interesting'. It is typical of Hearn that he should enjoy work with supernatural themes, but (unlike Yeats) find a non-supernatural justification for his enjoyment.

★   ★   ★

My concern here, however, is not particularly to develop these biographical connections, but to place Yeats and Hearn together in regard to ghosts. And my real excuse for considering them in this way is that I want to put their interest in the context of Japan. This is not the only context in which their ghostly concerns could be discussed, but by focusing on the topic of ghosts I think we can gain some new insight into the way Yeats developed what he called his Nō plays, just as we can gain some insight into the way in which Hearn made himself such an important commentator on Japan and Japanese culture.

   Hearn leaves us only one account of a successful séance (though he wrote several articles on the subject of spiritualism in Cincinnati); Yeats, on the other hand, left many. His first, and rather unsatisfactory experience was in 1885. Then from 1911, after an encounter with a medium (Mrs Chenoweth) in Boston, he began to attend séances actively. And in London in 1912, with Mrs Wriedt, he was lucky enough to have the experience of hearing 'an exceedingly loud voice' which came through a long tin trumpet 'standing on its broad end in the middle of the room'. Mrs Wriedt said the voice had come for Mr Gates. Yeats, who was always happy to cooperate in such matters, said 'this was evidently me' (Goldman 116).

   Yeats visited other mediums around England, and seriously

studied the automatic writing of Elizabeth Radcliffe – work that probably stimulated Georgie Hyde-Lees to try automatic writing after their marriage. And it was automatic writing by spirit controls that lay behind Yeats's two versions of *A Vision* and some of his most famous poetry. He lectured in enthusiastic vein to the London Spiritualist Alliance in 1914 (Kutch 114-35).

The ghosts which appear in late nineteenth and early twentieth century writing are no doubt within traditions that go back to Hamlet or Banquo, Alcestis or the Witch of Endor. But they were also a distinctive new phenomenon of an age worried by the death of the past. Although they were unreal in terms of common sense, they seemed to speak of greater reality. Ghosts verified people's roots in various places, in the houses or the countryside they loved, and yet their modern popularity was also connected with growing internationalism (since the ghost craze was trans-Atlantic), and the fashion for mediums and spiritualist societies was bound up with many of the techniques of modern publicity. There were so many ghosts – they were so active then – where, one wonders, have they all gone now?

The spiritualist craze started, according to Janet Oppenheim, in 1848 in America, in Hydesville, New York, when ghosts began to give messages to the young Fox sisters, Margaret and Kate, by banging on a wall. America remained important as a source of mediums, but they spread their activities fairly rapidly to England. Tricks were exposed, but many people were not entirely convinced by the exposures. 'Because mediumship is dramatisation', Yeats later said, 'even honest mediums cheat at times. . . and almost always truth and lies are mixed together. But what shall we say of [the spirits']. . . knowledge of events, their assumption of forms and names beyond the medium's knowledge or ours? What of the arm photographed [by Dr Ochorowicz] in a bottle?' (*Explorations* 365–6). Lafcadio Hearn would not have believed in Dr Ochoworicz's arm, since he wrote an article in *The Cincinnati Commercial* in 1875, in which he systematically discussed the kind of tricks that spirit photographers could play: over-printing on used negatives, holes in the developing tanks and the like ('Spirit Photography'). But Yeats

liked spirit photographs: he even had his own photograph
taken with a spirit aura. He is looking serious and
contemplative, in a creased jacket and wearing a bow-tie,
with a large round, rather surprised-looking, ghostly face
coming out of the top of his head (Goldman plate 1).

                        ★   ★   ★

For Hearn and Yeats, however, it was not just a question of
visiting spirit mediums for a joke, they had what amounts
almost to an obsession with the subject of ghosts. B.H.
Chamberlain says: 'No one could understand Lafcadio Hearn
who did not take into account his belief in Ghosts.' (*Japanese
Letters* lv) It is certainly true that in the United States, in the
West Indies, in Japan, Hearn is constantly writing about
ghosts. Some of his work on ghosts is in the form of exotic
folktales translated or edited from other sources (like *Stray
Leaves from Strange Literature*, 1884); some consists of anecdotes
recounted by informants in New Orleans or in the West
Indies. Yeats is similarly involved in collecting and publishing
Irish fairy tales and ghost stories. He insisted that the 'mystical
life' was the centre of all he did, and that his aim as a writer
was to reconcile 'spiritist fact with credible philosophy'
(Ellman 97, 294).

In Hearn's work the term 'ghost' does not just come up in
stories of the supernatural. He uses it widely to refer to people,
mountains, the 'world-Ghost', 'the supreme ghost', 'the Blue
Ghost', the 'ghostly facts' of the universe. Elisabeth Bisland, his
editor and friend (whom Hearn refers to as 'my dear, sweet,
ghostly sister') says 'the word "ghost" appears a thousand times
in Hearn's books, in endless association with all his thoughts'.
Nonetheless, Hearn is prepared to accept (unlike Yeats) that
most modern spiritualism is 'humbug'. He thinks the ghosts of
spiritualists are too domesticated and probably fakes. What he
means by 'ghost', on the whole, is that which gives us a deep
sense of emotional unity. Personal ghosts are an illusion
(*Japanese Letters* I, 475; II, 379, 382, 265).

Writers, however, Hearn thinks 'must seek their material in
those parts of the world where ghosts still linger'. They should
be in pursuit of ghost stories because, although such stories are

illusory, they reveal to us what we have in common with others, and something of our own 'primeval fears'. Hearn is extremely interested in the way supernatural fiction works, and comes to the conclusion that it is fundamentally based on 'dream-experience'. And within that dream experience he thinks the most common fear is *the fear of being touched by ghosts*' (*Japanese Letters* 215; *On Art* 115–28; 'Nightmare Touch', *Shadowings*).

Ghost stories, then, must not be dismissed, because they are based on dream-experience. Modern scientific theory can find an explanation for them in terms of our common unconscious lives. Ideas of reincarnation, Hearn thinks, can be related to scientific theories of heredity, or in Herbert Spencer's phrase, to 'organic memory'. For Hearn this is a 'dim inherited memory of experience in other lives' – though he stresses that the term 'memory' is used only in a symbolic sense: 'instinct' or 'intuition' might also be used. Since there is some kind of organic memory, the old ideas of metempsychosis, transmigration or resurrection were not simply false, 'they were rather foreshadowings of a truth vaster than all myths and deeper than all religions'. Behind everything is a nameless and unnamable force: 'we are, each and all, infinite compounds of fragments of anterior lives' (*Lectures* 8–9; *Oriental Articles* 110; *Gleanings* 89–90). The basic theory is perhaps a little confusing and confused, but it is a theory that attempts to use modern science to account for ancient ideas. It does not imply (as Yeats's comment on Hearn suggests) that he had found any *empirical* evidence for reincarnation in Japan.

Yeats himself is more determined to believe in ghosts and spirits of a personal type: 'We may come to think that nothing exists but a stream of souls.' Memory, however, is also a focus for him, and he says that in trying to explain modern theories of 'forgotten personal memory' he came on the theory of a 'Great Memory [containing images] passing on from generation to generation'. But this concept alone was not enough for him, because he found intention and choice within the organization of the images in the memory. (Hearn, by contrast, found only a 'dim inherited memory'. He does not see it as organized.) Yeats concluded that some of the memories in our great sea of memory were actually the memories of dead people who were still 'living in their memories'. In his view the dead were able to organize their own memories and, since we draw on these organized memories, they were 'the source [in us] of all that we call instinct'. The memories of the dead are in this sense within us – but shadows and materialization may also indicate their place outside us 'among walls, or by rocks and trees, that bring before their memory some moment of emotion while they still had animate bodies' (*Mythologies* 343–66).

There are obviously profound differences between these theories, particularly in their view of persons or individuals; but they move within similar terminology, and both writers conclude for their own reasons that accounts of ghosts and spirit-experiences are worth taking seriously.

Hearn and Yeats also found that the topic of ghosts could easily be linked to folklore, when it was happily brought into areas of wider concern, and even gained some sense of proximity to academic or scientific studies. When this was in turn linked to Japan – as Yeats said he had attempted to 'annex Japan to Ireland' (*Letters* 807) – then ghosts were given the added support of the prestige that surrounded Japanese art in the late nineteenth and early twentieth century. Ghosts in Japanese form were exotic: audiences would not be tempted to see them as comic frauds.

Japan is far more obviously important in the work of Hearn than in Yeats, but ghosts-plus-Japan have a productive effect on the work of both these writers. In Yeats's drama in particular, and in Hearn's travel writings, the conjunction allows a kind of creative freedom that was difficult to obtain otherwise. We can put together what we might call a productive triangle of ghosts, folklore and Japan – within which Yeats and Hearn are able to give their obsessive interest an artistic life.

★   ★   ★

We can trace the emergence of this productive triangle in Yeats's work through his association with Ezra Pound and their commentaries on the Fenollosa translations of Nō drama. Pound says:

All through the winter of 1914-15 I watched Mr Yeats correlating folklore. . . and data of the occult writers, with the habits of charlatans of Bond Street [i.e. spirit mediums]. If the Japanese authors had not combined the psychology of such matter with what is to me a very fine sort of poetry, I would not bother about it (*Classic Noh* 26).

In the introduction he wrote for Lady Gregory's collection of folklore, Yeats also brought in Swedenborg and other authorities on the supernatural; but the correlation Pound speaks of between Japanese drama and spirit mediums of Bond Street (or in Yeats's version, Soho and Holloway,) still figures importantly. In case we think this approach to the Nō is a fairly obvious one, it is instructive to contrast it with that of Arthur Waley – who attacks the Delphic mysteries of such critics and insists that 'the device of making an apparition the hero of the play was simply a dramatic convention' (26).

Yeats explains, however, that with the help of these plays he has invented a new form of drama. Much recent scholarship has been devoted to the work of tracing parallels between individual Nō plays and the drama Yeats went on to write, and I am not attempting here to add to it. Rather I want to shift the emphasis, and draw attention to the conjunction that Yeats himself makes with 'spiritism', or spiritualism, and the Nō.

★　★　★

In Yeats's 1914 lecture to the Spiritualist Alliance he insisted that Japanese Shintoism was 'nothing but simple Spiritism. There was no doctrine in Spiritism today that was not in Shintoism. It was in the beautiful philosophy of the Noh drama of Japan' (Kutch 127). (Hearn, by the way, also suggested that in the doctrines of Shinto 'We have. . . a conception resembling very strongly the Spiritualistic notion of ghosts' [*Kokoro* 268]). But if we examine the plays that Yeats wrote, those plays which he refers to as his own Nō plays (*Letters* 615), we may be surprised to find that in the first of them, and perhaps the most imporant – *At the Hawk's Well* (1917) – ghosts or mediums do not seem to appear at all. At least they do not appear in a guise that we can connect directly with the spirit mediums of Bond Street or Soho. The play is set in Ireland, and the story that Yeats uses is of Cuchulain's attempt to find a well of miraculous water. As Richard Taylor has suggested, Yeats may have picked up some ideas for this from the play *Yōrō* by Zeami, which was among the unpublished Fenollosa papers. Yet I think we must admit that the relationship is not close. The plot, as has been suggested, could equally have come from William Morris's *The Well at the World's End*. (Incidentally, Hearn also uses the story of a Fountain of Youth in the chapter called 'The Dream of Summer's Day' in *Out of the East* (1895) – though I would not suggest there is any connection with Yeats here.)

All the same, it will not do to play down, as Denis Donoghue or Helen Vendler have done, the relation between *At the Hawk's Well* and Japan. Yeats follows the Nō both in terms of what he sees as its poetic technique, and in the importance he gives to the climactic dance. In Yeats's introduction to the Fenollosa/Pound volume he writes: 'I wonder am I fanciful in discovering in the plays themselves . . . a playing upon a single metaphor' (160). He quotes the use of grass in *Nishikigi*, and the feather mantle in *Hagoromo*. In *At the Hawk's Well*, he seems to have used metaphors about eyes in a similar way: he focuses on the 'eye of the mind', the 'heavy eyes' of the guardian of the well, the 'glass look' in the eyes, the 'dazed and heavy' eyes, the 'unmoistened eyes', and at the end of the play 'hateful eyes', 'unfaltering, unmoistened eyes'.

The eyes of the guardian of the well are associated with a state of trance, and a kind of possession. The old man says:

And now I know why she has been so stupid
All the day through, and had such heavy eyes.
Look at her shivering now, the terrible life
Is slipping through her veins. She is possessed (*Variorum* 408).

The state of trance, or possession by spirits, is expressed in the famous dance of this hawk-like figure. As Katharine Worth points out, Yeats had been interested in putting dance into drama for some time, but it is in *At the Hawk's Well* that we finally and clearly find a dance which represents a form of spirit possession. And there is no doubt that it was Yeats's idea of specifically Japanese dance that led to this. Much has been made by some critics of the fact that Yeats's main source of information on dance was Michio Itō, who had been studying Western ballet in Paris, and disliked the Nō. But Itō had studied Japanese dance in his youth. He obviously did show some Japanese dance to Yeats, and Yeats was deeply impressed by the way Itō dancing seemed to inhabit 'the deeps of the mind'. Such dances, he thought 'enable us to pass for a few moments into a deep of the mind that had hitherto been too subtle for our habitation' (*Classic Noh* 143-4).

The Japanese-style dance in *At the Hawk's Well* was undoubtedly meant to show a figure in a state of trance. In Fenollosa's essay on the Nō he emphasizes that the 'most certainly Japanese element of the drama was the sacred dance in the Shinto temples'. He goes on to say: 'The ancient Shinto dance or pantomime was probably, at first, a story enacted by the local Spirit. . . Shintoism is spiritism' (*Classic Noh* 63). Fenollosa does not, I think, mean modern spiritualism here, his reference is to ancient Greek religious practices. Yeats, on the other hand, grasped at a connection that suited his own interests: and thus he could base the convergence of Nō and Western ideas on the figure of the spirit medium. The drama of the medium's possession, ritualized in a dance, provides for him a link between East and West.

Yeats's use of the dance, and its significance for him, can be related to Hearn's writings on Japan. Hearn was also profoundly impressed by a dance, the Bon-odori, that he saw in a mountain village when he was living in Matsue. He describes it in *Glimpses of Unfamiliar Japan* (1894):

> Out of the shadow of the temple a processional line of dancers files into the moonlight and as suddenly halts. . . figures lightly poised as birds. . . and so slowly, weirdly, the processional movement changes into a great round, circling about the moonlit court and around the voiceless crowd of spectators. . . Unto what, I ask myself, may this be likened? Unto nothing; yet it suggests some fancy of somnambulism,– dreamers, who dream themselves flying, dreaming upon their feet.
>
> And there comes to me the thought that I am looking at something immemorially old, something belonging to the unrecorded beginnings of this Oriental life. . . a symbolism of

motion whereof the meaning has been forgotten for
innumerable years. . . there creeps upon me a nameless,
tingling sense of being haunted. . . what is it? I know not;
yet I feel it to be something infinitely more old than I,–
something not only of one place or time, but vibrant to all
common joy or pain of being, under the universal sun (132-8).

This is deservedly one of Hearn's most famous descriptions
of Japan – one of the moments when Japan becomes all he
wants it to be: ghostly, beautiful, remote from the modern
Western world, exotic and yet somehow speaking of deeps of
the mind. The dance is birdlike, somnambulisitic (Yeats also
talks of 'somnambulistic' journeys in association with ghosts
[*Explorations* 47]) and it makes Hearn feel haunted. It is
perhaps ironic that in the case of both Yeats and Hearn a
Japanese version of ritual dance is necessary for the Western
writer to convince himself that a sacred universal 'commu-
nitas', a living world of myth, is still possible.

★   ★   ★

Yeats and Hearn come together in their view of Japanese
dance, but for Hearn the dancers are only one example of an
experience of what he calls 'Ghostly Japan'. These dancers are
not actually ghosts, they only seem to be ghostly to him.

In most cases, in Hearn's Japanese work, real communication with personal ghosts is imagined as something for other
people, not for Hearn himself. In particular, seeing ghosts is
possible for unselfconscious members of the kind of closed
community of the old Japan he so lovingly observed at Matsue
and so longed to enter. Hearn is constantly aware of how far
he is from the mental world which contains Japanese ghosts,
his 'incapacity to enter into the soul-life of this ancient East'. A
trained sociologist coming to the few remaining traditional
areas of Japan would find, he said 'the rule of the dead'. And
he would also recognize that 'between those minds and the
minds of his own epoch no kinship of thought, no community
of sentiment, no sympathy whatever could exist' (*Japan* 460,
383).

This kind of distance is not something Yeats emphasizes;
though of course he does not have personal experience of

Japan and he selects only a very limited area for his attention. When Hearn describes Japan for Western readers, however, he is always performing a balancing act for them: he has special insight and sympathy, but he is still an outsider. Between inside and outside he has somehow to try and keep his foothold, while still entertaining his non-Japanese audience. 'I ask nobody', he says to his readers 'to take for granted the possibility of the Iki-ryō [living ghosts], except as a strong form of conscience'. If he can place these ghosts firmly within the mental world of Japan, however, he can absolve them of the need for logic, consistency or verifiability that are demanded in the West; and he is extremely happy with such a position. 'The house now occupied by one of my friends used to be haunted', he tells us. It is not Hearn's own house of course; and, once he has made plain that this is not his own account he is giving, he can suggest that 'Iki-ryō, which are the ghosts of the living, may come at all hours; and they are much more to be feared [than the Shi-ryō, ghosts of the dead], because they have power to kill' (*Out of the East* 172-6). Does Hearn believe in all these vengeful spirits? Certainly not in a straightforward way. But since his friend believes in them, he can assure himself that they do have some kind of effect, some undeniable place in a real world of somebody's experience.

Hearn's admirers have often preferred to ignore his reservations and surround him with the aura of the ghostly. Nobushige Amenomori, for example, describes Hearn working at one o'clock at night alone in his study:

> It was not the Hearn I was familiar with: it was another Hearn. His face was mysteriously white; his large eye gleamed. He appeared like one touched with some unearthly presence (*Atlantic Monthly* 524).

Obviously, Hearn is here presented as a kind of spirit medium of the arts: but for Hearn himself inspired figures who can communicate directly with ghosts exist most comfortably within the setting of re-told folk tales. It is within a distant and legendary world 'Some centuries ago' that he frames the figure of Mimi-nashi-Hōïchi, the blind biwa player who chants the · story of the Heike battles to the ghosts of the Heike clan.

Hōïchi hears his ghostly audience 'murmuring praise': 'How marvellous an artist!' – 'Never in our own province was playing heard like this!' (*Kwaidan* 10). He represents an ideal artist for Hearn, someone in tune with the ghostly in several senses; but he is placed away from the reader's world, within a framework of literary effects, cultural explanations and footnotes. There is a marked difference between this and Yeats's introduction to *The Celtic Twilight*, where Yeats tells us: 'I have. . . been at no pains to separate my own beliefs from those of the peasantry' (1). Unlike Yeats, Hearn *did* separate his beliefs from those of the peasantry; though he also enjoyed pointing out how they might shadow one another at times.

                                    ★   ★   ★

Yeats would like to enter into negotiations with ghosts first and then sort out the implication afterwards. Japan, the Nō, folklore, ghosts and fairies can all be used by him: he is determined to ignore conventional barriers and categories of knowledge. He would also like to bring the question of how negotiations take place firmly back to his own contemporary world, as we see in *The Words upon the Window-Pane* (1934).

In this play, Mrs Henderson, a modern spirit medium who has travelled from England to Dublin to give séances, is interrupted by the ghosts of Jonathan Swift, Vanessa and Stella. They speak through Mrs Henderson, performing again the tragic struggles of their relationships – though she herself claims not to know who Swift is.

It has been pointed out that in some respects Yeats draws here on the Nō tradition: I would not disagree. But again I should like to shift attention from consideration of possible parallels, to the way in which Yeats's dramatic ghosts have become, in this play, the ghosts of ancestors. Although Swift and Stella are not literally Yeats's ancestors, at the time he wrote the play he was busy constructing a Protestant ancestral tradition for himself. Swift, Berkeley, Goldsmith and Burke were to be re-read and revived by Yeats, to represent an Anglo-Irish heritage threatened by the new Catholic Irish State. The emergence of the voice of Swift through the medium (which is in one sense what Yeats calls 'dreaming back') does also mean that the play, like a 'Mugen' Nō drama, raises the ghost of a heroic figure. (Though as Yasunari Takahashi has pointed out, unlike the real Nō, the ghost does not appear in person, and Yeats brings an element of Western-style conflict into the play. [*Cambridge Review* 172-6]). It becomes significant here that Yeats had emphasized how the ideas of Shinto and of modern spiritism can be considered together. Negotiating with ghosts in this play has become not just a glimpse of deep reality perceived through a trance-like dance, but a kind of Yeatsian ancestor-worship.

John Corbet, the young student in the play (who bears one of Yeats's own family names) says: 'I hope to prove that in Swift's day men of intellect reached the height of their power – the greatest position they ever attained in society and the State, that everything great in Ireland and in our character, in what remains of our architecture, comes from that day' (*Variorum* 941-2). The trance of the medium is thus linked to historical experience, and to the respect that should be given those ancestors who created 'everything great' in Ireland.

If Yeats was involved in a nostaligc search for ancestors in his later career, so of course was Hearn. In Hearn's case this meant looking more and more towards Greece, which he associated with his mother. His feeling for his own ancestors, however, also goes with a deepening sense of the significance of Shinto and ancestor-worship in Japan. Hearn had always given Shinto more respectful treatment than writers like B.H. Chamberlain, and in his final work *Japan: An Attempt at an Interpretation* (1904), he insists that from the ancestor-cult 'almost everything in Japanese society, derives'. Understanding the treatment of ghosts, is for him the key to understanding Japan. He compares the 'ideas of the old Greeks regarding the dead' and 'the ideas of the old Japanese'.

No doubt because Hearn himself came from a broken home, he was deeply impressed by what he calls the 'domestic worship [of Japan], which regards the dead as continuing to form a part of the household life, and needing still the affection and the respect of their children'. The bond with ancestral ghosts was originally one of fear, he suggests, but it has been replaced by a 'religion of affection'. '[The ghosts of the ancestors] are not thought of as dead. . . Unseen they guard the home, and watch over the welfare of its inmates: they hover nightly in the glow of the shrine-lamp; and the stirring of its flame is the motion of them. . . They were the givers of life, the givers of wealth, the makers and teachers of the present: they represent the past of the race, and all its sacrifices;– whatever the living possess is from them'. (28-9,44-5) He sees Japanese ancestor-worship not as superstition, but as something the West might profitably learn.

Despite radical differences in their personal concepts of ghosts, then, there is an interesting convergence here between these two writers: for both of them Japan (or at least their idea of Shinto in Japan) legitimizes reference to ghostly ancestors. They both deplore the neglect of their forbears – and are drawn in their writings to the Japanese rituals that embody respect for the dead.

★   ★   ★

It is clear, I hope, from these comparisons I have sketched out, that the topic of ghosts for both Yeats and Hearn is not a minor one in relation to their work. It is one that touches on their ideas of creativity, inspiration, the universality of emotions, and it is deeply involved with their creation of a tradition to which they would like to belong. As I have been attempting to show, they are both involved in a *series* of negotiations throughout their lives, and for both of them these negotiations touch at important points on Japan.

And yet we must admit that their negotiations with ghosts are not entirely happy. They want to negotiate, they take up their different positions from which to do so, but the ghosts do not, on the whole, want to respond. Even when they perform their dreaming back, like Swift in *The Words upon the Window-Pane*, communication is somehow blocked: Swift simply repeats again his terrible decline. In Hearn's world the ghosts may come, but they come to the Japanese, and not to Hearn. The kindly ancestral ghosts are not those of his ancestors. The circle which they look over and guard is one from which Hearn is excluded by his birth.

But in one important respect, of course, things have turned out rather better. These attempts at negotiation, or rather, this fascination with the prospect of negotiation, leaves behind it some of the most interesting, if some of the more problematic work, of the two writers. The triangle of ghosts, folklore and Japan – whatever its difficulties – has been a productive one from a literary point of view. The writers finally speak louder than the ghosts – even when the ghosts speak through trumpets.

7

LAFCADIO HEARN AND
USHAW COLLEGE

Louis Allen

Field-Marshall Viscount Montgomery's biographer, and one of Lafcadio Hearn's biographers, improbably, share a common feature: neither of them has a clue where County Durham is. Nigel Hamilton speaks with airy inaccuracy of the Field-Marshall, in war-time, going to shoot on the Yorkshire Moors in Durham; while Vera McWilliams refers to 'life in the Yorkshire hills near Durham'.[1] Let us set the record straight on what seems to be a topographical difficulty. Durham lies between Northumberland, England's northern-most county, on the edge of Scotland, and Yorkshire, England's largest county. In terms of rivers, it lies (or lay, before more recent boundaries) between the Tees and the Tyne, the former noted for the exploitation of iron and steel and the establishment of the world's first passenger railway (the Stockton and Darlington Railway, 1825), and the latter for shipbuilding. Both rivers have Japanese connections: in Darlington, on the banks of the Tees, lies the body of a young samurai from Shikoku, one of the companions of Baba Tatsui, who was drowned in 1873 at the age of 18 while apprenticed to a Middlesbrough shipbuilder. And the Tyne is, of course, the home of the Armstrong shipyards, where were built many of the ships of the Japanese fleet which defeated the Russians at the battle of Tsushima in 1905. It was here, too, that

Fukuzawa Yukichi called in 1862, accompanying the Bakumatsu mission to the Western world which he observed in *Seiyō Jijō*. Fukuzawa's lesson to young Japan – *Datsu-A Nyū-O* (leave Asia, enter Europe), is, interestingly enough, the precise contrary of the lesson preached to the Japanese people by a young boy who entered school in County Durham the year after Fukuzawa had passed through it: Lafcadio Hearn.

The school in question was the Catholic seminary, St Cuthbert's College, at Ushaw about three miles west of Durham City; usually abbreviated to 'Ushaw College'. It still stands, and is now both a seminary and a constituent college of Durham University; itself now home to a Japanese university which has founded in its grounds, in appropriate homage and with an appropriate sense of place, a Lafcadio Hearn Cultural Centre. In the nineteenth century, Ushaw did not merely train budding priests. It also functioned as a minor public school for the sons of Catholic families, with parents overseas, like Hearn's father, a surgeon in Her Majesty's service. In the days of expanding empire, such an educational system was inevitable, in spite of the heartbreaks it produced – witness Kipling's account of his childhood in England. Lafcadio Hearn undoubtedly went through similar emotional stress – at the start – though his immediate family was no further away than Dublin.

It would be wrong, however, to assume that Ushaw as a school, although situated in an area – half moorland, half coal-mining territory – not geographically dissimilar from the bleak background of Dickens's *Nicholas Nickleby*, had too much in common with Dotheboys Hall. It was, of course, intentionally a comfortless place. The only seating then, and for decades later, was backless wooden benches, whether in playrooms, classrooms or refectory. Even fifty years later the boys followed a regime of rising at 6.30 am, seven days a week, followed by Mass at 7.00 and breakfast at 7.45, consisting of bread (with a scraping of butter) and tea, the exception being Christmas Day, when a currant bun was to be had, and Easter Sunday, when everyone had two boiled eggs to celebrate the Resurrection. A solid dinner – beef and potatoes, but cod on Fridays – was followed by 'pod', a brown steamed pudding of suet, currants and spices. Strange as it may seem to us today, it is a fact that beer was also available in fairly copious amounts, as in many English schools at the time. In the evenings, supper was bread and cocoa. After 9.15 pm Benediction, Lights Out was at 10 pm for the seniors, though at 9.00 or 9.15 for the Junior House. Fooling around in the dormitories was a grave offence, punishable by birching ('tipping'). A central heating system had been introduced, but it was not very efficient, and there was no hot water for washing – an impossibly sybaritic concept.

Ushaw had its own nomenclature for dividing groups of pupils. The very beginners were in 'Underlow', divided into First, Second and Third Classes, leading to 'Low Figures'. 'Little Lads' comprised High Figures, Syntax and Grammar, and 'Big Lads' Rhetoric and Poetry. Further up the tree came Philosophers, High and Low, until ultimately the awesome height of Divines was reached by those about to enter the priesthood. The names recall the old medieval categories and were a very natural usage for a school of which the foundations went back to Cardinal Allen's establishment of the English College at Douai in Flanders in the year 1568 (Edmund Campion was a student there before joining the Society of Jesus). Ushaw had a long tradition of learning and piety and self-sacrifice: before the end of Elizabeth's reign, four hundred and fifty priests had run the gauntlet of imprisonment and death under the penal laws to keep alive the old religion in England. This does not mean that learning or the cultivation of the intellect or the imagination for themselves were highly prized. They were not. There was a strong anti-intellectual flavour about English public school education in the nineteenth century which Ushaw did not find in the least strange.

The reason Ushaw was situated where it was resulted from a series of trial-and-error experiments with other locations. The seminary at Douai had provided priests for what was known as the 'English mission' until the anti-clerical forces of the French Revolution drove staff and students back to England in 1795. Catholic emancipation was still thirty-three years away, but the English government's hostility to the Revolution, after the execution of Louis XVI in 1793, guaranteed a welcome to exiled French clergy, and, *pari passu*, to English Catholics compelled to study abroad. So Douai was uprooted, and a home found for it first at Crook Hall, 'isolated. . . in a cheerless district some ten miles to the W.N.W of Durham City';[2] then later at Ushaw in 1808. Rain, wind, and a typhus epidemic greeted the new students and staff, one of whom was the scholar and historian John Lingard, author of the first history of England to be based on primary documentary research. Throughout the nineteenth century, the seminary grew along with the increase in the Catholic population as a whole, new buildings were added to the original house, and chapels were designed for it in the newly fashionable neo-gothic mode by Augustus Welby Pugin.

In 1842, the wave of discontent running through the English school system reached Ushaw. The grounds for it were local – the change of curriculum to make it conform to the requirements of the new University of London, since it was intended to send students in for its examinations. But there was clearly a whole concatenation of causes for such violent protest: students excluded from refectory festivities on the feast of St Cecilia (22 November), 1842, went to the room of the Prefect of Studies and smashed it up, then marched around the House creating a general disturbance, hurling the portable fire pump against the refectory door, and sending one of their number – the College's official rat-catcher who knew his way around the gas pipes – along the Refectory roof to switch off the gas and turn the place into darkness. In the upshot, he slipped and put his foot through the refectory roof, and was barely saved from plunging through the ceiling into the diners below. Another student borrowed a pistol from a local villager for a deposit of ten shillings, and blasted off blank cartridges whenever a patrolling professor came into view. Another hurled a poker at the Prefect as he entered one of the playrooms. The revolt ultimately lost momentum, but not before the Vice-President, Dr Tate, had personally expelled one of the ringleaders by nobbling him in the chapel after Mass and despatching him home in a carriage which was waiting to drive him away.[3]

By the end of the decade the troubles were more or less forgotten. A visitation by certain higher clergy of the north of

England reported that the college superiors were 'perfectly satisfied with the willing, cheerful and ready obedience evinced by the students. . . the internal discipline, piety and studies of the College have proved most satisfactory. . .'. [4] But the revolt had one effect which lingered well into the twentieth century. A new prefect appointed in 1839 had abolished flogging. His overstrict successor, described as 'harsh and ungentlemanly' in his treatment of students, was no doubt one of the contributory factors in the revolt. But the lack of discipline the revolt showed meant that the birch was brought back, and flogging seems to have been a constant element in Ushaw life during Lafcadio's stay there in the 1860s.

Lafcadio arrived in Ushaw twenty years after the revolt, on 9 September 1863. It was the year in which Dr Robert Tate arrived, who had been both prefect and vice-president but preferred to both posts his former existence as a huntin' shootin' and fishin' country chaplain to the Vavasour family in Yorkshire. It was also a year in which not only the rapid development of Ushaw, but also of nineteenth-century English Catholicism as a whole, had come to an end. The worst excesses of the Gothic revival had by then made their mark on both Anglican and Roman Catholic architecture. The Catholic hierarchy had been restored in 1850. The converts of the Oxford Movement had been – some with ease, some with difficulty – absorbed into Roman Catholic life, and some of them were at the forefront of the Ultramontane movement which would culminate in the papal infallibility definition of the First Vatican Council. The revival of scholastic philosophy, the development of a Catholic social teaching, and the debate over Anglican Orders, lay in the decades to come. Robert Tate, therefore, presided over Ushaw at a period – 1863 to 1876 – of communal self-confidence, and also at a time when the endless wrangles between the northern bishops and the college authorities were more or less over.

The great influx of Irish Catholics as a result of the potato famine in Ireland meant that the large increase in the Catholic population required an increase in the number of its priests, so Ushaw grew with the demand, and flourished. The college had a face-lift. Central heating, however inadequate, had already been installed, but a natural history museum was

established, a reading-room was fitted out, a new dormitory
was built, and walks and gardens ornamented the front of the
college. New farm buildings were constructed – the college in
some respects was quite self-supporting – and in the mid-fifties
a laboratory and laundry were added, together with a new
infirmary. Four years before the young Hearn arrived, a
separate building to house junior boys was built in 1859.

In the still extant mark-books of Ushaw, the new student
from Dublin is always entered as 'Paddy Hearn'. His full name
is, of course, Patrick Lafcadio Hearn, and there is no doubt
that the use of his first name was wise: any boy sporting an
outlandish name like Lafcadio was likely to find himself
mercilessly ragged, but '"Paddy" meant that he was a good
fellow and one of the crowd'.[5] The safe orthodoxy of the
name was matched by the tacit appeal of mischief-making and,
in studies, a no more than average performance.

> He was always very much in evidence[6] and played many
> pranks of a peculiar and imaginative kind. I should say he was
> very happy here altogether, had any amount to say, and was
> very original. He was not altogether a desirable boy, from the
> Superior's point of view, yet his playfulness of manner and
> brightness disarmed any feeling of anger for his many
> escapades. He was so very curious a boy, so wild in the
> tumult of his thoughts, that you felt he might do anything in
> different surroundings.[7]

The near-cliché, of the mischievous boy who endears
himself to his school-fellows by his mischievous attitude to
authority, is reinforced by the fact that he does not shine
academically: little interest in mathematics, selective enthu-
siasms for history, fair to good Latin and Greek. But there was
one exception. From the beginning Lafcadio was always top of
his class in English composition, right until the moment he left
Ushaw at the age of seventeen, on 28 October 1867:

> Poor Paddy Hearn![8] I can see his face now, beaming with
> delight at some of his many mischievous plots with which he
> disturbed the College and usually was flogged for... he was
> always considered 'wild as a March hare' and the terror of his
> masters. He laughed at his many whippings, wrote poetry about
> them and the birch, etc., and was, in fact, quite irresponsible.[9]

Following Nina Kennard,[10] Elizabeth Stevenson also quotes
this passage, but strangely and incomprehensively alters the
word 'birch' to 'birth' which makes no sense of what precedes
at all; and she is forced to add a futile explanantion in square
brackets [Virgin birth], thereby attempting to make Lafcadio's
rebellion against authority into a rebellion against the religion
from which the authority derives. This rebellion would no
doubt in time take place; but in *this* context it is an
anachronism. Ushaw was no doubt partly responsible for
Lafcadio's alienation from the Catholic faith, which in turn led
to that conspicuous feature of his observations on Japan, a
dislike of those who tried to spread it – missionary priests;
thence to a dislike of Christianity as a whole.

There was something in the rich liturgical celebrations at
Ushaw which must have appealed to the nascent aesthetic in
him; as he was later to reflect on it from outside, 'the whole
poetry of the thing',[11] which was later to combine with the
interest in the ghostly and the supernatural of childhood and
adolescence, and to be developed in the West Indies and
Japan:

> Roman Catholicism in some Latin countries – with its vast
> world of ghosts, saints, evil and good spirits at each man's
> elbow, – its visions, its miracles, its skulls and bones enshrined
> in silver and gold, – its cruelties and consolations, – its lust-
> exasperating asceticisms that create temptations, – surely to
> understand it all one must have felt either the life of the pagan
> or polytheistic Orient, or understand profoundly the
> polytheism of the antique West.[12]

Understandably, it was the 'spookiness', not the spirituality
of Catholicism which caught his adolescent imagination,
mingled with descriptions of the agonies of Hell evoked by a
hysterical young cousin in Dublin,[13] and with the puritanical
view of religion which was the salient characteristic of his
great-aunt Sarah Brenane's convert Catholicism:

> Her faith was not Catholicism in the expansive, consecrative,
> humanist form, but it was anxious, puritanical, and concerned
> almost entirely with sin and death.[14]

It would, I think, be a mistake to think that Sarah Brenane's

Catholicism was personal and idiosyncratic. Stevenson's description of it would fit nineteenth-century Christianity as a whole, and it was combined with a rejection and fear of sexuality, symbolized perfectly by the action of a tutor employed by Sarah Brenane, in censoring Lafcadio's use of the family library. In an autobiographical fragment, 'Idolatry', quoted at length by Elizabeth Bisland[15] he describes the impact upon him of his first vision of the gods of antiquity, which he had been taught to look upon as goblins and devils:

. . . at last one day I discovered, in one unexplored corner of our library, several beautiful books about art, – great folio books containing figures of gods and of demi-gods, athletes and heroes, nymphs and fauns and nereids, and all the charming monsters – half-man, half-animal – of Greek mythology.

How my heart leaped and fluttered on that happy day! Breathless I gazed; and the longer that I gazed the more unspeakably lovely those faces and forms appeared. Figure after figure dazzled, astounded, bewitched me. . . And these had been called devils! I adored them! – I loved them! – I promised to detest forever all who refused them reverence!. . . Oh! the contrast between that immortal loveliness and the squalor of the saints and the patriarchs and the prophets of my religious pictures! – a contrast indeed as of heaven and hell. . . In that hour the mediaeval creed seemed to me the very religion of ugliness and hate. And as it had been taught to me, in the weakness of my sickly childhood, it certainly was. And even today, in spite of larger knowledge, the words 'heathen' and 'pagan' – however ignorantly used in scorn – revive within me old sensations of light and beauty, of freedom and joy.[16]

Then, inevitably, the books of drawings were discovered, and removed from the boy's reach 'the phantom of rapture forgotten'.[17]

When the books re-appeared on the shelves, they had been 'unmercifully revised. . .'

My censors had been offended by the nakedness of the gods, and had undertaken to correct that impropriety. Parts of many figures, dryads, naiads, graces, muses had been found too charming and erased with a pen-knife; – I can still recall one beautiful seated figure, whose breasts had been thus excised. Evidently 'the breasts of the nymphs in the brake' had been found too charming: dryads, naiads, graces and muses – all had been rendered breastless. And, in most cases, *drawers* had been put upon the gods – even upon the tiny Loves – large baggy bathing-drawers, woven with cross-strokes of a quill-pen, so designed as to conceal all curves of beauty, – especially the lines of the long fine thighs.[18]

Equally inevitably, the clumsy screening had its own counter-effect: the young Lafcadio spent hours trying to reproduce the original contours in pencil strokes, – which enabled him, he later thought, to understand how Greek art had idealized the human figure. His conclusion is clear enough: it was the pursuit of a beauty which had been hidden from him, that led him to reject the religion in which he had been brought up:

> Now after I had learned to know and to love the elder gods, the world again began to glow about me. Glooms that had brooded over it slowly thinned away. The terror was not yet gone; but I now wanted only reasons to disbelieve all that I feared and hated. In the sunshine, in the green of the fields, in the blue of the sky, I found a gladness before unknown. Within myself new thoughts, new imaginings, dim longings for I knew not what were quickening and thrilling. I looked for beauty, and everywhere found it: in passing faces – in attitudes and motions, – in the poise of plants and trees, – in long white clouds, – in faint-blue lines of far-off hills. At moments the simple pleasure of life would quicken to a joy so large, so deep, that it frightened me. But at other times there would come to me a new and strange sadness, – a shadowy and inexplicable pain.
> I had entered into my Renaissance.[19]

Ushaw's attitude to the physical charms of the gods and goddesses of antiquity would be little different from those of his vigilant Irish tutor, at any rate in its view of sexuality. But I cannot help thinking that the account in a letter to George Gould[20] of his confession made to Mr Wrennall[21], is derived, not from experience, but from a literary memory, a reading of Flaubert's *La Tentation de Saint Antoine*, which he was later to translate and to recommend to Basil Hall Chamberlain:[22]

> When I was a boy I had to go to confession, and my

confessions were honest ones. One day I told the ghostly
father that I had been guilty of desiring that the devil would
come to me in the shape of the beautiful women in which he
came to the anchorites in the desert, and that I thought I
should yield to such temptations. He was a grim man who
rarely showed emotion, my confessor, but on that occasion he
actually rose to his feet in anger.

'Let me warn you!' he cried, 'let me warn you! Of all things
never wish that! You might be more sorry for it than you can
possibly believe!'

His earnestness filled me with a fearful joy; – for I thought
the temptation might actually be realized – so serious he
looked. . . but the pretty succubi all continued to remain in
hell.[23]

A counterpoint to his fascinated fear of the supernatural was
a romantic obsession with ghosts and night, something he
shared with a fellow-pupil at Ushaw, Achilles Daunt, from
Ireland like himself: Kilcasan Castle, County Cork. They told
each other stories:

Knightly feats of arms, combats with gigantic foes in deep
forests, low red moons throwing their dim light across desolate
spaces and glinting on the armour of great champions, storms
howling over wastes, and ghosts shrieking in the gale – these
were favourite topics of conversation.[24]

Lafcadio did not lack for friends during his days at Ushaw.
But there was something missing. Not just the resolute plainness of nineteenth-century religion in its Catholic version of
Arnold's muscular Christianity (in contrast to the ornate
gothic of Pugin's chapel, and the splendours of Ushaw's choir)
but also the hostility to any beauty derived from sexuality,
were compounded with a resolute turning away from the
feminine element in life and society. This was natural enough
in an institution devoted to training celibate priests. More than
half a century later, when around forty maids of all work were
employed in the college – they were known as 'Betties' – for a
weekly wage of 4/6d and all found, the boys rarely if ever set
eyes on them.[25]

In terms not of sex but of natural companionship, Lafcadio
at Ushaw was therefore doubly deprived, held prisoner in a
motherless world. An exclusively male society, strict and

authoritarian in manner, and ultimately devoted to an ideal –
the ecclesiastical life – of which celibacy was an absolute
component, brought home to him ever more strongly the loss
of his mother.
There is some ambiguity here. Lafcadio never saw his
mother after 1856, when he was six years old. She has been
described as capricious and tyrannical to her children[26] and
Lafcadio remembers being slapped by her, but the cause seems
understandable enough:

> My mother's face only I remember, and I remember it for this
> reason. One day it bent over me caressingly. It was delicate
> and dark, with large black eyes – very large. A childish impulse
> came to me to slap it. I slapped it – simply to see the result,
> perhaps. The result was immediate and severe castigation, and
> I remember both crying and feeling I deserved what I got. I
> felt no resentment, although the aggressor in such cases is
> usually the most indignant at consequences.[27]

Writing to his brother, in adulthood, in an attempt to help
him recall their mother, it is the dark beauty that he recalls,
and his conviction that it is from her that his true nature
derives:

> And you do not remember that dark and beautiful face – with
> dark brown eyes like a wild deer's – that used to bend over
> your cradle? You do not remember the voice which told you
> each night to cross your fingers after the old Greek orthodox
> fashion, and utter the words Ἐν τὸ ὄνομα τοῦ Πατρὸς καὶ
> τοῦ Ἱοῦ καὶ τοῦ Ἁγίου Πνεύματος, [In the name of the
> Father, and of the Son, and of the Holy Ghost]. . .
> Whatever there is of good in me came from that dark race-
> soul of which we know so little. My love of right, my hate of
> wrong; – my admiration for what is beautiful or true; – my
> capacity for faith in man or woman; – my sensitiveness to
> artistic things which gives me whatever little success I have, –
> even that language-power whose physical sign is in the large
> eyes of both of us, – came from Her. . . It is the mother who
> makes us. . .[28]

Even his surrogate-mother, his great-aunt Sarah Brenane,
had given over her affections - and control over her fortune –
to another distant relative Henry Hearn Molyneux, in whose

house in England she finally settled; a house where Lafcadio was made less and less welcome, so that in the later years at Ushaw he spent not merely the terms but also some of the vacations in the by then almost deserted halls and corridors.

The power of that mother-image continued to haunt Lafcadio. It reappears most vividly in the Rip Van Winkle story of Urashima Tarō, who is taken by a sea-maiden to the kingdom of the sea, where he tastes all possible pleasures, but feels heavy-hearted when he thinks of his lonely parents waiting for him at home. The sea-maiden lets him return, bearing a box he is instructed not to open. The village is the same, but strangely altered, and Urashima finds his own monument in its graveyard. He opens the box, from which a cold white spectral vapour escapes, and learns that he has destroyed his own happiness. He can never return to the sea-kingdom, and he shrivels up and dies. Hearn sets this story against the background of a journey he made along the shores of Urashima, borne by a sprinting rickshaw-puller under the telegraph wires and the transparent sunlight, the sound of the wheels drowned by a deep booming, village drums asking the gods for rain. And his compassion for Urashima Taro turns inward upon himself, to the child he once was. He, too, has known the same metamorphosis from paradise. And the adult Hearn, carapace thickened by now against insult and indifference, sends his memory sliding past the coast of Japan, the hot Antilles, the bitter starving streets of Cincinnati, and the tall cold rooms, resounding chapel and woods of Ushaw College, to a childhood Eden over which his mother presides:

> I have memory of a place and a magical time in which the Sun and the Moon were larger and brighter than now. Whether it was of this life or some life before I cannot tell. . . the days were ever so much longer than these days. . . and every day there were new wonders and pleasures for me. And all that country and all that time were softly ruled by One who thought only of ways to make me happy. Sometimes I would refuse to be made happy, and that always caused her pain, although she was divine; – and I remember that I tried very hard to be sorry. When day was done, and there fell the great hush of the light before moonrise, she would tell me stories

that made me tingle from head to foot with pleasure. I have never heard any other stories half so beautiful. And when the pleasure became too great, she would sing a weird little song which always brought sleep.

At last there came a parting day; and she wept, and told me of a charm she had given that I must never, never lose, because it would keep me young, and give me power to return. But I never returned. And the years went; and one day I knew that I had lost the charm, and had become ridiculously old.[29]

For someone as devoted to the Eternal Feminine as Lafcadio, the loss of maternal affection must have been a great wound to the psyche. Yet neither the enforced alienation from his mother, for which Ushaw is not responsible, nor the beatings inflicted by Ushaw's Prefect, seem to have turned Lafcadio into an unhappy schoolboy, as accounts by his contemporaries make clear.

But the posed photograph of him at the age of 16 (between pp. xx and xxi of Elizabeth Bisland's Introduction to *The Japanese Letters of Lafcadio Hearn*) gives a totally different impression. The awkward seated pose, elbow uncomfortably on a side table, the stiff, heavy black suit and the glum, unsmiling face not looking directly at the camera, show that something untoward has happened. The clue lies, of course, in the right eye, the eye nearest the camera. The left eye is barely visible, but the right one is – ever so slightly – bulbous, seeming almost to protrude. That eye is the key to a change in Lafcadio's life: a casual accident at a game in college, which was to modify his whole existence.

Along with the college silver, a number of traditions, and a library of books, the exiled professors from Douai brought back to Ushaw certain traditional games peculiar to their institution.[30] Special ball courts were built in playing-fields next to the main House. One game was called 'Giant's Stride', and in it a knotted rope was used. During the game of Giant's Stride, in the year 1866, Lafcadio was struck in the eye by a length of knotted rope. The eye became inflamed, and in spite of an operation to save it, he lost the sight of that eye. 'Scar tissue formed', writes Elizabeth Stevenson, 'and whitened the surface of the cornea. The eyeball was not removed.'[31] To a sufferer from myopia, as Lafcadio was, the loss of an eye was perilous in more ways than one. To make up for it, he used his remaining eye punishingly – he was a voracious reader – and it began, little by little, to bulge from the socket.

The effect of this loss, and the gradual deformation which acompanied it, on such a susceptible and passionate nature, was traumatic. The conviction that he was socially – and sexually – unacceptable led to a withdrawal from society: 'He was sure he could not please, so his practice was to back off like an awkward crab... It was only sometimes with women of an entirely different background that he could forget he was not acceptable.'[32] The combative vivaciousness of the mischievous schoolboy gradually gave way to the diffident and solitary adolescent. The change was compounded by a quite Dickensian change in his fortunes. The ruination of his great-aunt's estate by Henry Molyneux, who had effectively elbowed the boy Lafcadio out of the succession, meant there were no more funds to keep him at Ushaw. He left on 28 October, 1867, at the age of seventeen, to live in the East End of London with a former servant of his great-aunt. Then, in the spring of 1869, he was packed off to a distant relative in the United States. It was there, in Cincinnati, that he found sexual acceptance, in the arms of a pretty young mulatto girl Mattie Foley. She was the daughter of a white plantation owner and a slave mother, illiterate, but a brilliant talker; in 1874 he married her, though the legality of the marriage was doubtful. A decade before Lafcadio left for Japan, Mattie married again.

Some friends shunned him after this marriage, but more important was the damage done to his eyesight by constant newspaper work and proof-reading. He could not read without pain, he wrote from Memphis to a friend, Henry Watkin, long after he had left Mattie behind, and confessed to him that he wept at night, just as he had done at Ushaw when he returned there after the holidays.[33] He was desperately afraid of going blind. In this way, the accident at Ushaw left its permanent mark on him. It is possible to see this, by contraries, as it were, in the way he later described the form and shape of the Japanese eye:

To me the Japanese eye has a beauty which I think Western

eyes have not. . . The most beautiful pair of eyes I ever saw – a
pair that fascinated me a great deal too much, and caused me
to do some foolish things in old bachelor days – were Japanese.
They were not small, but very characteristically racial; the
lashes were very long, and the opening also of the lids; – and
the feeling they gave one was that of the eyes of a great
wonderful bird of prey. – There are wonderful eyes in Japan
for those who can see. . .

There is a beauty of the Japanese eyelid, quite rare, but very
singular, – in which the lid-edge seems double, or at least
marvellously grooved, – and the effect is a softness and
shadowiness difficult to describe.

However, it seems to me that the chief beauty of a beautiful
Japanese eye is in the peculiar anatomical arrangement which
characterizes it. The ball of the eye is *not* shown, – the setting
is totally hidden. The brown smooth skin opens quite
suddenly and strangely over a moving jewel. Now in the
most beautiful Western eyes the set of the ball into the skull is
visible, – the whole orbed form, and the whole line of the
ball-socket, – except in special cases. The mechanism is visible.
I think that from a perfectly artistic point of view, the veiling
of the mechanism is a greater feat on Nature's part. . . that
which least shows the *machinery behind it* – the osteological and
nervous machinery – now appears to me to have the greater
charm.[34]

That is the human eye in Japan, passionately examined in its
mechanism and beauty by one who has the full and bitter
knowledge of the destruction of beauty in his own, nearly
thirty years before.

We can, therefore, select two factors in his life at Ushaw
which had a permanent effect on Lafcadio's life. One, internal,
conjugated with the fears of his Dublin childhood, is the
gradual sloughing away of belief in Catholicism, which is seen
as a destroyer of beauty; the other, external, is the accident
which partially destroyed his sight and left him ashamed of the
appearance he was sure he presented to the outside world,
particularly that side of it, the Eternal Feminine, which he was
so anxious to impress.

There is a corollary to his loss of faith, which will become
conspicuous in his view of Japanese history and the Japan of
the nineteenth century: his aversion to missionaries and

missionary activity. In part, this is based on his mistrust of change of any sort in Japan, as almost inevitably change for the worse; and, of course, the attempted missionary Christianization of Japan was one of the foremost instruments of change. This idea is expressed most unambiguously in the chapter 'Reflections' of his last work, *Japan: An Interpretation*:

> From the sociological point of view the whole missionary system, irrespective of sect and creed, represents the skirmishing-force of Western civilization in its general attack upon all civilizations of the ancient type, – the first line in the forward movement of the strongest and most highly evolved societies upon the weaker and less evolved. The conscious work of these fighters is that of preachers and teachers; their unconscious work is that of sappers and destroyers. The subjugation of weak races has been aided by their work to a degree little imagined; and by no other conceivable means could it have been accomplished so quickly and so surely. For destruction they labour unknowingly, like a force of nature. Yet Christianity does not appreciably expand. They perish; and they really lay down their lives, with more than the courage of soldiers, not, as they hope, to assist the spread of that doctrine which the East must still of necessity refuse, but to help industrial enterprise and Occidental aggrandizement. The real and avowed object of missions is defeated by persistent indifference to sociological truths; and the martyrdoms and sacrifices are utilized by Christian nations for ends essentially opposed to the spirit of Christianity.

This is, of course, the anti-Christian case of the Enlightenment, put in nineteenth-century terms. But behind the sociological reasoning lies also Lafcadio's antipathy to those missionaries who were his contemporaries in Japan, and who in their mode of life represented that Victorian puritanism and distrust of sensual beauty which he had recognized years before in his Rathmines tutor and in the Spartan restrictions of Ushaw; and from which he had turned with passionate relief to the warmth of Creole life in the West Indies, long before he thought of coming to Japan.

The aesthetic element also forms part of his critique of pre-nineteenth-century Jesuit missions in Japan. While conceding that Roman Catholicism, as monotheism, was a stage in advance of primitive ancestor worship, he claimed that it was only adapted to a society 'in which the ancient family had been dissolved, and the religion of filial piety forgotten'.[35] Neither Chinese nor Japanese society had reached that point, and 'the religion of the Jesuits' could never adapt itself to the social conditions of Japan. The repressive measures taken against it by Ieyasu 'signify sociologically no more than the national perception of supreme danger'.[36] They were a recognition that the triumph of Catholicism would involve the total disintegration of Japanese society.

Lafcadio stresses that not only the sociologist but also the artist should be glad of the failure of the missions, because it permitted the survival of the world of Japanese art, traditions, beliefs and customs. 'Roman Catholicism, triumphant, would have swept all this out of existence. The natural antagonism of the artist to the missionary may be found in the fact that the latter is always, and must be, an unsparing destroyer. . . Even could they have understood and felt the meaning of that world of strange beauty, – result of a race-experience never to be repeated or replaced, – they would not have hesitated a moment in the work of obliteration and effacement.'[37]

There was a strong personal element in this antipathy to missionaries past and present, and Lafcadio was sure the hostility was mutual. In his unhappy days at Kumamoto, he was convinced missionaries were conspiring against him, and that one of his school colleagues was spying on him and reporting him to them.[38] Earlier, he had been even more specific in a letter to Chamberlain about missionaries in Matsue:

> You ask about Matsue foreigners. If it is nothing very special I think I can get you whatever information you want. . .
> . . . Just now I can't remember the names of the beasts who were there before B –, but the story is not spoiled for that. They aimed especially at converting Samurai girls – because these were educated, and supposed to still possess some small influence. They were also very poverty-stricken, – desperate, starving; struggling between death and dishonour, – for Samurai girls had high notions of chastity. What missionaries wanted was native local proselytizers. They induced one girl by promises of employment to become a preacher for them.

Of course in becoming a convert, she became a social pariah. Her people cast her off; common folk despised her. She was an innocent sort of a girl, – talked simply and feebly, – betrayed in her very manner the necessity and compulsion. The people paid no attention to her. The missionaries dropped her as a useless instrument. Then no one would give her work or help. She became a prostitute. But even as a prostitute, her connection with proselytism had rendered her disreputable. So she was sold to an Osaka brothel.[39]

As if to achieve a balance between this logically inconsequential horror-story of missionary ill-treatment, Lafcadio continues in the same letter to reflect on what appears to be a muddled version of his Ushaw boyhood, seen at a falsifying remove of thirty years (Ushaw was an exclusively secular college, and had no Jesuit connections at all):

By the way, what you say about Rome awakes a chord. You know, I suppose, that my relatives tried once to make a priest of me. My father was an Episcopalian; but after his death in India, I fell into the hands of relatives who sent me to a Jesuit College.[40] By the Jesuit standard, I was a fiend incarnate, and treated accordingly. How I hated them. My impotent resentment used to relieve itself in the imagination of massacres and horible tortures. I hate them and have nightmares about them still. And yet at times, there comes to me a half wish to be a monk. This is all a romance, – the romance of the ideal monastery, with gothic ogives, libraries of vellums illumined by the stained-glass windows, etc., and rest from struggle. But the reality is Browning's 'Soliloquy of the Spanish Cloister'. Still, there is a world of romance in old Romanism.[41]

That he had left behind among his Ushaw comrades the impression of a bold adolescent sceptic is true enough. But what scepticism there was *at the time* was no doubt partly due to a desire to shock, as his friend and contemporary Achilles Daunt recalled:

He was of a very speculative turn of mind, and I have a lively recollection of the shock it occasioned to several of us when he one day announced his disbelief in the Bible. I am of opinion, however, that he was then only posing as an *esprit fort*, for a few days afterwards, during a week with the class in the

country, he returned to this subject in discussion with a
master, and I inferred from what he said to me that he was
quite satisfied with the evidences of the truth of the
Scriptures.[42]

According to Elizabeth Bisland, Lafcadio was convinced
that the Church, with persistent memory and far-reaching
hand, had never forgotten or forgiven his apostasy, nor failed
to remind him of the fact from time to time.

> This conviction remained a dim and threatening shadow in
> the background of his whole life; to all remonstrances on the
> subject his only reply was 'You don't know the Church as I
> do'; and several curious coincidences in crises of his career
> seemed to justify and confirm this belief.[43]

There is a grain of truth in this, as far as Ushaw is concerned,
and not only 'apostasy' is the cause. In the eyes of a Victorian
seminary, Lafcadio had committed not merely apostasy but
any number of other sins as well. He had lived with a woman
in Cincinnati (the 'marriage' came later), and, what was worse,
she was not a white woman; and when, later in Japan, he
married a Japanese wife, he not merely forsook his name and
nationality but also espoused her religion. Recalling the
imperial assumptions in Ushaw's psychology only a few short
years after Lafcadio's death, Mgr McReavy recalls the jingoism
of the day, and nowhere indicates that staff and students did
not share it:

> Britain was indisputably top-nation, alike in its wealth and in
> the unprecedented extent of its empire, a fact of life in which I
> had been trained at my father's knee to exult, almost as though
> I had shared in its achievement and benefitted greatly from it.
> Jingoism indeed was endemic, part of the national faith.[44]

Lafcadio's misdemeanours – insofar as they were noised
abroad – must clearly have aroused three separate and
powerful reflexes at his Alma Mater, religious, moral, and
patriotic. It is interesting that the College's official history,
published as recently as 1964, and replete with all sorts of
references to instantly forgettable minor ecclesiastics of the
North-East of England, makes no mention of Lafcadio
anywhere. The poet Francis Thompson, on the other hand,

who arrived there three years after Lafcadio had left, and lived
for a longer period the same squalid life of the streets that
Lafcadio knew in London and Cincinnati, finds a tiny place in
it. But during the decadent 90s Thompson had remained
within the fold, and so was mentionable.[45]
The omission of Lafcadio's name is all the more curious
since the history's bibliography lists an article by Martin Vasey,
a former pupil and later professor of English at Ushaw, who
published an article 'Ushaw Authorship' in the *Ushaw
Magazine* for 1940.[46] There is a whiff of hagiography about
it, and a good deal of it is pious literary archeology, though the
writer is humorous enough to detect in at least one of his
subjects, Fr Thomas Allen, a clerical poet, an almost
McGonagall-esque ineptitude:

> 'Tis Flora the Saracen seeketh fair haven,
> Are dark her fair features, her tresses are raven.
> Behold her fair forehead is wounded and ruddy,
> Her once comely countenance pallid and bloody.

It is not difficult to agree with a reviewer of Fr Allen's verse:
'We have seen worse; but not much.'[47]
Vasey forthrightly describes Lafcadio as the most outstanding of Ushaw's secular writers, devoting three pages to
him. The picture drawn is of a sentimental, morbid
personality, which is put forward as the explanation for
Lafcadio's associating Catholicism with unhappiness; a man
guided by feelings rather than intelligence who 'consequently[48] desired a more physical union with a material
godhead'.[49] Refusing to accept accounts of Lafcadio as an
'initiate' of Buddhism, Vasey echoes Lafcadio's own
description of himself as a pantheist, tracing this to the
familiar episode in *Exotics and Retrospectives* which he situates
at Ushaw:

> I remember when a boy lying on my back in the grass, gazing
> into the summer blue above me, and wishing that I could melt
> into it, – become a part of it. For these fancies I believe that a
> religious tutor was innocently responsible: he had tried to
> explain to me, because of certain dreamy questions, what he
> termed 'the folly and the wickedness of pantheism', – with the
> result that I immediately became a pantheist, at the tender age

of fifteen. And my imaginings presently led me not only to want the sky for a playground, but also to become the sky!⁵⁰

Vasey concludes that Lafcadio was 'an exception even of exceptions', and that his life 'seems to fly off at a tangent from the kind of life one expects from an Ushawman – the part played by his Alma Mater in shaping his career is extremely difficult to estimate'.⁵¹ The conclusion is easy to share, because the direction of the influence is largely negative: in almost everything that Ushaw tried to inculcate in him, Lafcadio went resolutely the opposite way. But one can surely affirm that Ushaw, where he lived the tempestuous years of adolescence, was the *locus* of immense and enduring changes in his life: internally, the hostile re-assessment of Christianity; and externally, the wound to body and psyche represented by that moment, in a casual game, which altered forever his whole way of considering his relationships with others.

APPENDIX

My contribution should end here, but I would like to add some notes, at a tangent to its main theme, which bear on the question of missionaries, and have a particular relevance to Matsue.

The notes derive from the transcription of a diary kept in Matsue and elsewhere in Japan between 12 February 1908 and 21 January 1909. The diarist, Gillian Mary Barclay, nee Birkbeck, was the young wife of a missionary, Joseph Gurney Barclay ('G' in the diary), born at Bixley, Norfolk on 25 October 1882; she married in 1905, went out to Japan three years later, and died on 15 May, 1909; she had given birth to a son. She came from a wealthy, cultivated background, and seems to have had a lively passionate nature. 'Gilly, the eldest, was, I think, the most remarkable of the family', writes Constance Sitwell of the Birkbecks in her memoir *Bright Morning*,⁵² 'with her pale vivid face and her ardent nature; she was the liveliest and most poetic of our crew as a girl, and as years went on became intensely religious; after her marriage she went to Japan and there she died when she was twenty-six.'

Constance Sitwell speaks of the love and friendship, and 'the extraordinary purity and freshness' of the Birkbeck household. It is clear that Gillian, in her tragically short missionary life, felt obliged to damp down her own ardent enthusiasm for the minor joys of life in the most unnecessary fashion. Like her husband Gurney, she was the descendant of a family of wealthy Quaker bankers who had entered the Church of England. Poor girl, she did not last long. After a year in Matsue she went to Kobe to give birth to her son, Roderick, on 22 February 1909 and was dead less than three months later.

She wrote up her diary at regular intervals and posted it home, along with her drawings and photographs. The typist made mistakes in transcribing Japanese names here and there (Miyajinia for Miyajima, for instance), where her writing must have been hard to decipher; and the illustrations have not come down with the transcript. In spite of this, the 200-page record is a fascinating glimpse of life in Matsue at the end of the Meiji period, and also sheds light on the motivation and character of one Protestant missionary, as well as the colleagues and converts who surrounded her.

Her comfortable English background, and a happy married life in Cambridge, did not prevent her from being socially aware, and she has an eye for suffering as well as happiness. Her wish to conform to the norms in dress and behaviour imposed by her fellow missionaries are no doubt genuine, but it is clear that common-sense breaks out now and then in the form of agonized (and occasionally exasperated) self-questioning. Like Lafcadio, she is intensely aware of the visual beauty of Japan. Like him, she notes trees, flowers, and butterflies; unlike him, the rest of Matsue's insect world she finds purgatorial in the hot summer months.

But my reason for adducing this piece of evidence about Meiji Matsue is to provide some reinforcement for Lafcadio's views of missionary behaviour; as well as to suggest that, in some respects, he has got them wrong. Gillian Barclay's observations show that whatever their essential goodness and dedication, they can be pharisaical towards the rest of the foreign colony, – referred to as 'the Community' –, particularly in Kobe or Karuizawa. They are also casuistically

puritanical in dress and deportment, and one can sense the
natural happiness and sense of beauty of a young girl full of life
being quenched by their disapproval.

Interestingly enough, Gillian gives no sign of ever having
heard of Lafcadio. She seems to have no idea that a writer on
Japan, by then very well-known, had lived in the town where
she spent such an eventful year. In one note she speaks of there
being no 'non-missionaries' for hundreds of miles, a reference
which might well have evoked a mention of the Hearn
family's former presence. After all, he had only been dead four
years when she arrived in Matsue.

There are, too, I'm afraid, occasions when sheer social
snobbery breaks through Gillian's observations on her fellow
missionaries:

> Somehow I think it is easier (she writes on 26 March 1908) to
> feel a real sister with the Japanese women than with the
> missionaries – perhaps not with the real missionaries – they are
> generally such saints that one doesn't see their outsides, and
> only feels unworthy to be their friend, but with the *half*
> missionaries – Mrs L. for instance – it is so difficult to listen
> patiently to the endless chatter of her small frivolous mind. She
> is about the same class as a village shopkeeper's wife at home,
> and her patronage is fearful! Her whole conversation consists
> of clothes (I will leave her attempts at finery – pale blue velvet
> trimmings, ragged white ostrich feathers, etc. - undescribed)
> her servant difficulties. . .
> . . . but this isn't very Sunday writing so I must stop.

But those who despise clothes are even more of a problem:

> Mr Wilkes came on board after breakfast, and a Miss Harrison,
> who I think is one of his workers, and at sight of her I rushed
> to put away the hat with flowers I had meant to wear, feeling
> quite ashamed of its frivolity! Clothes are an awful question
> altogether. (19 March 1908).

We come closer to Lafcadio-like but ambivalent exasperation
with the missionary style of living in an entry for 24 August
1908. There are two topics raised here at some length, the old
vexed question of clothes, and that of games; both, clearly, a
trap for the unwary innocent:

> I was very amused before we left England by the number of

people who asked which I was going to be out here, a missionary or Gurney's wife: and I said both. But how much simpler it would be to be one thing or the other! Easier still to do neither well. Everyone who has ever had a house knows what endless *time* as well as thought has to be spent if all is to go well, and out here much more so with Japanese servants, who can do nothing by themselves.

With such pressing needs all round one, the question must come, how much of this time is it right to spend?

Putting the question of food and cooking, which involve G's missionary efficiency, entirely on one side I mean all the little things that go to make a house comfortable, of which perhaps 'doing the flowers' is one of the smallest parts, not *necessary* things in any way as far as health goes, is time spent over them being spent the very best way for the cause of Christ?

. . . G. and I went once to luncheon with some missionaries, the best I think that we have met since we came to Japan, the most spiritually minded, unselfish, whole hearted, hard-working people you could find. I shall never forget their room, no pictures. . . no carpet, dining room, and drawing room all in one, and the furniture looking as if most of it had been made out of packing cases. I was taken upstairs to the dreariest of attics where few English servants would care to sleep, more packing case furniture and the hardest looking beds. Certainly the 'Not I' part of Gal. 2.20 was written all over that house, as the 'but Christ' is written in their shining faces, and as I got back into our drawing room the thought came that these people were living much nearer to the Master who 'has not where to lay His head' than we with all our sofa cushions.

Still Solomon's virtuous woman 'looked well to the ways of her household' and it is hard to imagine anything either ugly or untidy in that house: her own clothes too were 'purple and fine linen'. Oh! the question of clothes out here! At home it is all so simple, you pray before you go out shopping think of them very much while you are choosing them, try and find Christian clothes, and once bought all bother is at an end. Here by the keenest people everything pretty is thought wicked, changing at all in the evening (I don't mean into low frocks) worldly. One of our best friends out here told G. he thought it would be wrong even to possess evening clothes. It must take far more time to choose the ugly things most people wear: I don't think I have ever thought so much about clothes as since I came to Japan, one looks at every frill and scrap of lace with suspicion, hopes that trimmings won't be noticed, pulls off buttons and flattens down hats!

Her anxiety lest 'Babylonish garments' might hinder the Christian revival she longs for, Gillian is equally perplexed about holidays and games. G had brought his tennis racquet with him, but was told exercise, though a necessity, could more profitably be had from walks:

> . . . we never realized till we got here how strong the feeling was among a certain set (and they apparently the best and keenest) against tennis and all games, in fact all forms of amusement. We have actually heard prayers for those 'poor missionaries looking forward to a summer of pleasure'. . .

Not only clothes, furniture and games; jewellery was even more abhorrent:

(22 May 1908)

> I had been very uncomfortable about my jewellery ever since the morning before at Arima, when, just as I was going in to breakfast one of the missionaries stopped me and asked if I did not think I ought to give it up? I told her I had prayed about it, and did not think it in the least wrong for myself, and that the things I was wearing were not for ornament, but I loved them because of the people who gave them: also that I had asked Elizabeth and Jane if they thought it could do any harm at Matsuye, and they had both said no, and so had Miss Bosanquet, whom I had consulted when she stayed with us. She went on to say, however, that she was not the only person who had noticed my jewellery: others had talked of it too, and how very plainly I ought to dress, etc, etc. I felt very wretched about it, I thought my clothes had been very plain, nothing but grays and brown hollands, and occasionally dark green, the whole time, though *I can't* see that colours are wrong when God has made everything so beautiful He can't mind them. Please don't think me very wicked if I draw this picture of one of the Kobe missionaries, who scrapes back all her hair as tight as she can under a tam-o-shanter, and for someone who is anyhow 'elderly' I can't see that it is to the glory of God to look like that!

It is difficult not to sympathize with Gillian's feeble but

wistful theological attempt to justify pretty surroundings:

> I am beginning to think[53] that even one's natural instincts to make the house look pretty may become a temptation. Please pray that we may have wisdom in all these things. I am not sure what I think about any of them yet. A pretty house is much more resting than an ugly one. . . Then there are the richer Japanese to consider – they probably would not be hindered, and God might even use a nice house to attract them, with all those soldiers coming to Matsuye in October, ought we not to consider the officers' wives and those sort of people?

She is oppressed, too, by the contrast between the beauty of Japanese temples and the kind of churches the missionaries have been erecting:

> Ever since we sat in that lovely Shinto temple in Nagasaki I have wished so that as they became Christians, their temples could be turned into churches. It was so with the Sicilian heathen temples, and I don't see why it should not be so here. With these people's love of everything beautiful I don't know what they must think of the hideous little churches and mission rooms we build, all so utterly unjapanese. It seems to me that Christianity ought to be represented to them in as eastern a way as possible. I should have every church in the middle of a lovely garden where the people could sit and meditate.
> (8 April 1908)

However horrified he might have been by the take-over proposition, Lafcadio could hardly have disapproved of the thought behind it; and might well have been surprised at the sermon Gillian quotes with approval:

> In so far as we Europeanise these people in so far as missionaries we fail (12 April 1908).

She feels this particularly so for a people with such a natural sense of the beauty of objects:

> I am always thinking it was such a pity Ruskin never came here, he would have appreciated these people so, with their love of beautiful things. He would have been pleased too with their hatred of luxury, and the care and trouble they take with

the things they make. Each detail is perfectly finished, till sometimes they get so fond of what they have made they can hardly be persuaded to sell it! The very fact that the *linings* of their kimonos are made of far more beautiful and expensive stuff than the outside would have delighted him.
(2 April 1908)

Luxury, or at any rate comfort, was a source of grievance to her. A Japanese missionary who introduced her and Gurney to the Matsue congregation laid great emphasis on what they had left behind in England. This was a gauge of their missionary zeal and it was oddly capped by a stranger to the congregation who added his own contribution:

> The third (who) got up was a worker who had come from outside, not a Matsuye man at all: he was very funny and said it was one thing for us to give up our lives to Japan, but another thing to come here of all places, even the Japanese wouldn't come here if they could help it, and he hadn't at all wanted to come himself. Everyone knew that Matsuye was the most inconvenient place in the country, and what must it be for the foreigners etc. If the good man only knew it, its remoteness is its chief charm, and I have come to dread nothing more than the advent of the railway and the 'conveniences' that will bring.There is even a threat of tramlines too, imagine a tram in Matsuye!
> (28 May 1908)

But natural beauty does not blind Gillian to grave faults in Japanese society. Already on the boat which brought them to Japan they had come across a *karayuki-san* who had been sent home to die:

> On the ship coming out with us there was a poor girl, one of those who had either sold herself or been sold into slavery at Singapore. Now she is very ill, dying of consumption, so they were letting her go home.

Factory life, too, is as appalling as in early Victorian England:

> I think of all the factories in that great big Osaka, almost every one under English management: have we no responsibility there? The conditions are much the same as they were in England when Mrs Browning's 'Cry of the Children' was written, only here the wheels never stop either on Sundays or

by night: women and girls from eight years upwards, working in shifts of twelve hours each, a day shift and a night shift, changing I think about once a month. The description of the misery of these girls' lives is too sad to write about, and believing as they do that death is the end of all things, it is no wonder that they commit suicide in hundreds every year. . .

. . . imagine what it must be for them, they are boarded there and everything, one thousand going to sleep at night in the places the other thousand have just got up from. The government have made a law that all children over seven must go to school, so they have their own school inside the factory, to which the children are sent *out of sleeping time, after their twelve hours' work.*

(13 April 1908)

Problems with cooks, with insects, with puritanical colleagues, with 'horrible' Japanese tea and food, in the end make Gillian conclude 'This *is* an unmissionary diary. I have been reading it through, and it seems to be all about food, but as I said at Matsuye I lived among the pots and pans, and one can only write about what one is doing.' Fortunately, she writes about a great deal more, and her wrestling with her conscience and her outgoing sympathy for the women of 'the Community', who gamble, smoke and drink cocktails all Sunday from morning till night ('till their children do the same: little girls of eleven and twelve smoking cigarettes and sometimes quite drunk' – 17 January 1909) and are termed 'the ungodly' by her missionary friends, make her a warm and complex human being. One wonders if anyone in Matsue ever left a record of meeting her?

I have left a copy of the complete transcription of the diary with the Lafcadio Hearn Museum, in the hope that historians of Matsue and Shimane Prefecture may find her record of interest.

HEARN AND THE GASTRONOMIC GROTESQUE

Alan Rosen

A mong the great variety of topics treated in the works of Lafcadio Hearn, that of food and eating occupies a place of surprising prominence. As we know from his letters and his biographers, especially E.L. Tinker, Hearn's interest in food was much wider than that of the typical 'hungry' young writer. He was the compiler of a lengthy cookbook on Creole cuisine; he was the owner of a short-lived, low-priced New Orleans restaurant called 'The Hard Times', in which he served as waiter and manager. He is said to have divorced Althea Foley because, among other reasons, he did not like her cooking. He changed his living quarters in New Orleans just to be near Mrs Courtney's wonderful dining-room, and he even dedicated a copy of his third book, *Some Chinese Ghosts*, to her, or rather to her savoury, health-giving meals.[1]

In his letters of the period to Mr Watkin are his schemes to profit from the cheap cost of food in New Orleans, while his travel sketches sometimes devote hundreds of continuous lines acquainting the reader with the beauty and variety of exotic foods in the Martinique marketplace.[2] He also authored several newspaper articles on matters of eating, such as 'How to Eat Cheaply in New Orleans' and 'How to Eat Fruit'.[3]

His appetite was also well known. Letters describe some of the humorously large meals that he claimed to have regularly eaten, and those who knew him in New Orleans confirm it. In Tinker's words, Hearn was 'no mean trencherman', a man 'inordinately fond of good food', gourmand as well as gourmet.[4] Despite his rather small stature and lean look, especially in his youth, Hearn had an extraordinary interest in and capacity for eating.[5]

In his so-called 'gruesome' period,[6] when he became known as a master reporter of the sensational, the morbid, and the horrible, his sensitive and shockingly graphic treatment of distasteful subjects brought him a kind of respectful notoriety as a journalist. He described himself as having tastes 'whimsically grotesque and arabesque', as a believer in the 'Revoltingly Horrible or the Excruciatingly Beautiful', a worshipper of the 'French school of sensation' who 'revelled in thrusting a reeking mixture of bones, blood and hair under people's noses at breakfast time' and who was 'ever running down into vaults and out over graves'. Hearn's mention of breakfast-time here is revealing, for he often used the act of eating to create his startling effects. If a 'reeking mixture' under one's nose *at* breakfast was revolting, Hearn also knew that the ingestion of that mixture *for* breakfast was even more so. Thus, in his desire to amuse his readers, the gruesome ingestion of 'food' became an effective motif. It appears throughout his career in a variety of literary formats: in the news articles written in Cincinnati and New Orleans, in the early short fictional creations he called 'Fantastics', in the anecdotes he told his son Kazuo, in his personal letters, and in the essays and fiction written in and about Japan. In Hearn's writings, people (and sometimes creatures) eat a bewildering variety of seemingly unpalatable things and combinations of things, usually for different reasons and with different effects. The tone of the treatment may be as lighthearted as that in 'The Little Red Kitten' or as serious as that in 'Jikininki' (The Eater of Human Flesh). Sometimes Hearn's purpose is simply to nauseate the reader, but often the eating teaches something, metaphorizes a deep human truth, or exposes a hidden aspect of the human heart.

★   ★   ★

Grotesque eating first appears in a humorous political piece for the Cincinnati *Enquirer* called 'The English and the Anthropophagi' (27 November 1873) in which Hearn uses cannibalism to poke fun at the high-minded efforts of the British government and Christian missionaries to 'civilize' the Fiji Island man-eaters. Hearn dutifully reports the royal pedigree of a native chief recently declared king, a man of fatally impeccable blue-blooded background:

> His ancestors were lordly cannibals who had severally eaten some hundreds of people – who chronicled the number of their victims by ranging stones in ornamental rows – several of whom had died from constipation of the bowels by devouring too much 'long pig'.

Hearn goes on to paint a wonderful vignette of Christian missionaries protesting vainly as newly converted Fijians roast, boil and bake white prisoners for a huge banquet. Then with characteristic understatement and word play, Hearn goes on to satirize Fijians and missionaries alike:

> Calmly considered, the Fijis are a very nasty set of people. Notwithstanding the daring efforts of the missionaries, many of whom have paid the penalty of their heroic presumption by being *converted* into various dishes of different flavors, Christianity has made little impression upon the cannibal heart. (my italics)

Despite the best efforts of political and religious reformers, the Fijians' savage customs and barbarous habits stubbornly survive. In the interior of the islands, widows are strangled, old peoples' skulls are crushed, women not strangled at birth may well be buried alive, choked to death, or even cooked for the chief's dinner. Every one with an enemy 'anxiously longs for an opportunity to knock him on the head, and eat his tongue raw'. Hearn's treatment of cannibalism here is a stock one, comic-book stuff, its reality worlds away from the reader's experience. Cannibalism is humorous both as a parody of distinguished dining and in the consternation it causes to those who attempt to eradicate it. Like a nation of Tom Sawyers, the Fijians simply defy civilizing. Woe to the country that dares to annex Fiji, Hearn concludes; it will have its hands full.

A follow-up article, 'Cannibal Culture', appeared nearly a year later to announce that at last Fiji had been annexed. Punning on the 'Herculean task' awaiting the new governor, Sir Hercules Robinson, and on 'chiefs [who] grew fat on each other's valiant warriors', Hearn recycles certain elements of the original article: the pedigree of the chiefs who died of constipation from devouring too much 'long pig', the portrayal of the missionaries as nothing more to the natives than gastronomic ingredients to be 'baked and digested there', and the felicitously expressed observation – repeated almost word for word – that 'the Fijian slips out of his Christianity when he slips out of his trousers'. Such recycling of material suggests, if not what elements the readers enjoyed, then at least the parts Hearn or his editors *thought* were the most successful. In the first article on Fiji, Hearn had created the premise for a political situation comedy in which refined, well-mannered adults try valiantly but in vain to 'civilize' a wild brood of savage children. In the sequel, the formula is fundamentally the same with nothing really new except that annexation is no longer a prospect but a fact.

In between the publication of these two articles, another on cannibalism appeared, this time in a context culturally closer to the reader's experience. 'Greeks, Jews and Cannibals' (29 December 1873) recounts a 'melo-drama' that Hearn had read about in a recent issue of the *Jewish Chronicle*. Noticeably less flippant in tone and purpose, this article satirizes the ignorance of the anti-Semitic Greeks and Turks of the small Asia Minor village of Kilmasti Casaba. Despite occasionally wringing a bit of humour out of their pathetic situation, Hearn's genuine sympathy for the story's Jews is apparent. One day, a six-year-old child was discovered to be missing.

> Of course, in Kilmasti Casaba there was but one way of accounting for the disappearance of a child – the Jews must have kidnapped it for anthropophagical purposes.

Hearn relates the subsequent massacre of the local Jews by the townspeople. Even after the real murderer (a wealthy young Turk) was discovered and convicted, many villagers still clung to the belief that the Jews were guilty. Hearn then describes several more historical incidents in which Jews were wrongly

accused of killing Gentile children allegedly to eat their flesh
or to use their blood in secret rituals. Again, Hearn's
fundamental interest lies not so much in the 'cannibals'
(amusing though they may be) as in the people who believe
themselves religiously or culturally superior. In this article, it is
the alleged anthropophagi themselves who appear to be the
moral superiors.

★ ★ ★

After changing employers and now writing for the Cincinnati
Commercial, Hearn produced between September 1875 and
July 1876 a second series of newspaper articles, far more
graphic than the first, exploiting the gastronomic grotesque.
The first, and perhaps the best, was 'Haceldama', in which two
kinds of grotesque appetite – that of hogs and that of people –
are subtly contrasted to illuminate the idiosyncrasies of human
nature. Ostensibly an investigative news report comparing the
sordid inhumanity of the Gentile slaughterhouse with the
enlightened humanity of its Jewish counterpart, 'Haceldama'
achieves its purpose through a contrast of diet.[8] You are what
you eat – not only physically, but also morally and spiritually.
We are not moved to pity by the slaughter of a hog, writes
Hearn, because the loathsomeness of what it eats reveals the
loathsomeness of what it is:

> The rotting bodies of the dead, the foulest ordure, the most
> offensive carcasses, are not less palatable to the hog than the
> most savory vegetable; and a nice fat baby, a fowl, and even its
> own new-born young, are greatly relished by this cannibal
> creature.[9]

In the Gentile slaughterhouse these animals are employed as
scavengers, 'fattening on the blood and entrails which pass
down to them through the offal gutter'. These hogs rarely
squeal – 'they only grunt out their deep satisfaction, their sense
of repletion and their regret that their cavernous bellies are not
larger'. Beyond the immediate effects of revolting the reader,
Hearn has in mind a loftier literary purpose: to equate their
low-mindedness, of which their disgusting eating habits are
only the manifestation, with that of the Gentile butchers. The

hogs' gluttony conveys a moral obtuseness, a blind self-indulgence, which Hearn expects the reader to see as the animal counterpart to the Gentile slaughterhouse workmen. The Gentile butchers' pleasure in torturing a helpless, frightened cow is, for Hearn, the moral equivalent of the hog:

> Then a great yellow-haired brute of a man, with very large calves and very ugly feet, seized a pritch and put out the poor cow's left eye . . . And the brawny butcher brought down the axe, not on the right spot, but on the bleeding eye . . . The human heart would have heaved in horror at a cry of such anguish . . . But the butcher only laughed, and swung the ax again in the most unscientific, bungling and brutal way.

Such men, says Hearn, 'would be more fitly employed in those horrible cannibal markets spoken of by recent African travellers, where human flesh is sold by weight, and human legs and arms dangle in the booths . . . The fiend who can laugh at the tortures of a blind cow, would certainly find rare amusement in severing a human throat . . . And how amusing it would be to pry out a human eye with a pritchet'. Hearn's implication is that, like the hog, which enjoys eating its own babies, these men would enjoy slaughtering other people for food.

It is again through a gastronomic comparison that Hearn portrays the superiority of the Jewish butcher, the Shochet, whose clean, competent, scientific, and above all humane manner of killing simply produces the 'tenderest, freshest, healthiest of all' meat. Hearn then turns the reader's attention from eating the meat to drinking the blood. While the blood that flows from animals butchered by the ax is rather sickening, 'black and thick and lifeless', that of the kosher animals looks 'brightly ruddy and clear as new wine'. 'It tastes like new milk from the cow,' says the Shochet, and Hearn begins the piece's remarkable climax:

> The Shochet passed by with his long knife. 'I am going to cut a bullock now,' he observed, 'if you want a glass of blood.'
> A large tumbler was rinsed and brought forward, and the throat of the bullock severed, and the glass held to the severed veins. It was filled in an instant and handed to us, brimming over with the clear, ruddy life stream which warmed the vessel

through and through. There was no odor, no thickening, no consequent feeling of nausea; and the first mouthful swallowed, the glass was easily drained.

Relishing his role as the ghoulish gourmet, Hearn turns the rhetoric of the first part of the article on its head, now describing the drinking of pure blood as if it were the ultimate in fine dining:

> And how did it taste? Fancy the richest cream, warm, with a tart sweetness, and the healthy strength of pure wine . . . It was a draught simply delicious, sweeter than any concoction of the chemist, the confectioner, the winemaker – it was the very elixir of life itself . . . No other earthly draughts can rival such crimsom cream, and its strength spreads through the veins with the very rapidity of wine.

The hyperbole is typical of Hearn, but here the gushing prose serves an important thematic purpose. For it is in the taste that Hearn has invested the proof of his argument: moral depravity, cruelty, and bungling inhumanity are pollutive, unhealthy, and ultimately nauseating, whereas respect for life and pity for suffering are the wellsprings of a higher pleasure, symbolized by the clean, clear taste of the earth's most delicious beverage.[10] It is significant, too, that the Shochet himself does not drink the blood, even though he believes it to be tasty and healthful; he is shown to be a man governed by principle and religious duty rather than by appetite. Hearn turns the pig's indiscriminate appetite into the gastronomic equivalent of the Gentile butcher's piggish brutality, and he contrasts that animal not with the cow or the lamb but with the Shochet, whose mind and method embody the very antithesis.

★   ★   ★

Hearn's next treatment of grotesque eating followed soon in an article for the *Commercial* entitled 'Notes on the Utilization of Human Remains', 7 November 1875. Here the level of disgust successfully achieved in 'Haceldama' is raised by a simple change in the menu from animal blood and entrails to the human body, thus introducing the *Commercial*'s readers to the Hearn treatment of cannibalism that had appeared three times in the *Enquirer*. For *Commercial* readers, Hearn's article provided a wealth of historical and anthropological detail. The tone throughout is deliberately textbookish and matter-of-fact, serving only to intensify the repugnance of the details. 'Human brains have been in all ages esteemed a great delicacy by cannibals,' he writes, thus introducing a lengthy discourse on the many uses, culinary and otherwise, of human brains, bones, flesh, and blood. Writing about the sixth siege of Paris, Hearn again uses eating to shock by relating the atrocities brought about by hunger:

> The bark of trees, the skins of animals, rats, and even the leather of old shoes, were devoured by the starving . . . As in the days of Titus, mothers fed upon the flesh of their children; the dead bodies lying in the streets were riven asunder and devoured by crowds of starving men . . . Then the Spanish Ambassador of the League advised that the bones of the dead should be disinterred from the public cemeteries, ground into a bone-flour . . . and made into bread. The tombs gave up their dead . . . and the slimy worms robbed of their food.

This description carries a double impact, the disgust of the diet itself reinforced by the ghastly fact of its coming from half-rotted, dead-and-buried corpses. That all this was the result of a 'holy' war could only have intensified Hearn's increasingly anti-Christian views.

'These things naturally lead us to the very ancient subject of cannibalism, in which bones, blood, brains, marrow and all figure quite extensively,' he continues, drawing on his previous articles to pepper the account of the South Seas cannibals with such culinary tidbits as 'all cannibals agree [human flesh] tastes like first class pork, but has a bad effect upon the bowels'. Further immersing the reader in gory tales and facts of human atrocity, he reiterates its connection with religion:

> The Mexican priests were also wont on certain occasions to knead a paste, made of maize and human blood, into the figure of an idol, which was eaten as a sacrificial rite—something after the fashion of the Roman Catholic 'communion.' The hearts of victims were frequently eaten

by the priests, who tore them, still palpitating, from the breasts of their captives.

At this point, in case the reader's capacity to respond was diminishing, Hearn introduces a few instances of torture-induced cannibalism: starved prisoners-of-war forced by their captors to eat the flesh torn from their living leader with red-hot pincers, and 'the forcing of a prisoner by torture to devour a part of his own flesh'.[12] He also tells of a seventeenth-century 'royal English physician' who prescribed the following:

> a 'mummial quintessence', to be made of flesh from the thighs of 'a sound young man dying a natural death about the middle of August,' which 'mummial quintessence' was to be eaten with spirits of wine and salt; also, a recipe for a wonderful tonic, to be made from the blood of a sound young man dying in springtime.

So much for any feelings of cultural superiority felt by his American or British readers.

Hearn was also extremely interested in the medicinal aspects of diet. He published an article called 'The Creole Doctor' in the *New York Tribune* of 3 January 1886 in which he gives the recipes for dozens of strange remedies such as lettuce-leaf tea, geranium-leaf tea, and coffee with lemon juice. He was fully aware that to the sophisticated Northern readers, some of the Creole recipes must have sounded quite as repulsive as his previous accounts of the gastronomic grotesque: 'For tetanus cockroach tea is given. I do not know how many cockroaches go to make up the cup; . . . and cockroaches fried in oil with garlic for indigestion.'[12] Hearn loved to shock the squeamish whenever he could, challenging their sheltered vision of reality with descriptions of the strange things he believed were hidden under the rocks in their mental gardens.

★   ★   ★

In Hearn's fictional writing, the first instance of disagreeable dining occupies a small but essential place in 'The Little Red Kitten', one of his so-called 'Fantastics', which appeared in the *Daily Item* on 24 September 1879. A humorous treatment of a kitten's eating habits, it signifies Hearn's first fictional attempt at using strange eating to create laughter rather than nausea:

> It ate beefsteak and cockroaches, caterpillars and fish, chicken and butterflies, mosquito-hawks and roast mutton, hash and tumble-bugs, beetles and pig's feet, crabs and spiders, moths and poached eggs, oysters and earthworms, ham and mice, rats and rice pudding—until its belly became a realization of Noah's Ark. On this diet it soon acquired the strength to whip all the ancient cats in the neighborhood.[13]

Through clever selection and imaginative juxtaposition of the food items, Hearn manages to create a tone of delightfully entertaining disgust. Notice how each pair of food items contains one normal (to humans) and one abnormal dish, and how the order of these dishes alternates with each successive pair to re-enforce the element of surprise from which the amusement derives. Here Hearn uses the device of cataloguing, the creation of an elaborate, imaginatively composed list, to produce a particular rhetorical effect.[14] Later, in his Martinique sketches, he expanded this device to create descriptive catalogues of foodstuffs that go on unbroken for literally hundreds of lines.[15]

Also at about this time (16 November 1879) Hearn wrote another gastronomically humorous piece in answer to a request for a good recipe for tartar sauce. Elaborating on the pun, he creates a tiny masterpiece of tone. 'Catch a *young Tartar*: for the old ones are very tough and devoid of juice . . . Having killed, skinned and cleaned the Tartar, cut off the tenderest parts of the hams and thighs; boil three hours, and then hash up with Mexican pepper, aloes and spices . . .' The concerned attitude and careful attention to practical details such as taking care to 'escape the observation of the police authorities' and to dispose of the remains 'judiciously' hark back to Jonathan Swift's 'A Modest Proposal'. Unlike Swift, however, Hearn's theme is culinary, not political; he ends with an alternative recipe using egg, mustard, olive oil, vinegar, parsley, and cucumber, for those who may be too much 'in a hurry' to try the first.[16]

★   ★   ★

The last major treatment of the motif in Hearn's American
journalism was 'A Strange Tale of Cannibalism', which
appeared in *The Times Democrat*, 15 October 1882. Here again
he uses descriptions of revolting diet, but this time they serve
mainly to punctuate a larger story of human fear and suffering.
The actual degeneration into cannibalism is described with a
brevity that shocks by the very dryness of the treatment:

> For days subsequently that little band of human skeletons
> struggle vainly to leave the well–compelled by infernal thirst
> and heat to return after having marched a few miles under the
> sun; –lizards and sand insects are eaten alive; reason weakens
> and looses its grasp upon the reins of passion. An Arab sent out
> for assistance is shot and eaten by his comrades. Two more are
> subsequently murdered. The survivors devour the bodies; and
> a new phase of horror commences. Those who had marched
> on in advance return upon hearing the shots; they partake of
> the repast; they even kill another of the weaker ones and eat
> his flesh . . . There is little flesh on those starving bodies–the
> bones are crushed and devoured.[17]

As subject matter, this is all familiar territory for Hearn, but his
treatment is new. Here plot is paramount, and the literary
purpose of the cannibalism is to enhance the story's tragic
elements, to arouse sorrow and pity rather than disgust. The
most horrifying aspect, Hearn points out, is their fear of
themselves: 'they fear at night to sleep . . . dreading each other
more than death; –fearing the sunset . . . fearing the tepidness
of night tempting the weary to close their eyes, –fearing the
furnace-glow of dawn heralding another day of horrors'.
    In the final paragraph, Hearn tries to delineate the
psychological dimensions of the incident's human misery, of
which the grotesque diet is but one manifestation, lavishing his
descriptive powers on two intermingled hells–the outer hell of
the desert landscape and the inner hell of the survivors' minds:

> When the reader pictures to his mind the unutterable
> misery of that march though a waste fantastically desolate as a
> lunar landscape, –under a sky whose very clouds are flying
> sand, –under a perpendicular sun, whose beams scorch like
> molten iron, –against a wind whose heat flays the face,
> excoriates the hands, shrivels even the water-skins upon the
> backs of the dromedaries; –and when he imagines the silent

struggle about the oasis, −the murder of sleepers at the well, − the frenzy of mutual hatred inspired by cannibalism, −the emaciation that rendered it almost impossible to obtain three days' food from nearly twelve adult bodies, −the crunching of bones when starvation had consumed the muscles of the victim, −the thirst that blackens the lips and makes the tongue crack open and stifles speech in the throat, −it is indeed difficult to conceive how men can pass through such experience and remain sane!

It is another catalogue, an inventory of the natural, mental, and physiological ordeals endured by these men, with cannibalism as both cause and result of human abasement. Up until this news article, Hearn had discussed cannibalism either anthropologically, performed by people who enjoyed it and practised it as a vital part of their culture, or historically, as a facet of human warfare, a cruel weapon of torture or subjugation, performed by people who were forced to do it. Here the enemies are the desert and the human heart, each brutal and frightful in its own way, and cannibalism is treated psychologically, as a symbol of Conradian horror.

The tale ends with an example of how that horror and fear progressed into insanity for one of the members:

> The most pitiful case of all seems that of the poor spahi left alone for nearly a week at the well, who took flight whenever his ghoulish companions came back for water, and returned by stealth in the night to gnaw the bones of the dead.

A man who prefers the company of dead men's bones to his former companions is indeed tragic in his pathological paranoia, and yet, Hearn seems to imply, he has simply learned too well the harsh lessons cannibalism has taught. In his final story about cannibalism, 'Jikininki', Hearn once again shows the pitiful side of the eater of human flesh who, like the poor spahi, appears only at night to devour the corpse in solitary despair.

★   ★   ★

In Japan, Hearn published only one sustained treatment of grotesque eating, 'Jikininki', one of the *Kwaidan* written near the end of his life. But in his stories to Kazuo, in his letters, and occasionally in his published work, the motif reappears briefly again and again to illustrate a human fault or virtue, or to symbolize a human condition. In several places, incidents of bizarre eating are used to display courage and self-sacrifice.

In the essay 'Of Ghosts and Goblins' near the end of *Glimpses*, Hearn tells the 'queer tale' of a beautiful samurai girl who required each of her many would-be suitors to pass a mysterious test of their love and courage. But upon being put to the test, all the high-ranking wooers had run away terrified. Finally, there came one poor but true-hearted samurai youth, and he, too, was put to the test. Long after midnight, she came dressed all in white and led him to a freshly dug grave. Digging furiously, she hit the coffin and opened it to reveal the corpse of a child.

> With goblin gestures she wrung an arm from the body, wrenched it in twain, and, squatting down, began to devour the upper half. Then, flinging to her lover the other half, she cried to him, '*Eat, if thou lovest me! this is what I eat!*'

Without hesitation the young man eats, saying how good it tastes and asking for more, for the arm was actually made from the finest confectionery. The test of courage passed, the delighted girl laughs and says, 'I will marry you; I can love you: you are a *man!*'

A similar tale of manliness tested through grotesque eating appears in a letter of March 1899 to Mitchell McDonald. Here, however, the ghoulish atmosphere is totally absent, and instead of a corpse in a coffin we have a 'hairy caterpillar in a salad at a banquet':

> The lady of the palace had ladled the salad and the caterpillar into the plate of some admirable commodore, and saw what she had done when it was too late. The seaman caught her horrified eye, held it, and smiling, swallowed the caterpillar unseen by the other guests. After the banquet, the beauty came to thank him—out of the innermost rosy chamber of her heart—when he is reported to have said: 'Why, Madam, did you think that I would permit your pleasure of the evening to be spoiled by a miserable G—d d—d caterpillar!'[18]

Hearn considered this commodore to be 'a better man out and

out than Cyrano' [de Bergerac], and saw in this story of chivalry, nobility, and self-sacrifice the essence of true manly heroism.

As for womanly heroism, Hearn tells the moving story of a Japanese wife, again involving an incident of repulsive eating:

> A peasant went to consult an astrologer what to do for his mother's eyes: she had become blind. The astrologer said that she would get her sight back if she could eat a little human liver—taken fresh from a young body. The peasant went home crying, and told his wife. She said: 'We have only one boy. He is beautiful. You can get another wife as good, or better than I, very easily, but might never be able to get another son. Therefore, you must kill me instead of the son, and give my liver to your mother.' They embraced; and the husband killed her with a sword, and cut out the liver and began to cook it, when the child awoke and screamed. Neighbours and police came.[19]

For Hearn, the story's significance lay not only in the pitiable ignorance of the peasants but also in the remarkable sense of wifely duty, in the 'idolatrous self-devotion to a mother'. Such devotion, he felt, was all the more poignant for having been utterly foolish and was unimaginable in Western culture. Though both this and the caterpillar incidents share a similar theme centering around an act of grotesque eating, they offer strikingly contrastive portraits of cross-cultural behaviour that Hearn was surely aware of: The European nobleman's act of self-sacrifice is, after all, relatively trivial, momentary, a heroic twinkle in an enlightened and highly cultivated society. Its world is fundamentally rational, polite, and bright, the world of romantic comedy. The party's fun saved, a little wine soon washes away the bad taste while the lady's gratitude and the commodore's example of chivalry shine happily on. By contrast, the world of the Japanese peasant in this incident is irrational, ignorant, and dark, the world of tragedy. Instead of a hostess's face saved, a woman's life is destroyed, needlessly. While deploring the ignorance, Hearn could not have helped but admire the depth of devotion and self-sacrifice in that peasant woman. The self-sacrifice of the European nobleman, he surely knew, paled before that of the Japanese country wife.

★ ★ ★

For his son Kazuo's English lessons, Hearn created or re-created little fables which he wrote down in a notebook or dictated for Kazuo to copy. Among these, the most frequent motif appears to be that of unusual eating which leads to death. One of the lessons in natural history dictated by Hearn seems calculated to arouse a pleasant thrill of fear in the seven-year-old boy:

ABOUT CRABS

There are crabs which eat men . . . They live near the sea-shore in hot countries. If a man goes there alone millions of crabs attack him, and bite him and tear him, and gnaw the flesh from all his bones, –as the rats devoured Bishop Hatto.[29]

This is a leaner, cleaner version of the gruesome reporting Hearn was famous for in his own youth. Simplified for the child, the style itself is stripped to the bone–spare, undecorated. There are virtually no adjectives; strong, plain verbs alone do all the work. Compared with Hearn's earlier treatment of the gastronomic grotesque, the economy and compression of detail seen here offer an extreme example of the stylistic change Hearn's writing underwent as his art matured.

In another story for dictation, Hearn told of a strange plant that ate meat. A man kept it and fed it every day until it became monstrous, daily requiring 'more meat than a hungry lion'.

Well, one day when the man went to feed the plant, his foot slipped, and he fell upon the plant. Immediately, the horrible plant wrapped its long, snakelike arms around him, just like a great cuttlefish, and began to eat him.

The man's servants heard his screams, but they could not free him. With an ax they managed to chop through the roots, but the man was dead, 'poisoned and crushed by the monstrous plant'.[21]

Other stories were created to warn Kazuo of the mortal dangers of improper diet. One told about men in Swiss prisons who ate only meat and drank only wine. 'The meat and wine are very good. But the wicked men soon get sick and die. It is very bad to eat only one thing.' Another was about a little boy (Kazuo?) who loved oranges but who ignored his father's warning and ate a seed: 'That seed took root in his dear little stomach, and grew up into a little tree; and the branches went into the throat of the boy, and choked him, so that he died.'

In addition to tales illustrating the fatal consequences of wrong eating there are stories about magical eating. One recounts an incident in the life of a warrior named Sigurd who, being very hungry after slaying a terrible dragon, 'cut out the dragon's heart, and made a fire, and cooked it. When it had been well roasted, he tasted it. Then a strange thing happened. He heard the birds singing; and he knew what they said. He understood the language of birds'.[22] Just then Sigurd heard the birds singing words to the effect that someone was about to kill him. He turned, saw the enemy, and killed him first, thus saving his life. Hearn's unexpected moral of the story? 'If you want to know the language of birds, you must eat the heart of a dragon . . . Try!' And since this story was part of Hearn's ongoing battle with Kazuo over English lessons, the deeper moral might have been this: It is wonderful to know a foreign language, but skills like that do not come easily. We must do frightfully difficult things and make great efforts to realize our dreams.

In 'The Story of the God Thor', another fiction for Kazuo's copybook, Hearn uses a magical eating and drinking contest to teach a lesson in humility. Here the grotesque element involves quantity rather than quality, and the narrative is closer to parable than to fable. The little god Thor visits the city of the giants and is challenged to a contest of drinking, eating, and wrestling. Though he claims that he can drink and eat as much as any man, he fails to drain a cup of ale by more than a tenth of an inch, and then he is embarrassingly out-eaten by a little boy-servant in a roast-beef eating contest:

> So they began; and Thor ate very fast. But the little boy ate much faster. And Thor ate only the meat; but the little boy ate the bones and the meat and the plates and the knives and the forks and the table-cloth and the table.

In the final humiliation, Thor is easily out-wrestled by a very

old woman. But as he leaves, sad and ashamed, the king reveals
the truth: 'When we gave you that cup, we really gave you the
whole sea to drink. Even a god cannot drink up the sea.' The
true name of the boy-servant is Fire, also called 'the Hungry
Ghost'. The old woman's true name is Old Age; 'and even the
gods cannot overcome Old Age'.

The story is not, however, Hearn's own creation, as
Kazuo's textual annotation has it; rather it is a simplified
version of an episode from the Prose Edda of Nordic
mythology.[23] In the original, Thor is so infuriated by the
king's revelation that he turns to strike him, but Hearn leaves
this off, ending with a sense of wonder at the hidden truth.
Hearn's transformation of the original into a child's parable
seems to have been more for amusement than for instruction,
an adventure centering around an episode of magical dining.

It is interesting to note the similarity between this tale and
parts of the *kwaidan* 'Horai':

> The people of Horai eat their rice out of very, very small
> bowls; but the rice never diminishes within these bowls, –
> however much of it be eaten, –until the eater desires no more.
> And the people of Horai drink their wine out of very, very
> small cups; but no man can empty one of those cups, –
> however stoutly he may drink, –until there comes upon him
> the pleasant drowsiness of intoxication.

This part of the legend, Hearn writes, is taken from old
Chinese books, and is untrue: 'For really there are no
enchanted fruits which leave the eater forever satisfied . . . nor
any bowls which never lack rice, –nor any cups which never
lack wine.' But there is something even more wonderful: the
atmosphere, composed not of air but of ghost, of the substance
of countless souls: 'Whatever mortal man inhales that
atmosphere, he takes into his blood the thrilling of these
spirits. They change the senses within him . . .' Hearn renders
this atmosphere as the extension of food, invisible nourishment which mixes with the blood, intoxicating the spirit. It is
the mystical version of an idea expressed in a letter of 1884
from Grand Isle: 'One does not need any wine here; the sea air
is wine enough.'[24]

A similar story of mysterious, invisible nourishment appears

in 'In Cholera-Time' from *Kokoro*. There an infant is always
kept very close to his dead mother's *ihai* or mortuary tablet in
his crib, in accordance with her final wishes: 'From what time
I die till three full years be past I pray you to leave the child
always united with the Shadow of me: never let him be
separated from my ihai, so that I may continue to care for him
and to nurse him—since thou knowest that he should have the
breast for three years.' The poor father, who could not afford
to buy milk, fed the child nothing but rice gruel and *ame*
syrup. When the narrator comments that the boy looks rather
healthy despite the lack of milk, he is quickly reproached by
his servant: 'That . . . is because the dead mother nurses him.
How could he want for milk?'

In 'Jikininki' (The Eater of Human Flesh) Hearn again
dramatizes the link between the world of the dead and that of
the living, with supernatural eating again occupying a central
place. The effect produced by these common elements,
however, could hardly be more different. Instead of heart-
warming feelings aroused by mother-love, Hearn strives for
the heart-chilling ones of a tortured ghost condemned to
devour human corpses. Instead of the dead world providing
nourishment to the living, the living world provides it to the
dead. Instead of a contented, well-nourished baby, we are
concerned with the tortured ghost of an ancient priest. Hearn,
by now an expert, renders the horrible eating scene with
power and economy through the eyes of the living priest,
Muso:

> But when the hush of the night was at its deepest, there
> noiselessly entered a Shape, vague and vast; and in the same
> moment Muso found himself without power to move or
> speak. He saw that Shape lift the corpse, as with hands, and
> devour it, more quickly than a cat devours a rat, —beginning at
> the head, and eating everything: the hair and the bones and
> even the shroud. And the monstrous Thing, having thus
> consumed the body, turned to the offerings, and ate them also.
> Then it went away, as mysteriously as it had come.

The conciseness is certainly a hallmark of Hearn's mature style,
but it is more than that. After all, effective though it may be,
the eating of the corpse is not the central event of the story.

That event, elaborated and dramatized with dialogue not in
the source, is the confession of the priest-ghost to Muso:

> 'Ah! I am ashamed!–I am very much ashamed!–I am
> exceedingly ashamed!'
> 'You need not be ashamed for having refused to shelter me,'
> said Muso. 'You directed me to the village yonder, where I
> was very kindly treated; and I thank you for that favour.'
> 'I can give no man shelter,' the recluse made answer, –'and
> it is not for the refusal that I am ashamed. I am ashamed only
> that you should have seen me in my real shape, –for it was I
> who devoured the corpse and the offerings last night before
> your eyes . . . Know, Reverend Sir, that I am a *jikininki*, –an
> eater of human flesh. Have pity upon me, and suffer me to
> confess the secret fault by which I became reduced to this
> condition.'

Here, as in 'Yuki Onna' and the other *kwaidan*, Hearn
emphasizes the chilling revelation of a seemingly normal
human being's true other-worldly identity. But this is a ghost
with a painfully keen conscience. As a priest, the physical
aspects of cannibalism are far less important to him than the
moral; it is the *shame* of it that tortures him.

For the first time in Hearn's treatment of it, cannibalism is
presented as a moral judgement, a divine punishment for
earthly sinfulness. Appropriately, we are given insight into the
cannibal's psychological state, hearing from the flesh-eater
himself how he feels. It is also the first and only time that
Hearn treats cannibalism in the context of the supernatural
world. The two priests are alter-egos, mirror images, standing
on either side of death, brought into moral confrontation with
each other through the existence of the corpse. The living
priest is in the room with the corpse due to his sense of
charity, the kindness of his heart; the ghost is there due to the
lack of that very kindness when he was the priest of this
village. His self-proclaimed impiety is that he performed his
priestly duties for the dead 'only as a matter of business; –I
thought only of the food and the clothes that my sacred
profession enabled me to gain'. Now, he must literally take the
dead into his being; they have literally become his food.

In 'A Strange Tale of Cannibalism' Hearn also aroused our
pity for the cannibals by describing their physical and mental

suffering. Horrible as it was, though, it was earthly and finite, unconnected to the spiritual world; death, their ultimate fear, would have mercifully ended all their suffering. In 'Jikininki', however, the ghost is already in the world beyond and thus cannot hope to die. He is condemned to relive his shame through acts of cannibalism repeated ad infinitum, unless, through the kindness of another priest, a Segaki service to 'feed hungry ghosts' is performed for him.[25] Whether or not this rite is successfully performed Hearn does not tell. The story ends with the sudden disappearance of the ghost and his hermitage, leaving Muso alone in the mountains again, kneeling by an ancient tomb that seems to be that of a priest.

★   ★   ★

Though Hearn never lost a certain fascination for the gastronomic grotesque, his literary interest in it in his later years was generally as a metaphor. The physical acts of eating so frequent in his tales for Kazuo and so central in 'Jikininki' usually came not from Hearn's imagination but from his sources, and they no longer engaged his full attention. Passing up opportunities for descriptive detail, Hearn used these acts as springboards for higher, more abstract considerations. When he did employ the culinary grotesque as metaphor, it was most often associated with the life of the mind and the role of the suffering artist. The menu was the human mind, brain, or heart.

Hearn once advised a friend not to write for a New Orleans paper: 'To send it any essay would be to fling a jewel into the sewer, –to give Chateau Margaux to a dog, –to feed a buzzard with Charlotte Russe . . . equivalent to feeding a big baboon with human brains.'[26] Brains, both as food and as an organ that eats, appear in several of his Japanese letters as well. To Chamberlain, he complained that 'Our brains eat up our lives and the life of the world–and yet are starved or fed with ornamental bric-a-brac.'[27] That is, to educate a human brain to contribute to society consumes the better part of a lifetime, and still the brain is left virtually empty or malnourished by trivia. And again to Chamberlain two years later:

The mind, in my case, eats itself when unemployed. Reading,
you might suggest, would employ it. No: my thoughts
wander, and the gnawing goes on just the same. What kind of
gnawing? Vexation and anger and imaginings and recollections
of unpleasant things said and done.

Hearn is effectively equating himself with the most piteous
examples contained in his earlier treatments of cannibalism: his
mind gnawing at itself is reminiscent of that solitary figure at
the end of 'A Strange Tale of Cannibalism', in deep mental
torment, alienated from all human companionship, and
literally gnawing at the bones of former friends. Even after
another two years had passed, the metaphor Hearn used to
describe his mental condition was the same: 'Would I, being
independent, become idle? I don't think so; but I know that
some of my work has been done just to keep the mind from
eating itself–as does the stomach without food.'[28]

Towards the end of his life, Hearn became so absorbed in
the life of the mind and the world of imagination that he was
sometimes oblivious to eating in the real world, putting sugar
in his soup and forgetting what he had just eaten.[29] This is
confirmed by an amusing account from Setsuko:

> It was our custom for the three children to go upstairs and
> shout, 'Papa, come down; supper is ready!' Hearn always
> replied, 'All right, sweet boys!' and looked so delighted,
> sometimes almost dancing about. But there were occasions
> when he was working so hard that even the children's
> announcement would not bring any response, and they could
> get no answer, 'All right!' At such times we might wait and
> wait, but he would not appear in the dining-room. Then I
> would go up myself, and say, 'Papa-san, we have been waiting
> a long time, and all the things will taste bad. I wish you would
> hurry up. All the children are waiting.' Then Hearn would
> ask, 'What is it?' I would reply, 'What's the matter with you?
> This will never do; it is dinner-time. Won't you take some
> dinner?' 'I? Haven't I had dinner yet? I thought I had finished
> it. That's funny!'[30]

To keep the mind from eating itself, Hearn fed it with literary
work, often forgetting the need to feed his body as well, a
higher hunger absorbing him.

But if work could nourish, it could also cannibalize. One of

Hearn's most eloquent expressions of the pain of being a writer is contained in the essay 'Kusa-Hibari' from *Kotto*. Structurally, it is one of Hearn's most finely crafted pieces, exploring the relationships between the writer and his pet, between human being and tiny insect, master and slave, audience and performer, deepening their relationship until by the end they can be seen as essentially the same: two mortal souls, two hungry artists, two self-destructive victims of their own talents. The insect's cage is a kind of microcosm of Hearn's isolated study room–a larger 'cage'–which is kept heated to 75 or more degrees F to keep both insect-singer and human-writer warm and able to produce their respective nightly songs. Even the insect's dependence on a piece of cucumber to be put daily into the tiny cage is roughly analogous to Hearn's dependence on the insect's song to be heard each night in his workroom. It is partly because of this implicit, shared identity that the ending achieves its power, but it is also partly because of the grotesque result of physical hunger:

> And then to think of the little creature hungering and thirsting, night after night, and day after day, while the thoughts of his guardian deity were turned to the weaving of dreams! . . . How bravely, nevertheless, he sang on to the very end–an atrocious end, for he had eaten his own legs! . . . May the gods forgive us all–especially Hana the housemaid!
>
> Yet, after all, to devour one's own legs for hunger is not the worst that can happen to a being cursed with the gift of song. There are human crickets who must eat their own hearts in order to sing.

Here Hearn raises the horror of self-cannibalism to its highest level–from eating one's own physical substance, the legs, to eating one's emotional and spiritual repository, the heart. Out of the gruesome, naturalistic details of early works like 'Haceldama' and 'Notes on the Utilization of Human Remains' Hearn seems here to have distilled a metaphor to convey the sometimes sickening gastronomy of the artist's psyche. The motif he had used so graphically and sensationally as a news reporter in America had deepened and matured in Japan to become, in the later years, the metaphor he used to express his own inner demons.

Of all the gastronomic horrors Hearn had written about, none was more disturbing to him than cannibalism, and none more piteous than self-cannibalism: nourishment as death. But at this late stage of his career, physical eating engaged his imagination only in so far as it pointed towards a moral or spiritual dimension of a piece of writing, and he came to view self-cannibalism in a detached, philosophical way as nothing less than a fundamental law of all life. In 'Ululation', from *In Ghostly Japan*, he synthesized his Spencerian and Buddhist learning into the concept of a ghoulish gastronomy underlying the entire natural world:

> Only by eating each other do beings exist! Beautiful to the poet's vision our world may seem—with its loves, its hopes, its memories, its aspirations; but there is nothing beautiful in the fact that life is fed by continual murder—that the tenderest affection, the noblest enthusiasm, the purest idealism, must be nourished by the eating of flesh and the drinking of blood. All life, to sustain itself, must devour life. You may imagine yourself divine if you please—but you have to obey that law. Be, if you will, a vegetarian: none the less you must eat forms that have feeling and desire. Sterilize your food; and digestion stops. You cannot even drink without swallowing life. Loathe the name as we may, we are cannibals; —all being is essentially One; and whether we eat the flesh of a plant, a fish, a reptile, a bird, a mammal, or a man, the ultimate fact is the same.

That all living things must kill to live is the law of nature, the inescapable law of survival in classic Spencerian terms. It was Buddhism, however, which taught Hearn that all life is essentially the same substance, recycled and reborn again and again in various forms according to the laws of re-incarnation, thus making us all inadvertent cannibals of our own flesh:

> And for all life the end is the same: every creature, whether buried or burnt, is devoured—and not only once or twice —nor a hundred, nor a thousand, nor a myriad times! Consider the ground upon which we move, the soil out of which we came; —think of the vanished billions that have risen from it and crumbled back into its latency to feed what becomes our food! Perpetually we eat the dust of our race—*the substance of our ancient selves.*

The sharp distinction between gourmet and grotesque dining which he had exploited for humour or for shock value in his earlier writings first blurred and then virtually disappeared: all eating, he had come to believe, was fundamentally grotesque, an unavoidable form of self-cannibalism. Eating humans, or anything else for that matter, was neither amusing nor disgusting to him any more; it was simply an inescapable fact of life. He had come to the sobering realization that as a human being he was condemned to eat the bodies of his own and other creatures' former selves; and that as an artist, he was further condemned to devour his living heart and soul. As a starving immigrant in Cincinnati, he had craved enough food to survive; as a young reporter in New Orleans he had craved large quantities of cheap but delicious food; and as a seasoned writer and thinker late in his Japan career, his only hunger was for mental food. From a man of stomach, to a man of the palate, to a man of the spirit, Hearn's changing relationship to food and his imaginative use of its grotesque aspects in his writing constitute a significant dimension of his life and work.

LAFCADIO HEARN'S *YOUMA*: SELF AS OUTSIDER

Naoko Sugiyama

B efore coming to Japan, Lafcadio Hearn stayed in the United States and then in the French West Indies, first as a journalist and eventually establishing his career as a writer for American audiences. In his American years, he showed considerable interest in exotic and marginal subjects. Early in his career as a newspaper reporter in Cincinnati, Hearn dealt with cultures different from the mainstream of Western tradition, such as black culture, as well as Chinese and Jewish cultures. He was not unique in doing so. In this era in American literary history, American readers were interested in exotic topics and welcomed local colour literature, especially works with Southern topics and dialects. It was rare, however, for white authors to treat black characters, especially women, as whole human beings, much less as central characters. As Barbara Christian points out in her *Black Women Novelists*, the racial stereotypes of the late nineteenth century presented black women as black, ugly, fat, sexless mammies or sensuous animal-like temptresses.[1] If they were treated with any seriousness, or if they had any good characteristics, for example, physical beauty or intelligence, such characteristics were often attributed to the portion of white blood in their veins.

Compared with many of his contemporaries, Hearn treats

different cultures in an amazingly pluralistic way. Hearn was too much of an observer, though often a romantic one, to taint his sketches with the stereotypical images of non-Anglo-Saxons which abounded in his contemporary American literature. This is particularly true when he describes black characters, especially black women. 'Dolly', one of the better known pieces of Hearn's Cincinnati period, includes a description of a beautiful young black woman, which shows us that Hearn was quite capable of aesthetic appreciation of the beauty of black bodies. In this sense, Hearn was free from the racial bias of many of his contemporaries. What he said of a Creole on Martinique Island, that 'aesthetically, his "colour prejudice" had no existence' is true of Hearn himself (*Youma*, 268).

At the same time, Hearn did hold to a racist ideology under the name of 'science' and 'the theory of evolution', and seems to have tried to create a novel according to it. In fact, in the abstract, there is no denying that he had a biased view towards black people. For example, in his essay called 'The Race Problems in America', written for the *Kobe Chronicle* in 1894, he says that black people are as 'ignorant as cattle' and implies that mulattos are shrewd troublemakers (36). It is noteworthy, however, that his essays on the subject of race are always ambiguous and indecisive, very unlike his essays of literary criticism.

These two contradictory aspects of Hearn are paralleled by his mixed feeling about race matters with regards to his own ancestry. In one of the letters to his brother, Hearn idealizes the image of his Greek mother, whom he calls 'Oriental', and goes so far as to say that 'whatever there is good in me, . . . came from that dark race-soul of which we knew so little' (*The Writings of Lafcadio Hearn*, XIII,10). On the other hand, he identified himself with 'the Westerner' and implied now and then that he believed in a hierarchical world order in which the white Anglo-Saxon race is on top and darker races are inferior.[2]

Youma, the novel written during the two years Hearn spent on the island of Martinique, is significant for a number of reasons. First of all, it is a good example of how Hearn succeeded in presenting authentic black characters in a sympathetic way. Another and more important aspect of this novel is that Hearn not only created black characters who were not stereotypical, but that he succeeded in doing so in spite of the racist framework he used. The fact that Hearn created a black character with whom he identified in spite of his racial ideas is one of the most fascinating aspects of *Youma*. *Youma* contains various contradictory ideas about race and, from today's point of view, the conflict of these ideas ironically spotlights the contradiction and hypocrisy of the racial ideology Hearn used.

And given this conflict, *Youma* is important in that it presents the question of Hearn's own standpoint. The question of which of the two voices we find in this text is authorial: which has more authority, and which is closer to Hearn's own point of view. I am going to argue that, in creating his black heroine, Hearn not only subverted his own assumptions about race, but also subverted his own standpoint as a member of the superior race, a standpoint which had never been stable in the first place, because of his strong attachment to his 'Oriental' mother and because of his incomplete formal education as a Westerner. I believe that he was able to do so because of his lifelong experience as an outsider and because of his tendency to identify with the cultural Other.

Youma seems a very straightforward and simple story, and from today's ethical, if not aesthetic, point of view, a rather appalling one due to its almost pro-slavery assumptions. It is basically the story of the life and death of a black slave woman, whom a white mistress has raised along with her own daughter as though the two were sisters. After the white daughter marries and dies young, leaving a baby in Youma's care, Youma takes care of the baby as her nurse. She falls in love with another slave but because of his lower status, her mistress does not allow her to marry him. In a slave uprising, Youma is confined with her small charge in the big house with white people, and chooses to stay with the child and burn to death in spite of her lover's passionate plea to desert the child and escape.

Written according to the traditional novel format, *Youma* starts with an explanation of background and setting. The introductory part describes the social situation of Martinique where the story takes place. There is a description of the slave nurse, or the 'da' in Martinique Creole, and her social situation. The narrator explains that 'da' is 'a product of slavery ... the one creation of slavery perhaps not unworthy of regret' (263). She is regarded as one of the family and as she grows old, she is treated with respect and affection by her white family. When she dies, a splendid funeral takes place. A 'da' is highly valued because she is loyal, affectionate, and 'herself at heart a child', and therefore between herself and a child there is 'absolute harmony between their natures–a happy community of likes and dislikes–a perfect sympathy in the animal joy of being' (262). In short, a black woman makes a good nurse because she is like a child herself. We should note that this childishness is attributed more to her race than to her sex, because here a 'da' is compared with a white mother who 'might be more loved' with the child's 'mental expansion' (262). Through this ideological framework, the authorial voice gives the novel not only its structure but also coherence.

From the beginning of Chapter 1, however, what we find is the story of Youma, a young woman of colour, whose characteristics and inner feelings are contrary to the characteristics attributed to her in Hearn's introduction. It is the story of a captive young woman, who falls in love with a captive young man, but refuses to accept fulfilment of her love and freedom because of her strong faith, sense of responsibility, and her sisterly love towards her dead white friend Aimée. According to the framework, Youma should be childlike and content with her situation as a 'da', devoting all her affection to the white family she serves. Therefore, it is in a way natural that she should choose to stay with the whites to die. In the story itself, however, the racist assumption of the framework is forgotten. Youma is the heroine of the story in her own right. Her virtues are evaluated, not from a Western point of view, but according to a black people's value system. For example, her physical beauty is described as 'beautiful ... like a shapely tree, like a young palm', the common way Martinique black people describe a beautiful woman (312). When she fights a big serpent to protect herself and the child, the highest praise she received is that she is 'sévè' (=severe), which is 'the negro's strongest adjective to qualify courage' (299). Youma is by no means childlike–she is a responsible woman who has a strong character and strong faith, and though she deplores her state of captivity, she consciously sacrifices herself in order to keep her oath to her dead friend and to God. In fact, Youma is two stories, one given by the ideological framework, and the other which I have here been calling the 'story'. Although these two stories proceed simultaneously and have the same ending, they contradict each other.

The assumption of the framework that Youma is content in her position and treated by whites like one of the family is subverted at the very beginning of the story. Youma is raised with Aimée, the daughter of her mistress, as if she were her sister. But Aimée is educated by a tutor and then sent to a girls' boarding school, while Youma is kept illiterate and stays at home. When Youma recollects the bitter moments of her experiences, the narrator explains:

> Youma's existence was confined by her duty as a nurse–compressed into the small sphere of a child's requirements . . . For the da there were no pleasures. The responsibilities of such a place–requiring nothing less than absolute self-sacrifice . . . Youma had scarcely ceased to be a child, when she found herself again senteneced to act, think, and speak as a child–for the sake of a child not her own. Her maginificent youth dumbly protested against this perpetual constraint. (310)

It is also noteworthy that it is Aimée, not Youma, who is the more emotional and excitable of the two. When Aimée leaves for school, it is Aimée who is upset while Youma stays calm, although they are both grieved at the parting. Thus again the assumption that black people are more childish and emotional than whites is subverted.

The assumption of the framework is that black people are childish and savage by nature. The love story of Youma and Gabriel again contradicts this assumption. Madame Peyronnette, who owns Youma, and M. Louis Desrivières, who owns Gabriel, are both shocked and appalled by the idea of the union of these two, since from their viewpoint, Youma is superior to and far more delicate than Gabriel because of her upbringing as a domestic slave and the moral influence she has received from white people. Desrivières recognizes Gabriel's merits, but nonetheless thinks that Gabriel is unsuitable for Youma. Madame Peyronette, who owns Youma, simply regards Gabriel as 'a common negro' (308). The reader is informed of Gabriel's superior qualities such as intelligence, calmness, physical strength, and love of independence. In the state of captivity, he courageously refuses to be broken by the slave system and secretly plans to escape and become legally and financially independent. The reader is also informed that Gabriel respects and loves Youma in a sensitive and considerate way. Youma rightly appreciates these characteristics in Gabriel and starts feeling the unfairness of the system which denies her the right to determine what is best for her.

Yet the framework interprets this tragic love story according to its ideology, and describes Youma's feeling towards Gabriel as dark and savage (309). The framework also interprets Gabriel's courage and love of independence critically: the narrative voice attributes Gabriel's yearning for liberty to the 'savage traits of his race', 'the hatred of all constraint–reasonable or unreasonable . . . which makes black people prefer hungry liberty to any comfort obtainable by hired labour' and thus, confuses laziness and lack of discipline with love of freedom and independence and indignation towards exploitation (330).

These aetmpts to redefine the tragic love story as that of a contented slave woman, ironically articulate the essential problem of concepts such as 'savage' and 'the traits of the savage race'. If people like Youma and Gabriel fall in love, because they are savages, and if one deplores slavery and exploitation and wishes to escape because one is a savage, then it is clear that there is something essentially wrong with these concepts. In other words, because of the contradiction between these two stories, another contradiction comes into focus–the binary opposition between black and white, with the hierarchical concept of white supremacy, on which the framework depends. It is the contradiction between the framework and the story itself which makes the reader uncertain what viewpoint she or he is supposed to have, and which makes us realize that this uncertain stance is probably Hearn's own. We should note that Hearn explains in a letter that he was motivated to write this novel by two events: one–a historical event–the slave uprising of 1848, in which a slave nurse was burned to death with white people; the other is an episode of a slave woman who fought with a serpent (*The Writings of Lafcadio Hearn*, XV, 79). The slave uprising confirmed Hearn's negative image of blacks, and the episodes of the slave nurse and of the serpent gave him the idea of a heroic figure which he felt essential to write the story.

One particular episode in the story illustrates this uncertain stance. It occurs when Youma tells Aimée's daughter Mayotte a story called 'Dame Kélément'. We should pay attention both to the text itself and to the context in which it is told. What is important about the text is that it is a story concerning identity and identification. In this story of a witch and a little girl, as soon as the little girl identifies the witch by her true name, the witch is compelled to disappear and her magic loses effect. As Hearn collected many folk-tales during his Martinique period, it is unlikely that his choice to use this particular story in this context was merely accidental. It seems to suggest that Hearn sensed the danger of identifying oneself with any particular position. If he identifies himself with the voice of the framework, the story of the wonderful heroine Youma will be impossible. If he identifies with Youma or Gabriel, then the framework of the novel itself will be dismantled.

The context in which Youma tells this story to Mayotte is thus; Mayotte, envying black children who are, unlike herself, allowed to play in the sun, expresses her desire to be black. Unable to persuade Mayotte that white is better and more beautiful than black, Youma tells the story to soothe the child. However, this subversion of the hierarchical black and white dichotomy in Mayotte's mind is not successfully reversed by the story. The effect of the story on Mayotte is a confusing one.

> . . . Mayotte's morning visits to the river with Youma had furnished her with material for the imaginative scenery of the last part of this foolish little story, which delighted her so much that she made her nurse repeat it over and over again. She had seen the crawfish show their heads above the pools; she had

caught the titiri in her little hands; . . . Dame Kélément, she fancied, must have had a face like old Tanga's when angry; and the little girl who lost her way in the woods must have looked just like a certain little black girl whom Tanga often had to scold, and who used to cry in the most extraordinary way: 'Ai'e-yai'e-yai'e-yai'e-yai'e!' (293, 294)

While interpreting the story by identifying the setting and the characters with her own environment and the creatures she sees everyday, Mayotte nevertheless excludes herself from it. When a nurse tells a little girl a story about a little girl who goes through an adventure and lives happily ever after, one would expect the child to identify with the heroine of the story, or at least imagine someone like herself. However, here Mayotte imagines the heroine to be like 'a certain black girl' like whom she will never be able to become.

Mayotte is in the position of the Other, an orphan and an outsider in the midst of black people, feeling excluded and inferior. She cannot think of herself as the heroine of the story though it is told especially for her.

This situation of Mayotte is Youma's own in the larger context of the story. When Gabriel tries to make Youma realize the evil of slavery and asks her, 'Do you believe slavery is a good thing–a right thing, Youma?,' she cannot answer directly except to say 'I think it is wicked to be cruel to slaves . . . But since the good God arranged it so that there should be slaves and masters . . .' (329). Here, in the story of which God is the story-teller, Youma cannot think for or of herself as the heroine of the story though Gabriel urges her to do so. It is not surprising that Hearn himself, an orphan and always an outsider, could identify himself with these characters. Mayotte's position as a listener to the story is Hearn's own as well, since Hearn actually collected the folk-tales from the Martinique black people. This episode of the story-telling of 'Dame Kélément' indicates the way Hearn, the Story-teller, the writing subject, had the tendency to yield to the text and to identify himself with the Other. This episode illuminates the moment in which Hearn's Western self disintegrates.

This uncertain stance enabled Hearn to create authentic black characters and at the same time made him fail to keep his position as the author, or the Western self. He had to become pluralistic and to praise differences without being hierarchical. As I stated earlier, he tended to take a Western point of view in discussing racial matters. However, when he wrote about actual non-white people who were heroic in their own right, those with whom he felt sympathy, Hearn could not write about them without subverting the hierarchical order of races. In other words, he failed to create a coherent world order in which his works could be neatly integrated.[3]

However, it seems that this is the very reason that he is not accused of appropriation as are some authors who deal with non-Westerners or minority groups. This tendency of letting go of his own stance as a Westerner, as is shown in *Youma*, is the characteristic of Hearn which eventually led him to become such a beloved writer in Japan. He could not be a superior Westerner writing in place of ignorant non-Westerners incapable of writing their own story for themselves, nor could he be simply an interpreter explaining the exotic to his fellow Westerners. But he was a writing self whose Western self disintegrated in the process of telling stories about non-Westerners.

In conclusion, I would like to quote from Robert Scholes' essay 'The Left Hand of Difference' which analyzes the deconstructing effect of Urshula LeGuin's science fiction classic, *The Left Hand of Darkness*. Urging the importance of deconstructing the Aristotelian hierarchical binary oppositions such as dark/light, right/left, man/woman, Scholes argues that LeGuin captures the moment in which 'we' become the aliens or the Other, and that by seeing the Other in ourselves we may learn to love what is different in ourselves, since, as the left hand of darkness is light, 'the left hand of difference is love' (128). Hearn, because of his love of the people he was writing about, seeing the Other in himself and himself in the Other, deconstructed the hierarchical world order, the hierarchical distinction of the self and the Other, and consequently created texts which appreciate the differences in different peoples and cultures.

TRAVEL SKETCHES OF LAFCADIO HEARN

Hiromi Kawashima

Hearn's travel sketches underwent a certain change during his years in Japan. A clue to this change can be found in his relations with Pierre Loti.

Lafcadio Hearn and Pierre Loti were born in the same year. At the age of nineteen they both made a start in life; Hearn left Europe alone and went to the United States, while Loti chose to travel around the world as a young officer in the French Navy. In 1885 Loti came to Japan, and spent the summer in Nagasaki. The experiences during this stay resulted in his famous *Madame Chrysanthemum*. He visited Kyoto, Kamakura and Nikko in the autumn of that year, and described his observations, which were brought together later in *Japoneries d'automne*. When his 'Kioto: La Ville Sainte' appeared in the *Nouvelle Revue* on 1 March 1887, Hearn translated a part of the essay into English quickly enough to introduce it on 3 and 17 April in two instalments in the *New Orleans Times Democrat*. Loti was thus introduced to English readers for the first time.

Hearn had been keeping his eye upon this French writer. He praised Loti's writings in one of his letters to H.E. Krehbiel in 1886, and affirmed: 'No writer ever had such effect upon me; and time strengthens my admiration. I hold him the greatest of living writers of the Impressionist School; and still he is something more . . .'[1] Hearn had made more than twenty

translations from Loti for two New Orleans papers before he
translated 'Kioto'. They are passages from the earlier works.
Loti's writings are characterized by an atmosphere all of its
own. Hearn seems to have been interested and attracted by his
exoticism.

When we read Hearn's translations from Loti, we realize
that Hearn's love for Loti's works is inseparable from his love
for the foreign scenes described in them. He especially loved
colourful tropical scenes. Hearn admitted that his likes and
dislikes about the works was swayed by his attachment to the
land described in them. He confessed that his dislike of grey
skies, fog and ice caused him to find less pleasure in the works
set in northern countries, such as *My Brother Yves* and *The
Iceland Fisherman*.[2]

On translation in general Hearn expressed his view in those
days as follows:

> . . . the path of the translator is hard . . . One who translates
> for the love of the original will probably have no reward save
> the satisfaction of creating something beautiful, and perhaps of
> saving a masterpiece from desecration by less reverent bards.[3]

To Hearn, to translate a writer is the expression of his great
esteem for the writer, where he sought the satisfaction of re-
creating the writer's beautiful world which he found so
fascinating. His sympathy and admiration towards the writer
urged him to translate and introduce his works. Translation
from Loti, therefore, is no exception. It seems that nobody
could surpass Hearn in the love of the original.

'Kioto: La Ville Sainte' is an interesting account of the old
city. Loti entered Kyoto by train, and narrates his experience
at the hotel, his visit to Yasaka, Kiyomizu, the palace of
Taiko-sama, Daibutsuden, Kitano-tenjin, and Sanju-san-gen-
do. For his English readers Hearn selected three of the topics.
Under the title of 'In the Palace of Taiko-sama' he translated
Loti's experience of walking though mysterious chambers. In
'The Big Bell' a good natured Japanese family from the
country who laughed with Loti are sketched, and Loti says:

> What a country this Japan, – where everything is oddity, and
> contrast![4]

The third piece, 'A Nightmare in Daylight' relates a legion of gods in the gloom of Sanju-san-gen-do. Here Loti exhibits his peculiar ability in description:

> In the midst, in the place of honour, – upon the open flower of a golden lotos, vast as the base of a tower, – sits throned a colossal Buddha of gold, – before a golden nimbus deployed behind him like the oustpread tail of a monstrous peacock. He is surrounded, guarded, by a score of nightmare-shapes, – something in likeness of human form, exaggeratedly huge, – and seeming to resemble at once both demons and corpses. When one enters through the central door, which is low and sly-looking, one recoils at the sight of these shapes of an evil dream, almost close to one.[5]

We notice that Loti has his favourite vocabulary in dealing with Japan; such as 'little', 'odd', 'mysterious', and 'strange'. The parts which Hearn chose are very typical of Loti, because Hearn was charmed with his exotic and romantic style. Loti was good at taking in foreign scenes intuitively, and showing them in his inimitable mysterious mood. Hearn tried to convey the deep impression he got from his works, by faithfully translating them. In this sense Hearn's translations from Loti's 'Kioto' represent the first step towards the travel sketches of Japan by Hearn himself.

In April 1890, Hearn came to Japan. Soon after arriving at Yokohama, he visited Kamakura and Enoshima. The opening of his first travel sketch in Japan, 'A Pilgrimage to Enoshima', is very impressive:

> Kamakura. A long, straggling country village, between low wooded hills, with a canal passing through it.
> . . . a sense of melancholy, of desolation unspeakable, weighs upon me as we roll along the bank of the tiny stream, between the mouldering lines of wretched little homes with grass growing on their roofs. For this mouldering hamlet represents all the remains of the million-peopled streets of Yoritomo's capital, the mighty city of the Shōgunate, the ancient seat of feudal power . . . Here still dwell the ancient gods in the great silence of their decaying temples, without worshippers, without revenues, surrounded by desolations of rice-fields, where the chanting of frogs replaces the sea-like murmur of the city that was and is not.[6]

Before leaving for Enoshima, he alludes to the deserted scene again:

> As we leave the temple of Kwannon behind us, there are no more dwellings visible along the road . . . But still, at intervals, some flight of venerable mossy steps, a carven Buddhist gateway, or a lofty torii, signals the presence of sanctuaries we have no time to visit: countless crumbling shrines are all around us, dumb witnesses to the antique splendour and vastness of the dead capital . . .[7]

Reading these passages, we find that there exists something which inevitably reminds us of Loti. 'Melancholy', 'tiny', 'little', 'decaying', 'desolations', 'the dead capital' – all these are, we recall, Loti's favourite words.

Not only the words and expressions, but also its whole tone closely resembles that of 'Toilette d'Impératrice' by Loti. Loti repeated that Kamakura was a dead capital, and Hearn took it over. They are also quite alike in construction, having a lot of subject matter in common; an ancient city which is now a desolate village, the Dai-Butsu which suddenly comes into full view at a turn, the wayside shrines of some unknown gods, and ancient, weather-worn, time-discoloured images of some deity. They both conclude with the mention of taking their leave in a locomotive, a symbol of Western civilization.

It is true that there exists a difference between Loti and Hearn in the way they each feel towards what they see, especially towards gods and towards Japanese people. This difference is significant. But, at the same time, there are surprisingly many factors in common. I wonder whether Hearn followed Loti's example purposely.

'Toilette d'Impératrice' first appeared in August 1888, when Hearn was in the West Indies. The book *Japoneries d'automne* was published in March 1889, but the copy Hearn owned is the 1893 edition. We should suppose, consequently, that Hearn had read 'Toilette d'Impératrice', but had no copy at hand when he wrote about Kamakura.

In any case, Hearn was looking at Japan from a point of view not very far from that of Loti. It has been pointed out that his travel sketches written during his early days in Japan are rather romantic. I take the view that the charm of this unfamiliar country became the greater for Hearn, under the influence of Loti: he saw Japan at first as Loti did. Hearn might have ended as a mere follower of Loti, if he had just stuck to this line.

While Loti remained a traveller to the last, Hearn decided to stay much longer in this country. In 1892 he visited Kyoto and wrote to Mason:

> . . . I can't say that I liked Kyōto as much as I expected. First of all, I was tremendously disappointed by my inability to discover what Loti described. He described only his own sensations: exquisite, weird, or wonderful. Loti's 'Kioto: La Ville Sainte' has no existence. I saw the San-ju-san-gen-do, for example: I saw nothing of Loti's – only recognized what had evoked the wonderful goblinry of his imagination.[8]

Hearn realized then that Loti's Kyoto has been the reflection of his sentiments and taste, rather than what Kyoto really was. Visiting Kyoto himself, Hearn found that what had attracted him was just the image of foreign lands reflected on Loti's mind. Accordingly, I regard this letter as the diverging point of the two writers. Once he failed to see the objects the way Loti had showed him to see them, his admiration began to cool down. New works by Loti seemed to him less fascinating. In 1893 and 94 we find many letters in which Hearn assumed a critical attitude towards Loti.

> . . . I fear Loti's nerves are played out. His work has become morbid of late.[9]

> He saw outwardly and on the surface only.[10]

> There is very, very great art in Loti – very wonderful art . . .Nevertheless, I must confess I dislike Loti very much . . .[11]

Besides, Hearn disapproved of Loti as a man for his lack of moral sense.

Meanwhile, Hearn praised another writer very highly; that is, Rudyard Kipling, an English journalist, who later became famous as the author of *The Jungle Book*. He visited Japan twice; in 1889, at the age of twenty-three, and three years later, in 1892. Since it was much later that his books on Japan

were published, Hearn seems to have read his writings as soon
as they appeared in newspapers. When Chamberlain wrote to
Hearn that he went to Kamakura, Hearn answered in the
following manner:

> I hope Mason has preserved for you the pretty lines of
> Rudyard Kipling about the Daibutsu at Kamakura. I enjoy
> him – not the poetry of the effort, but the prose of it. It is
> delicious. Alas! I had written my commonplace stuff about the
> Daibutsu long ago; – long before. Would I could atone for it
> now![12]

Kipling's letters to *The Times* are rather brisk and vigorous, and
contain some unforgettable expressions, though they must
have been writted in haste, as items of ephemeral journalism.

Hearn admired Kipling and confessed that he felt small and
stupid beside Kipling, while asserting, on the other hand, that
something was the matter with Loti. He says that Loti's
writing depends for its value upon super-sensitiveness to
impressions, and adds:

> Kipling's little sketch of Kamakura is truer art; perfectly
> controlled, subtle, didactic.[13]

Here we notice a change in Hearn's taste and his policy in
writing. His own work on Kamakura proved unsatisfactory to
himself after reading Kipling. He even calls his own writing
commonplace. Thus, his parting from Loti coincides with his
enthusiasm for Kipling, who writes calmly with profound
knowledge. Perfectly controlled, subtle, didactic – these are
the words Hearn used to comment on Kipling. They must
have become also the ideal style for Hearn himself.

After the visit in autumn 1895, Hearn took up Kyoto at last
in 'Notes of a Trip to Kyoto'. Eight-and-a-half years had
passed since he translated 'Kioto' by Loti. Perhaps Hearn was
at a loss in 1892 when he was greatly disappointed to find
nothing Loti had described in the city, but now, he was well
prepared to face the challenging task, as it were, of treating
Kyoto in his own way. Let us go over several points where his
intention is clearly seen.

In the first place, he attaches great importance to the city
and its people of his day, instead of the long history it has. It

seems that he even disregards or neglects its long history as an old capital. We may safely judge that it is partly because he deeply regretted his former attitude towards Kamakura. As we have seen, he had kept a rather fixed image of Kamakura as an ancient capital. This time he made a trip to see the eleven hundredth anniversary of the foundation of Kyoto, but he ignores the chance to refer to the history, and instead pays attention to the people of the present generation, such as those who marched in the procession, and the spectators. Though he used, in a private letter, the expression 'Holy Kyoto', he never used it in 'Notes of a Trip to Kyoto'. He avoids such expressions as Loti preferred.

As for subjects, Hearn does not mind taking up the same ones as Loti did, but he treats them in a way which forms a striking contrast to his rival. For example, both Hearn and Loti open their sketches with the scene of the train for Kyoto. In the case of Loti, the author is described as a weary foreigner, who is raised out of sleep in the train by an old lady, and gets off alone in European clothes which stand out clearly from the rest. In the case of Hearn, the author joins the passengers and the Japanese are described as a people who know how to divert themselves; this indication has direct bearings on the main theme of the piece. Both Loti and Hearn sketch festival lanterns. While Loti described them as strange and ominous, Hearn made careful observation of them and perceived Japanese ingenuity there. Hearn must have selected these subjects in order to make a distinction between Loti and himself.

As a whole, Hearn seems to have taken special care not to depend upon exotic atmosphere. He paid due respect to Loti's strong points even after he lost sympathy with Loti, saying, 'Only in exotic subjects he excels all others living . . .'[14] Loti repeats that everything is oddity and contrasts; this impression Loti entertained serves as a unity in his work. Hearn, on the other hand, averted the route Loti had taken; he tried to be original. When he wrote on Kamakura, he put in some legends about the temple, but the unity could be attained easily, because, as we have already seen, there was a fundamental image. Now that he had chosen not to rely on romantic exoticism any longer, he needed a new unity for writing on Kyoto. While Loti likes to treat foreign, colourful, strange and striking scenes, Hearn had begun to turn to something deeper. What he watches and treats is the sentiment universal to all people. This is what he attends to. He sought something common to all, and set it as a central unifying theme.

What binds Hearn's work on Kyoto then? He chose pleasure and beauty. From the beginning to the end, he keeps contemplating on it. Thus his travel sketches became more than mere records of travel or of impressions on Japan. His pursuit of unity led him to a unique style of travel sketches.

In the city of Kyoto there are many sights to see and describe, if one wishes. As a matter of fact, Hearn's letters show that he visited Kiyomizu and other places. But the experiences told in 'Notes of a Trip to Kyoto' are strictly confined to those which serve to cultivate his thoughts. He carefully arranges material and constructs an effective essay.

He though that Kyoto was most beautiful at night. He did not fail to write a paragraph of aesthetic and philosophical contemplation in relation to it:

> . . . the quick vanishing of all that composes of a Japanese festival-night really lends a keener edge to the pleasure of remembrance: there is no slow fading out of the phantasmagoria, and its memory is thus kept free from the least tinge of melancholy.[15]

We must note that melancholy is one of Loti's most favourite words and Hearn affirms here that the memory of a Japanese festival night is free from melancholy. This is a moderate, but definite disapproval of Loti's world, one may say. Hearn chose pleasure and beauty; a fine contrast to Loti's favourite mood. This symbolizes Hearn's separation from Loti.

Hearn was an ardent lover of exoticism at heart. He started to write on Japan, at first, as an extension of his admiration which he felt during his period in America. As he learned to see this country with his own eyes, he grasped the true character of the writings of Loti. Therefore, he substituted insight for impressions. Exotic feeling was replaced by more extensive learning. This tendency is exhibited in other travel essays by Hearn, but I have to leave this point for another occasion.

11

HEARN'S 'YUKI-ONNA' AND BAUDELAIRE'S 'LES BIENFAITS DE LA LUNE'

Yoko Makino

'Yuki-Onna' ('The Snow-Woman') is one of the best known and popular stories of Lafcadio Hearn. Although included in *Kwaidan* (1904), a collection of Japanese weird tales completed in the year of his death, the story of 'Yuki-Onna' is not only horrifying but also beautiful and fantastic.

While we have a definite original text for Hearn's other retold ghost stories, we have none for 'Yuki-Onna'. In his foreword to *Kwaidan*, Hearn says that he developed the tale from a legend which a peasant living in the district of Musashino had once told him. Since Hearn did not write it down, we cannot retrieve the original legend, despite many attempts to do so.

My aim here is to analyze 'Yuki-Onna' as a literary text and to point out another source of inspiration—namely, Baudelaire's poem 'Les Bienfaits de la Lune'. This investigation will reveal Hearn's particular image of time, which—projected into the climactic scene—creates intrinsic elements of horror and beauty.

In his short story, Hearn presents two woodcutters, Mosaku and Minokichi. Mosaku is an old man and Minokichi a young one. On a cold winter evening, walking home from the forest, they are overtaken by a snowstorm and have to spend the night in a small hut by the river. That night, 'Yuki-Onna' appears. She kills old Mosaku, but she lets Minokichi live—on the condition that he not tell anyone what he has seen. A year later, Minokichi meets a beautiful girl named O-Yuki (which means snow), and he marries her. They have a happy family, but one night Minokichi tells his wife that long ago he has seen the Yuki-Onna. O-Yuki suddenly reveals herself to be the snow-woman and leaves Minokichi forever.

In *Kwaidan* 'Yuki-Onna' is not a typical ghost story. The snow-woman is not an apparition of a dead person, and although she may be a frightening supernatural being who freezes men to death, she is so beautiful that she fascinates Minokichi even as he confronts death.

The most impressive parts of the tale are contained in two sections, the opening scene where Yuki-Onna first appears, and the final scene where she shows her true self.

The first scene takes place in the hut. In the snowstorm, Minokichi has been lying awake for a long time, shivering, but at last he falls asleep:

> He was awakened by a showering of snow in his face. The door of the hut had been forced open; and, by the snow-light (yuki-akari), he saw a woman in the room—a woman all in white. She was bending over Mosaku and blowing her breath upon him;—and her breath was like a bright white smoke. Almost in the same moment she turned to Minokichi, and stooped over him. He tried to cry out, but found that he could not utter a sound. The white woman bent down over him, lower and lower, until her face almost touched him; and he saw that she was very beautiful—though her eyes made him afraid. For a little time she continued to look at him;—then she smiled, and whispered: 'I intended to treat you like the other man. But I cannot help feeling some pity for you— because you are so young ... You are a pretty boy, Minokichi; and I will not hurt you now. But if you ever tell anybody—even your own mother—about what you have seen this night, I shall know it; and then I will kill you ... Remember what I say!'
>
> With these words, she turned from him, and passed through the doorway. Then he found himself able to move; and he

sprang up, and looked out. But the woman was nowhere to be seen . . . Mosaku was stark and dead.[1]

The vividness rather than the fearfulness of this scene makes it impressive: the white light in the dark; the face turning around; the woman's slow approach; and her face as she bends over the man.

The narrative that follows, however, is plain and straightforward. In a quiet tone, it tells us that Minokichi becomes ill from the shock, and that a year later, on a winter night, he meets a girl with whom he falls in love. Her mysterious beauty and youth remain just the same even after many years have passed and she has borne ten lovely children. Throughout, Hearn records no conversation; he gives a distant view.

But after this tranquil, adagio-like interlude he presents the dramatic conclusion:

> One night, after the children had gone to sleep, O-Yuki was sewing by the light of a paper lamp; and Minokichi, watching her, said:
>
> 'To see you sewing there, with the light on your face, makes me think of a strange thing that happened when I was a lad of eighteen. I then saw somebody as beautiful and white as you are now—indeed, she was very like you'
>
> Without lifting her eyes from her work, O-Yuki responded:
>
> 'Tell me about her . . . Where did you see her?'
>
> Then Minokichi told her about the terrible night in the ferryman's hut—and about the White Woman that had stooped above him, smiling and whispering—and about the silent death of old Mosaku . . .
>
> O-Yuki flung down her sewing, and arose, and bowed above Minokichi where he sat, and shrieked in his face:
>
> 'It was I—I—I! Yuki it was! And I told you then that I would kill you if ever you said one word about it! . . . But for those children asleep, I would kill you this moment! . . .
>
> Even as she screamed, her voice became thin, like a crying of wind;—then she melted into a bright white mist that spired to the roof-beams, and shuddered away through the smoke hole . . . Never again was she seen.[2]

If we compare this scene with the first, we find many common elements: Monokichi gazing at his wife's face, which is lit up beautifully and fearfully white in the darkness by the lantern light; an air of tension as she bends over her husband; fatal words being exchanged; and at last the woman vanishing, leaving the man alone.

These two scenes clearly correspond to each other in structure, but they rely on two important devices to create the central image and the text's literary impact. One is the strong basic composition, and the other is the repetition of this composition.

Most readers of this tale will likely experience sorrow rather than fear, and not just sadness at the protagonist's loss of his family but something that touches the very core of the soul. To understand this distinction, we need to determine where Hearn derived his central image.

In most cases, we know that Hearn created his Japanese tales from an original text. But in the case of 'Yuki-Onna' the original has not survived in written form, and the original legend cannot be specified in detail. Yet we can benefit from folklore studies. By Hearn's time, in the middle of the Meiji era, there were many snow-woman legends in Japan, especially in districts with heavy snowfall. These legends were all very simple, though, and none is similar to Hearn's tale. In most, the snow-woman is either a spirit or personification of snow, seen only from afar, which probably reflects primitive animism; or she is a comical character who visits a village house and, when invited to the fireside, melts away to the surprise of the family.

The uniqueness of Hearn's tale reveals that the legend he heard from the Musashino peasant was also a very simple story, and that the author got his inspiration from a different source. But what was this other source?

Significantly, Hearn refers to the Yuki-Onna legend repeatedly before coming to Tokyo—that is, before hearing it from the Musashino peasant. For example, in one of his earliest works on Japan, an essay entitled 'Of Ghosts and Goblins' (included in *Glimpses of Unfamiliar Japan*, 1894), he recounts how he learned of the existence of Yuki-Onna:

> It had snowed heavily in the morning; but now the sky and
> the sharp still air were clear as diamond; and the crisp snow

made a pleasant crunching sound under our feet as we walked; and it occurred to me to say: 'O Kinjuro, is there a God of Snow?'

'I cannot tell . . . But there is the Yuki-Onna, the Woman of the snow.' 'And what is the Yuki-Onna?'

'She is the White One that makes the Faces in the snow. She does not any harm, only makes afraid. By day she lifts only her head, and frightens those who journey alone. But at night she rises up sometimes, taller than the trees, and looks about in a little while, and then falls back in a shower of snow.'

'And what is her face like?'

'It is all white, white. It is an enormous face. And it is a *lonesome* face.'[3]

The Japanese legendary snow-woman here is a snow spirit with a big white face, but she does not harm men.

Hearn also refers to the snow-woman in a letter to his friend Basil Hall Chamberlain dated 5 February 1893:

European art does not seem to me to have ever caught the Soul of the Snow as the Japanese art has—with its fantasticalities, its wizardisms. And the Japanese Fancy has its 'Snow-women' too—its white spectres and goblins, which do no harm and say nothing, only frighten and make one feel cold. I can see the beauty of snow now, but still it makes me shiver. I think the Yuki-onna sometimes when I am asleep, passes her white arm through a crack of the amado into my sleeping room, and in spite of the fire, touches my heart and laughs. Then I wake up, and pull the futons closer . . .[4]

Again, Hearn explains that Yuki-Onna is a spirit of snow who does no harm. But the letter reveals that he had been deeply impressed by the legend, and that he was trying to find something similar to the snow-woman legend in Western literary tradition. Significantly, the core scenes in 'Yuki-Onna' are already present—namely, his imagination of a white woman coming into a room at midnight.

These facts suggest that Hearn may have been strongly influenced by some Western inspiration. I believe this inspiration came from a prose poem by Baudelaire: 'Les Bienfaits de la Lune' ('The Moon's Blessings').

As is well known, Hearn was proficient in French, and when he worked for local newspapers in America, he introduced many contemporary French writers and their works, including Baudelaire. But Hearn seemed to be especially attached to 'Les Bienfaits de la Lune', for he not only translated it and wrote a short essay about it for his American readers, but he also presented the entire work to his Japanese students, praising it as a masterpiece. This happened some twenty years later, when he was supposed to be lecturing on English, not French literature.

This is the poem in Hearn's translation:

> The Moon, who is caprice itself, looked through the window while thou wert sleeping in thy cradle, and exclaimed: 'That child pleases me!' And she softly descended her stairway of clouds, and passed without sound through the panes of glass; then she stretched herself above thee, with a mother's supple tenderness, and she put her own colours upon they face ... The Moon filled the whole room, like a phosphoric atmosphere, like a luminous poison; and all that living light thought and spoke: 'Thou shalt eternally endure the influence of my kiss; thou shalt be beautiful after my fashion; thou shalt love all I love, and all that loves me—water, clouds, the silence, and the night; the waters formless and multiform; the place where thou shalt never be; the lover thou shalt never know; monstrous flowers; the perfumes that give delirium; the cats that stretch themselves upon pianos, and moan like women, with a hoarse sweet voice ... the immense tumultuous sea-water, ... the sinister flowers that resemble the censers of some unknown religion, the perfumes that confuse the will, the wild and voluptuous animals that are emblems of their madness.'[5]

We can easily recognize a dramatic construct common to that of the first, impressive scene of 'Yuki-Onna'. Moonlight, just like snow, creeps into a dark room at night, and mysteriously lit up in such light, a personification of the moon appears. She is a beautiful but frightening figure, all in white. she comes to the baby who is lying in the cradle, lowers her face, and, kissing it, speaks to it in half blessing, half cursing words. From that moment on, her words control the destiny of the child. And the infant, whose cheeks turn pale, is both frightened and fascinated, just as Minokichi was by Yuki-Onna.

The goddess in Baudelaire's 'The Moon's Blessings' is characterized as a typical fin-de-siècle 'femme fatale'. The woman has a double face: one beautiful and tender, the other destructive and dangerous. She is also the ruler of a powerless young man's destiny.

By comparing Hearn's 'Yuki-Onna' and Baudelaire's 'The Moon's Blessings', we can find a definite similarity between the two mysterious characters. In Hearn's imagination the snow-woman legend of Japan was probably mingled with the 'femme fatale' figure, which was a prevailing literary fashion of the late nineteenth century. For this reason Hearn may have adopted Baudelaire's moonlight scene.

Hearn's 'Yuki-Onna' is not merely a translation of a Japanese folktale; it is a union of two different literary traditions: East and West. The unique characterization of Hearn's Yuki-Onna, which stands apart from all other Japanese snow-woman folktales, is best understood through the 'femme fatale' because this figure reveals the essential meaning of Yuki-Onna for Minokichi: fate. Simply put, Yuki-Onna determines Minokichi's fate.

There is nothing strange or surprising in the identification of a female personification of snow with the fin-de siècle 'femme fatale'. As is well known, the figure is often connected with water forms, such as rivers, lakes, the sea, and fountains. The elusiveness, transformability, and ambivalence of water greatly influenced people during this period. Snow, of course, has all those attributes, perhaps in their most extreme form.

Hearn had his own personal reasons for especially liking 'The Moon's Blessings' among the many 'femme fatale' figures in European literature. In his essay entitled 'Spring Phantoms' (*Item*, 21 April 1881), he condenses the whole poem into just seven lines:

> The moon, descending her staircase of clouds in one of the 'Petits Poèmes en Prose', enters the chamber of a newborn child, and whispers into his dreams: 'Thou shalt love all that loves me—the water that is formless and multiform, the vast green sea, the place where thou shalt never be, the woman thou shalt never know.'[6]

Here Hearn omits such modifiers as 'phosphoric' and 'poison', which the original uses to describe the moon goddess. In Baudelaire's text, the moon destines the child to be attached to many things, including 'the night, cat, monstrous flowers, delirious perfume, and voluptuous animals'. But in his essay, Hearn mentions only four of them: 'the water, the sea, the place where you shall never be, and the woman you shall never know'. It would seem that only these four were significant to Hearn.

He sums up his interpretation of the poem as follows:

> For those of us that were blessed or cursed at birth, this is perhaps the special season of such a dream—of nostalgia, vague as the world-sickness, for the places where we shall never be; and fancies as delicate as arabesques of smoke concerning the woman we shall never know.[7]

Hearn here has his own fate in mind, his own longing for the land of Greece, and for his Greek mother, from whom he had parted early in his childhood. He probably identified with the infant asleep in the cradle and saw his own loving but afflicted mother in the opening scene of 'The Moon's Blessings'. Accordingly, he identified his own personal history with that of Baudelaire's child. Such an identification may well account for Hearn's attraction to this poem.

Hearn had a strong desire for the eternal woman and for the happy family life of which he had been deprived. And his interpretation of the fate promised by the moon goddess was, as we have seen, a fate true to his vision of an unseen land and woman. All this, however, was ten years before he came to Japan.

In addition to similarities, we need to acknowledge an important difference between 'Yuki-Onna' and Baudelaire's poem: the meaning of fate as shown by the woman. This meaning is connected with the textual fact that in 'Yuki-Onna' the crucial scene is repeated: herein, I believe, lies the secret of the story.

'Yuki-Onna' obviously belongs to the universal folktale type of a 'hetero-species marriage' between a human being and a non-human. In this type of folktale, the non-human wife or husband inevitably leaves the other. There seem to be two ways in which the marriage is broken.

In tales in which the human knows the original form of his wife (such as in the Japanese Hagoromo legend, or in Hearn's own retold tale 'The Bird Wife'[8]), the wife escapes and the marriage is broken when the human husband is caught off guard and carelessly hands over the wife's means of returning to her own world (such as her heavenly robe or feather-wings). But in other stories in which the humans know nothing of the true nature of their spouses, their happiness is ruined when the human violates a taboo prearranged by the other. Such well-known tales as 'Tsuru-Nyobo' ('The Crane's Wife'), the 'Miwayama Legend' of Japan, and the 'Lohengrin' legend of Germany belong to this second type. So does Hearn's 'Yuki-Onna'.

As we can see in the 'Tsuru-Nyobo' folktale, the crane wife makes her husband promise never to look at her while she is weaving cloth, but the husband gives way to his curiosity and cannot help peeping into the forbidden room. In the 'Miwayama Legend', the husband—who secretly visits the wife every night—will not reveal his identity. So the curious wife sews a long thread to his garment, and following it she sees what she should not have discovered. In the 'Lohengrin' legend, too, the handsome knight who appears mysteriously to receive a bride forbids his wife to ask him whence he came. The spouse, however, cannot keep herself from asking this fatal question.

In these tales, the humans defy the taboos because of their curiosity about their mates' identity. In other words, the tales share the taboo related to the inviolability of an unknown region and to an awareness of a social norm: the taboo is characterized by the individual's concept of space. If so, is this also true of Hearn's 'Yuki-Onna'?

Let us recall the two pivotal scenes. On the night of the snowstorm, the snow-woman bids Minokichi 'not to tell anyone what he saw that night'. Years later, however, one winter night, when Minokichi is watching his wife O-Yuki sew by the light of a paper lantern, he cannot help recalling the fearful vision he had long ago. Minokichi tells her: 'To see you sewing there, with the light on your face, makes me think of a strange thing that happened when I was a lad of eighteen. I

then saw somebody as beautiful and white as you are now—
indeed, she was very much like you . . .' At this moment,
Minokichi is superimposing his wife's face, lit up by the
lamplight, on the white face of Yuki-Onna emerging in the
snow light, an unforgettable vision imprinted in his memory.
In other words, he is trying to compare the past with the
present, and by telling O-Yuki his feelings, he is trying to
reconfirm his memory and revive the past in the present.
Thereby, he violates the taboo.

O-Yuki suddenly raises her head, and her countenance
turns into that of the snow-woman. 'Yes, it was I!' she
screams, in answer to Minokichi's attempt to revive the past.
At this point, O-Yuki rises, draws near, and bends over him,
staring into his face. Here we see the composition of the
encounter scene repeated symbolically. It symbolizes a
resurrection of the past. And thus the happiness of Minokichi
and O-Yuki, which was based on a subtle balance between
reality and vision, collapses under the weight of the taboo.

The taboo in 'Yuki-Onna' is clearly related to the
individual's effort to cope with the memory of the past. In
other words, the taboo is characterized by the concept of time,
not space, and it is here that Hearn's 'Yuki-Onna' differs from
the 'hetero-species marriage' folktales.

The fate imposed upon Minokichi by the beautiful but
dangerous 'femme fatale' in the beginning of the story
consisted in never questioning, never confirming the past. The
snow-woman reprieves Minokichi from impending death,
changes herself into a gentle fairy wife and bestows on him
years of happy family life. But when Minokichi violates the
taboo and tries to confirm the past, his spouse must vanish into
a mist. Here we see that the fate declared by the Yuki Onna
runs counter to that of Baudelaire's moon goddess. Whereas
the moon goddess commands the poet to be true to a
particular vision throughout his life, the Yuki-Onna requires
Minokichi to cut his bonds with his unforgettable vision of the
past. Hearn modifies the original meaning of Baudelaire's
poem.

Having lost his mother early in his childhood, Hearn was
never freed from the memory of this experience. His travels to
the West Indies, his coming to Japan, his interest in non-

Western folktales: all this was affected and motivated by his yearning for the bygone happy years in Greece. But it was at the age of 40, when he came to Japan and especially to Matsue, where he got married and for the first time enjoyed a warm family life, that he could finally see his own childhood objectively. Never before had he been able to think about what his past experience meant to him and about the role which memory plays in life.

In Japan, Hearn must have begun to feel a strong reluctance and fear to pursue and face the past straight on in spite of his restless desire to do so. He must have felt deeply the double, ambivalent significance that memory has: its idealized charm, its fearful futility that gnaws at the heart.

In 'Yuki-Onna', this past is taboo, and the man is caught in the trap of memory. We see the deep perspective of time added to a simple folktale. The translucent atmosphere that dominates the whole story is not only due to the stage effect of snow or to the literary style of the author. It is due, I believe, to the fantastic, cosmic extension that time bears in the individual heart. And the vague sorrow with which the reader is left at the end is the pathos essential to all memories.

Lafcadio Hearn's 'Yuki-Onna' was seemingly written in order to introduce an exotic Japanese folktale. But 'Yuki-Onna' is not a simple, retold version. It is a union of East and West, a combination of an old legend and the fin-de-siècle epoch. Moreover, Hearn has revealed here a more fundamental aspect of the meaning of life through a psychological, introspective drama. The author has projected his own drama into a folktale now read mostly by children— one which has the unique power to penetrate, unconsciously, the imagination of everyone.

12

LAFCADIO HEARN: JAPAN'S PROBLEMATIC INTERPRETER

Yuzo Ota

L afcadio Hearn, who was born in 1850 in one of the Ionian Islands as a son of an Irish father and a Greek mother, took an early interest in the Orient partly because, as he explained to an American lady, he was 'Oriental by birth and half by blood'.[1] After eventful years spent in Europe and America, he arrived in Japan in 1890, and soon began to write articles and books on Japan. He married a Japanese woman and eventually became naturalized in Japan. When Hearn died in 1904, an obituary in the *New York Times* made the following claim about him: 'To a greater extent, probably, than any other Occidental Lafcadio Hearn succeeded in bridging the gulf which separates East and West. If ever a Westerner understood the Japanese it was he . . .'[2]

By the time of his death, Hearn had lived in Japan for roughly fourteen years and had published more than ten books on Japan. Through these books, he had become *the* interpreter of Japan for the Western audience. Evaluations of Hearn's importance as a Japan interpreter, similar to that of the obituary in the *New York Times*, were legion around that time. For example, reviewing four books of Hearn's reissued by Little, Brown & Co of Boston, a reviewer wrote in the *Chronicle*, a San Francisco newspaper: 'The late Lafcadio Hearn penetrated nearer the heart of the Japanese people than any other foreigner, because he lived their life and had keen sympathy with them. He knew the language almost as well as a native . . .[3] The title of a 1992 new anthology of his writings from Japan, *Lafcadio Hearn: Japan's Great Interpreter*,[4] indicates that Hearn continues to be understood as he was at his death. However, we should not accept such a positive evaluation without a careful examination. For example, did Hearn really know 'the language almost as well as a native', as the reviewer of the *Chronicle* and many others believed? Definitely not. In a letter of 1902, Hearn himself, who had lived in Japan for more than twelve years at that time, said: 'At present I have no acquaintance even with the Japanese language: I cannot read a Japanese newspaper.'[5] The photographic reproduction of some of the rare letters written by Hearn in Japanese show that his written Japanese was at the level of a Grade 1 or Grade 2 primary pupil in Japan.[6] Hearn's near native fluency in Japanese is nothing but an illusion created through his skilful use of Japanese assistants. One of the recipients of the rare Hearn letters written in Japanese testifies that Hearn 'was extremely afraid lest the world should get to know the level of his real knowledge of Japanese and made his letters written in Japanese strictly confidential'.[7]

Another illusion about Hearn which he himself was in no haste to destroy was the view that he was a great lover of Japan. It is true that during the first several months of his stay in Japan, Hearn was full of enthusiasm for the country. 'I feel indescribably towards Japan,'[8] said Hearn in a letter written in 1890 shortly after his arrival in Japan. However, it did not take long before disillusionment set in. In 1894 when Hearn reread his notes from 1890 immediately following his arrival in Japan, he was appalled by his own naive misplaced enthusiasm for Japanese things and people and wrote, 'I find I described horrible places as gardens of paradise, and horrid people as angels and divinities.'[9]

In his own eyes and in the eyes of many other people, Hearn was a rebel against his own civilization. However, like many other rebels, Hearn had internalized much of the values of his own culture and civilization. We can see this by looking at Hearn in Japan. For example, even during his Matsue days (1890–91), more or less unanimously regarded as the happiest period of his Japan years, his happiness diminished over time, because his soul was, after all, 'Western', as he admits in a letter in which he complains about excessively formal relationships among men in Japan:

> There is no such thing as clapping a man on the back and saying, 'Hello!, old boy!' There is no such thing as clapping a fellow on the knee, or chuckling a fellow under the ribs. All such familiarities are terribly vulgar in Japan. So each one has to tickle his own soul and clap it on the back, and say 'Hello' to it. And the soul, being Western, says: 'Do you expect me always to stay in this extraordinary country? I want to go home . . .'[10]

The extent of his acceptance of the Japanese values and customs was usually exaggerated in the popular image of him. Nobushige Amenomori, one of the few real Japanese friends Hearn had, writes that 'Hearn never took Japanese food except when travelling in the interior' and cites Hearn's own characterization of himself as 'a man, who although a Japanese in name, remains a barbarian in manners and total ignorance of etiquette'.[11] His alienation from the Western society, if real, by no means guaranteed his happy integration into Japanese society. Dr Pepellier who befriended Hearn during his Kobe years (1894–96) was struck that 'his knowledge of the Japanese vernacular was very poor for a man of his intelligence, who, for nearly four years, had lived almost entirely in the interior, surrounded by those who could only talk the language of the country'.[12] Perhaps, his bafflingly poor command of Japanese despite his obvious linguistic talent, which had made him a competent translator of French literature during his American days, was a reflection of his real alienation from Japanese society.

Hearn apparently thought it wise not to betray his disillusionment with Japan in his books. However, he revealed his true sentiments about Japan freely in his personal letters which he did not intend to publish. So, the publication of his collected letters, beginning with *The Life and Letters of Lafcadio Hearn*, ed. Elizabeth Bisland, in 1906, was something of a revelation. Especially, this was the case with the publication of *Some New Letters and Writings of Lafcadio*

Hearn, ed. Sanki Ichikawa (Tokyo: Kenkyusha, 1925). when it was reviewed in the *New York Times*, the heading read 'Did Lafcadio Hearn Hate Japan? His Letters to Japanese Friends Reveal Resentment, Disillusionment and Despair.'[13]

Hearn's first book on Japan titled *Glimpses of Unfamiliar Japan* published in 1894 contributed more than any other book to establish his reputation as a great Japan interpreter. It continues to be regarded by many as his most important book on Japan. The widespread high evaluation of the book by his contemporaries (one reviewer described it as 'not only one of the most interesting, but one of the most just, sympathetic and reliable books that have yet been published on modern Japan'[14]), however, makes a strange contrast with the low evaluation of the book by Hearn himself, who wrote in 1898: 'When I want to feel properly humble, I read "Glimpses of Unfamiliar Japan" – about half a page; – then I howl, and wonder how I could ever have written so badly, – and find that I am really only a very twenty-fifth-rate workman and that I ought to be kicked.'[15]

His own dissatisfaction with the book was not simply a matter of poor workmanship. He had also come to doubt the validity of his own rosy picture of Japan and the Japanese given in that book even before it was printed. 'I am beginning to think I was a great fool to write a book about Japan at all,'[16] confided Hearn to Basil Hall Chamberlain, one of the greatest Japanologists of his generation, in a letter of 1893, the year before the publication of *Glimpses of Unfamiliar Japan*. In the same letter to Chamberlain, he could not suppress his suspicion that 'my book is all wrong'.[17] His sceptical attitude towards his first book on Japan stayed with him. In a letter of 1902, Hearn dismissed *Glimpses of Unfamiliar Japan* as a book 'written before I really began to understand, not Japan, but how difficult it is to understand Japan'.[18]

Seen in the light of what I have just said, much of the contemporary reviews of Hearn's books on Japan appear to have been written by reviewers who were not adequately equipped to evaluate Hearn's significance as a Japan interpreter due to their ignorance of Japan and the Japanese language. The reviewer of *Glimpses of Unfamiliar Japan* for the *New York Times* who was full of enthusiasm for the book claimed that, 'It

is not necessary to have seen Japan to be convinced, or rather
to know, that in this book are no mistakes or misunderstand-
ings',[19] a claim which is too absurd to be taken seriously.
Clearly, Hearn's reputation in the West as the Interpreter of
Japan was not particularly well founded.

Now I would like to turn to the examination of Hearn's
place as a Japan interpreter in Japan. Today, although there is a
fairly strong interest in Hearn outside Japan as shown in the
publication of several studies on Hearn in recent years,
including, Robert A. Rosenstone, *Mirror in the Shrine:
American Encounters with Meiji Japan* (Cambridge, Mass.:
Harvard University Press, 1988), Jonathan Cott, *Wandering
Ghost: The Odyssey of Lafcadio Hearn* (New York: Alfred A.
Knopf, 1991), Carl Dawson, *Lafcadio Hearn and the Vision of
Japan* (Baltimore: The Johns Hopkins University Press, 1992),
and Paul Murray, *A Fantastic Journey: The Life and Literature of
Lafcadio Hearn* (Sandgate, Folkestone, Kent: Japan Library,
1993), Japan is indisputably the centre of interest in Hearn.
However, this was not always the case. Actually, until the
mid-1920s, relatively few Japanese were interested in him.

When the planned publication of the first complete works
of Lafcadio Hearn in Japanese translation was advertised in the
4 May 1926, issue of the *Tokyo Asahi Shimbun*, a major
Japanese newspaper, Hasegawa Minokichi, the head of Dai-
ichi-shobo, the publishing firm in Tokyo undertaking their
publication, contrasted Hearn's immense reputation abroad
with the almost complete lack of interest in him on the part of
the Japanese.[20] This lack of interest in Hearn may appear
curious, but it is not difficult to understand. As I showed
elsewhere, during Hearn's lifetime the Japanese, intent on
modernizing their country, tended to repudiate their past and,
accordingly, had no common ground with Hearn a lover of
the so-called Old Japan, who was hostile to New Japan which
was emerging through the modern transformation of Japan.[21]

Nevertheless, Hearn eventually became *the* Japan interpreter
for many Japanese just as he had been *the* Japan interpreter for
many Western readers a few decades before. One of the factors
contributing to Hearn's gradual emergence as the Japan
interpreter for the Japanese from the 1930s, was undoubtedly
the further transformation of Japan from the period when

Hearn lived there.[22] In his writings on Japan, Hearn focused his attention on the vestiges of what he called Old Japan which had a strong exotic appeal to himself and to his readers in the West. In 1890, the year of his arrival in Japan, even Tokyo, 'the most horrible place in Japan' according to Hearn, was a place of considerable exotic interest for a foreign tourist from the West, as Basil Hall Chamberlain points out in his widely read guidebook on Japan, *Things Japanese*, which appeared in that year: 'But after all the chief sight of Tōkyō to one fresh from home is Tōkyō itself – the quaint little wooden houses, which brick structures in foreign style have only partially replaced, the native dress which western fashions and fabrics have not yet completely driven out, the open air life of people, the clatter of clogs, the *jinrikishas*, the dainty children – dressed, powdered and rouged for a Sunday outing . . .'[24] As years passed, with the further progress of urbanization, industrialization and modernization in general, Japan, especially big cities like Tokyo became increasingly similar to what Western visitors were accustomed to at home, and the exotic charms of Japan diminished for them. On the other hand, unlike the Japanese of the late nineteenth century for whom the remnants of Old Japan were still too familiar and abundant to attract their special attention or interest, some of the Japanese of 1930s began to feel nostalgia for it.

Thus, time was ripe for the discovery of Hearn by the Japanese; Tokutomi Sohō, a prominent liberal journalist of Meiji Japan who had become a conservative ideologue, talked about the Japanese discovery of Hearn in a newspaper article of 1931.[25] In it he says, 'It is more appropriate to say that Japan has discovered Hearn than to say that Hearn discovered Japan.' and 'Japan has discovered in Hearn a good discoverer [of Japan].' What Tokutomi Sohō meant to say by these somewhat curious statements was apparently that Hearn's writings on Japan interpret Japan in the way the Japanese themselves want it to be interpreted.

Around that time the Japanese were beginning to reject Western values and emphasize their uniqueness. This tendency intensified after the outbreak of the Manchurian Incident of 1931 as Japanese international isolation deepened. Hearn's writings on Japan were in large measure in harmony with the conservative nationalisms which were becoming more and more dominant. In this period which lasted until 1945, not only communism and socialism but also democracy, liberalism and individualism became targets of vehement attack in Japan as Western ideologies. However, Hearn was not guilty of any of them. Although Hearn's life was individualistic, in his writings he voiced strong reservations about Western individualism, which is reflected, for example, in his appreciative use of a very long quotation from an essay written by a very conservative Japanese thinker attacking the Western principles of liberty and equality.[26]

Hearn's negative evaluation of the influences of Western individualism on the young generation in Japan can also be seen in his statements, such as 'They are becoming infected with the Western moral poison. They are beginning to love their wives more than their fathers and mothers; – it is much cheaper.'[27] Unlike Chamberlain, Hearn was not critical of Japanese chauvinism. He encouraged xenophobic sentiments on the part of his students: 'I do not try to check their feeling about foreigners. I rather encourage it. I encourage it because it is patriotic, because it is just, because it indicates national recuperation.'[28] He encouraged emperor worship too. He called 'the desire to die for His Imperial Majesty, your Emperor' expressed by many of his students at Matsue Middle School where he first taught 'holy' and urged them in his farewell talk 'never [to] suffer that noble wish you expressed to pass away from your souls'.[29] Hearn was no lover of democracy in Japan, either. He apparently thought that a 'military autocracy,' suited them best.[30] 'The only hope for Japan is a return to autocracy,'[31] he said. Tributes, such as, 'Now the Western material civilization is about to set, and the Eastern spiritual civilization is just about to rise. It is the time for us to listen to the voice of this prophet [Lafcadio Hearn] proclaiming the dawn of the beautiful Eastern culture'[32] and 'At this time of the awakening of the national consciousness we have, more than ever, much to learn from this national treasure, *The Complete Works of Lafcadio Hearn*,'[33] taken from an advertisement for a new reprint of Hearn's complete works in Japanese translation, published in 1930 on the eve of the Manchurian Incident, suggest how well Hearn fitted into the age of militarism and conservative nationalism. We may see its reflection in the fact that a Japanese military man said to Hearn's eldest son shortly after Pearl Harbor, 'The spirit of your honoured father must be really rejoicing at the great success of our attack on Pearl Harbor. Have you already paid a visit to his tomb to report on this?'[34]

Apart from our reservations about the ideological content of Hearn's writings on Japan, there are a few additional factors which make us hesitant to accept his increasingly great reputation in prewar Japan as a genuine reflection of the intrinsic value of his works. One is that many of the people who contributed to enhance Hearn's fame in Japan by translating his books into Japanese, by editing his lectures for posthumous publication, by writing their reminiscences of Hearn, and so on, were his former students. In advertisements for Hearn's works published in Japan we often find a statement to the effect that the translators or the editors did the work out of their deep sense of gratitude to their former teacher.[35] In the climate prevailing in prewar Japan as suggested by such a statement, it would have been virtually impossible for critics or scholars to submit the works of their former professor to honest, critical scrutiny. An even greater obstacle for Hearn's honest appraisal in prewar Japan was the sentiment that not only some individual Japanese (his former students) but the whole Japanese nation owed him a sense of gratitude. As an advertisement for *New Letters and Writings of Lafcadio Hearn*, ed. Ichikawa Sanki (1925) furnishes an example,[36] Lafcadio Hearn in prewar Japan was often presented as a benefactor of Japan.

This view, however, does not withstand critical scrutiny. During his stay in Japan, Lafcadio Hearn worked as a teacher most of the time, though he also worked as a journalist briefly during his Kobe period. His real calling, however, was that of a writer. Whether judged by what he did as his profession or as his calling, it is difficult to see him as a benefactor of Japan. He taught English at a middle school in Matsue from 1890 to 1891 and at a higher school in Kumamoto from 1891 to 1894 despite his conviction that indiscriminate teaching of English was very harmful to Japan. 'I must honestly confess that I approve the abolition of English studies. They should be permitted to those only gifted with a natural capacity for languages; and their indiscriminate, foolish, wholesale, topsyturvy teaching has been a great aid to national demoralization.' wrote Hearn in a letter written very likely in 1894.[37] 'Setting the whole Japanese nation to study English (the language of a people who are being forever preached to about their "rights", and never about their "duties") was almost an imprudence',[38] writes Hearn also in *Kokoro*, his third book on Japan.

Reflecting his ambivalence towards his own culture, Hearn was sceptical about the value of what he was doing as a teacher of English in Japan. Similar ambivalence and scepticism towards his profession persisted even after he started teaching English literature at Tokyo University in 1896 because of his avowed dislike of the subject ('I hate English literature'[39]) and his avowed conviction about the futility of teaching English literature in Japan ('I think it is a great mistake to teach English literature in Japan'[40]).

It is clear that his teaching activities in Japan had nothing to do with any altruistic objective of serving Japan. This was the case even to a larger extent with his activities as a writer. He wrote books on Japan because writing was what he enjoyed most and what formed the core of his sense of identity. The epithets for Hearn, such as 'the greatest benefactor of Japan'[41] tell us more about the Japanese who used them than about Hearn – their nagging sense of cultural inferiority, their craving for recognition by the West, and so on. At any rate, to call Hearn a benefactor of Japan simply because he sometimes painted flattering pictures of Japan and the Japanese would be almost tantamount to degrading Hearn to a mere propagandist. Occasionally, in some of his letters, Hearn does sound as if he had really been a propagandist in the employ of the Japanese government. For example, in a letter of 1903 written shortly after his contract with Tokyo University had not been renewed, he declares: 'So the long and the short of the matter is that after having worked during thirteen years for Japan, and sacrificed everything for Japan, I have been only driven out of the service and practically banished from the country.'[42] However, there is no evidence to suggest that Hearn wrote for any reasons other than his own.

The label of a benefactor must have impeded an honest

appraisal of Hearn's works in prewar Japan. To point out his shortcomings as a writer would have been an act of ingratitude towards a benefactor. Hearn was almost always called *bungō* (a great writer) or *dai-bungō* (a great *bungō*) in prewar Japanese newspaper and magazine articles.[43] Hearn himself would never have accepted such an epithet. He was keenly aware of his own limitations as a writer due, largely, to 'my absolute ignorance of realities'.[44]

After 1945 much of the characteristics of Hearn's writings on Japan which had made him the favourite interpreter of Japan in the eyes of the Japanese since 1931 were no longer qualities to recommend him to his reader even in Japan, let alone in the rest of the world. It is somewhat surprising that Hearn continues to be popular as a Japan interpreter both in Japan and outside Japan. His popularity is helped by persistent misconceptions about him, such as his being a great lover of Japan and a man who understood Japan better than anybody else.

In connection with the misconception that Hearn understood Japan better than any other Westerner, it should be pointed out that Hearn himself never claimed that he understood Japan or the Japanese. This was connected with Hearn's strong belief in the inborn racial differences between Japanese and Westerners.[45] Hearn was no believer in essential homogeneity of mankind, unlike some other major interpreters of Meiji Japan, such as Edward S. Morse and William Elliot Griffis. His rejection of the idea of essential homogeneity of mankind was fixed before his arrival in Japan. During his American days he published articles evincing a keen interest in the life of black and coloured people. Though often written with sympathy, they show that Hearn never accepted the idea of racial equality.[46] He also insisted that the Japanese were really different from the Westerners. For him the Japanese were 'another and inscrutable humanity, – another race-soul, strangely alluring, yet forever alien to your own'.[47] Hearn was pessimistic about the possibility of mutual understanding between individuals belonging to different races who are not kindred. 'Varying enormously in races so widely removed as English and Japanese it is impossible to believe that any feeling in one race is exactly paralleled by any feeling in the other,'[48] said Hearn, for example. Consistent with such view, to the end Hearn himself felt that he hardly understood the Japanese.[49]

It is not difficult to imagine what kind of preconceived ideas about the Japanese Hearn passed on to his Western reader through his writings on Japan. A reviewer of one of the volumes of Arthur Waley's epoch-making translation of *The Tale of Genji* by Lady Murasaki could not help expressing his astonishment because the Japanese world revealed by Waley was so different from what Hearn had led him to expect: 'We have been told so often, especially by Lafcadio Hearn, that the Japanese are not for us, that it is doubly astonishing not only to understand every syllable of Lady Murasaki's extraordinary narrative, but to recognize that it parallels much of our own experience.'[50] In fact, Waley and Hearn were at the opposite ends of a spectrum as Japan interpreters.

In Waley's translation of Japanese prose works, such as *The Tale of Genji*, the characters speak English which sounds natural as English. Faithful to one of his guiding principles concerning the art of translation, Waley, in fact, made 'the characters say things that people talking English could conceivably say'.[51] Hearn was radically different in this respect. To cite an extreme example, in a chapter titled 'In the Cave of the Children's Ghosts' from *Glimpses of Unfamiliar Japan*, there is a passage which describes how a curious crowd gathered around a hotel to see the only foreigner staying at the hotel. This is how Hearn translates the words of the landlord who rebukes the crowd:

'You-as-for! outrageousness doing,–*what* marvellous is?
'*Theatre* is not!
'*Juggler* is not!
'*Wrestler* is not!
'*Honourable-Guest* this is!
'Now august-to-eat-time-is; to-look-at *evil* matter is.
Honorable-returning-time-in-to-look-at-as-for-is-good.'[52]

It is clear that no native speaker of English could conceivably speak in this manner. To give another example, in the chapter titled 'The Dream of a Summer Day' from *Out of the East*, Hearn's second book on Japan, the dialogue in Japanese

betwen the narrator 'I' and the ricksha man (*kurumaya*) in
Japanese is translated in the following manner:

> ... I cried,–
> 'O kurumaya! the throat of Selfisness is dry; water desirable is.;
> He, still running, answered:–
> 'The Village of the Long Beach inside of–not far–a great gush-
> water is. There pure august water will be given.'[53]

This manner of translating spoken Japanese words has the
effect of making the Japanese appear strange and exotic.
Waley's way of translation, on the other hand, makes even the
tenth- or eleventh-century Japanese living under very
different conditions appear natural and in many ways quite
like the reader. What is involved is surely not just the
difference of techniques of translation. Rather it reflected a
fundamental difference in their understanding of the Japanese
as other people.

Unlike Waley who was very likely a believer in the basic
homogeneity of mankind, Hearn was convinced that the
Japanese were not only vastly different from Western people
but that their difference was hereditary and innate. For
example, 'Even as a Japanese infant inherits such ability to
handle a writing-brush as never can be acquired by Western
fingers, so does it inherit ethical sympathies totally different
from our own.'[54] writes Hearn in *Glimpses of Unfamiliar Japan*.
The fact that he knew only the second half of the Meiji period
(1868-1912), a period of great change after the fall of the
Tokugawa shogunate, made it difficult for him to detect even
palpable errors in some of his interpretations involving the idea
of innate and hereditary difference. For example, Hearn who
was strongly impressed by the devotion to the Emperor on the
part of his students jumped to the idea that it was 'in their
blood, – inherent as the impulse of the ant to perish for its little
republic, – unconscious as the loyalty of bees to their
queen'.[55] However, people, such as Chamberlain and Baelz
who had observed Japan from the early Meiji period through
the late Meiji period knew better. Baelz's diary entry for
'Tokyo, November 3, 1880' reads, 'The Emperor's birthday.
It distresses me to see how little interest the populace take in
their ruler ...'[56] His limited knowledge about Japan on

account of his virtual illiteracy in Japanese also made it difficult for him to detect errors in his own interpretations. For example, indirectly in support of his idea that the Japanese have a weaker sexual instinct in comparison with Westerners, Hearn mentions in his essay titled 'Of the Eternal Feminine' in *Out of the East* 'the reserve of Japanese literature regarding that love which is the great theme of our greatest novelists and poets'.[57] Yet, anyone who has read the greatest masterpieces of Japanese literature, such as the *Manyoshu*, the eighth-century anthology of Japanese poetry, and the *Tale of Genji*, knows that such reserve exists only in Hearn's imagination.[58]

'The ideas of this people are not our ideas; their sentiments are not our sentiments,'[59] said Hearn in *Japan: An Attempt at Interpretation* published in 1904, his last book on Japan which Hearn himself edited. According to the same book, 'to think like a Japanese' meant 'to think backwards, to think upside-down and inside-out, to think in directions totally foreign to Aryan habit'.[60] Far from 'bridging the gulf which separates East and West,' Hearn seems to have done his best to convince his reader that the gulf was, in fact, insurmountable. In that way, he seems to have impeded the mutual understanding between Japan and the rest of the world. For, we communicate with other people poorly, if at all, as long as we stick to the view that communication with them is impossible. Hearn himself who felt to the end that he did not understand the Japanese may be cited as a case illustrating this.

Paradoxical as it may seem, is it not his emphasis on the virtual impossibility of understanding the Japanese which is one of the important factors that explains Hearn's continued popularity as a Japan interpreter both inside and outside Japan? Hearn's interpretation fits into preconceived ideas on the part of many of the Western readers as reflected in phrases, such as 'inscrutable Orientals' and 'the mysterious East' and thus was and is easily digestible. It also fits into the deep-rooted assumption on the part of many of the Japanese readers that Japanese culture is so unique that only the Japanese can understand it properly. His writings flatter their desire to be thought to be unique and different from the world.[61] The continued popularity of Hearn gives us a lot of food for thought.[62]

13

THE WESTERN APPROACH TO SHINTO: LAFCADIO HEARN, BRUNO TAUT AND ANDRÉ MALRAUX

Masaru Toda

When Lafcadio Hearn came to Matsue to begin his teaching career in 1890, he found that Shinto, the ancient native religion of Japan, was still powerful and predominant all over this 'Chief City of the Province of the Gods'. It was not just as he had expected. According to what he had read and heard about Shinto, it should have been dead or dying.

Basil Hall Chamberlain, his best friend in Japan who had provided him with the job in Matsue, wrote in the 1891 edition of *Things Japanese*:

> Shintō, which means literally 'the way of the gods', is the name given to the mythology and vague ancestor and nature-worship which preceded the introduction of Buddhism into Japan. . .
>
> We would here draw attention to the fact that Shintō so often spoken of as a religion, is hardly entitled to that name. . . It has no set of dogmas, no sacred book, no moral code. . .
>
> By the introduction of Buddhism in the middle of the sixth century after Christ, the second period of the existence of

Shintō was inaugurated, and further growth in the direction of a religion was stopped. The metaphysics of Buddhism were too profound, its ritual far too gorgeous, its moral code far too exalted, for the puny fabric of Shintō to make any effective resistance. All that there was of religious feeling in the nation went over to the enemy. The Buddhist priesthood diplomatically received the native Shintō gods into their pantheon as avatars of ancient Buddhas, for which reason many of the Shintō ceremonies connected with the court were kept up. . .

The third period in the history of Shintō began about the year 1700, and continues down to the present day.It has been termed the period of the 'revival of pure Shintō.'. . . The great scholars Mabuchi (1697–1769), Motoori (1730–1801), and Hirata (1776–1843) devoted themselves to a religious propaganda – if that can be called a religion which sets out from the principle that the only two things needful are to follow one's natural impulses and to obey the Mikado. This order of ideas triumphed for a moment in the revolution of 1868. Buddhism was disestablished and disendowed, and Shintō was installed as the only state religion, the Council for Spiritual Affairs being given equal rank with the Council of State, which latter controlled things temporal. . . But as Shintō had no root in itself – being a thing too empty and jejune to influence the hearts of men – Buddhism soon rallied. The Council for Spiritual Affairs was reduced to the rank of a department, the department to a bureau, the bureau to a sub-bureau. The whole thing is now a mere shadow. . .[1]

This was supposed to be the best short history of Shinto and Chamberlain was a top specialist on the subject. The problem was, however, 'the whole thing' was not 'a mere shadow'. And his view was neither unique, nor original.

The Asiatic Society of Japan was founded by American and European residents in Japan in 1872. It started with over 100 members, including 77 British and 24 Americans. It had 42 merchants, 21 diplomats, 19 Japanese Government employees and 12 missionairies. Ninety per cent of them were living in the Treaty Port of Yokohama.

'The Shintô Temple of Isé', the first paper on Shinto ever written in English was read by a British diplomat at the meeting of the Society in 1874. Ise Shrines, the most sacred place of Shinto or 'the Mecca of Japan',[2] were unknown to Europeans until 1872, when the Japanese Government gave Ernest Mason Satow, a 31-year-old interpreter at the British Legation in Tokyo and one of the pioneers of modern Japanology, the opportunity of visiting them.

Although four years had passed since the Meiji Revolution, Shinto remained a major mystery and attracted a great deal of attention. After his reading a lot of questions were asked. Members began to exchange their personal views and critical comments. In fact, it was the first international symposium on the Japanese native religion.

The President of the Society was James Hepburn (1815-1911). After thanking Satow for his lecture, Hepburn recorded the fact that '. . . as for himself he had earnestly endeavoured to find out what there was in it, but had long given up, unable to find anything to reward his labour; – excepting a small book of Shintô prayers, he had not been able to find any book on the subject'.[3]

Satow agreed with his opinion that Shinto contained no moral code, and added: 'Shintôism, as expounded by Motoori, was nothing else than an engine for reducing the people to a condition of mental slavery, and this was the reason why such a high rank was assigned to the Department of Shintôism by the Mikado's government, in placing it on a level with the Council of State shortly after the revolution in 1868.'

Satow's boss, British Minister to Japan Sir Harry Parkes (1828-1885), expressed '. . . the disappointment which he in common with others had felt in being unable to learn what Shintôism was. Japanese in general seemed utterly at a loss to describe it, but this circumstance was intelligible if what was once an indigenous faith had been turned in later days into a political engine. . . If it had worked great results or had ever taken deep hold on the religious feeling of the Japanese people it would scarcely have been superseded so completely as it had by Buddhism'.

The Rev. Dr Samuel Brown (1810-1880) repeated the same opinion, but with much more hatred and eloquence, which greatly impressed Chamberlain. He noted that '. . . so far as he could learn Shintôism was in no proper sense of the term a religion. It would be strange, if during a residence of more than fourteen years in Japan, he had not endeavoured to inform himself upon this subject, but, as had been said by the President, Dr Hepburn, his search for information in the literature of the country had been but poorly rewarded, unless he counted the discovery of the emptiness of Shintôism as a compensation for his pains. The Japanese books in which he had hoped to find something that would command his respect, had utterly disappointed him. The *Kojiki* is the only work that professedly treats of the subject *in extenso*, but it hardly repaid the trouble of perusal. . . The *Kojiki* contains no system of morals, discusses no ethical questions, prescribes no ritual, or points to any god or gods as objects of worship. All essentials of a religion are wanting in Shintôism, and it is difficult to see how it could have ever been denominated a religion at all. . .

'Wherever it may have originated, Shintôism is, as a religion, hollow, empty and jejune beyond any other that is known among men. It is certain, that the Japanese government in attempting to substitute Shintôism for the long prevalent Buddhistic faith, has undertaken a Herculean task. Buddhism appeals to men's religious susceptibilities and has long been the popular faith, but Shintôism has nothing in it that comes down to men's hearts, and it is futile to attempt to make it the substitute for that religion to which the people have been accustomed for ages, and which is intimately interwoven with the whole social fabric. The government tacitly confesses that Shintôism is a vapid lifeless thing when it sends men to preach throughout the country, and provides them with texts taken from no Japanese sacred-book but borrowed from Confucius and Mencius. The endeavour to revive the interest in this would-be religion must end in entire failure.'

Those verdicts, particularly the Rev. Brown's unforgiving one, exerted a strong influence on Chamberlain. One can compare Chamberlain's '. . . Shintō so often spoken of as a religion, is hardly entitled to that name. . . It has no set of dogmas, no sacred book, no moral code', with Brown's '. . . no system of morals. . . no ethical questions. . . no ritual. . . All essentials of a religion are wanting in Shintôism, and it is difficult to see how it could have ever been denominated a religion at all'. Perhaps Chamberlain's words

'Shintō had *no root* in itself – being a thing too *empty* and *jejune* to *influence the hearts of men*. . .' might have been a paraphrase of Brown's '. . . it is, as a religion, *hollow, empty* and *jejune* beyond any other that is known among men. . . Shintôism has nothing in it that *comes down to men's hearts*. . .'[4] It may be a beautiful paraphrase, but would not be worth further examination, for both are telling us nothing but a typical reaction of the nineteenth-century Western intellectuals to an alien faith.

Starting from this symposium, the mysteries about Shinto were solved, one by one. Chamberlain translated the *Kojiki* in 1882, eight years before Hearn's arrival. Satow contributed his exhaustive commentaries on *Norito*, the ancient prayer book of Shinto, to the *Transactions of the Asiatic Society of Japan* during the years from 1878 to 81. His colleague in the British Legation, William Aston, published his translation of *Nihongi* later in 1896. Shinto was neither unnoticed, nor disregarded by the Western Japanologists. On the contrary, it had been the focus of their attention for more than a decade, carefully studied, then put away as 'trash'.

Hearn came to Matsue when Shinto was practically hidden behind those 'studies'. Soon after his visit to the Great Shrine of Izumo (or Kizuki) he contributed an article to *A Handbook for Travellers in Japan*, which cheerfully disagreed with the dismal tone of the symposium:

> The buildings, which are in the unornamented style of pure Shintō, impress the beholder by their great size and solidity and the majesty of the approaches under the successions of colossal *torii*. The services are conducted by priests gorgeously arrayed in white and purple robes with gold figuring. The chief priest, who is supposed to be the eighty-second descendant in a direct line from the god Susa-no-o, used to be styled *Iki-gami*–that is a god upon earth. . . . From 200,000 to 250,000 pilgrims visit the Great Shrine yearly. All day long the sound of the clapping hands to call the attention of the god, is unbroken like the sound of a cataract.[5]

Later, he rewrote the scene in his essay 'Kitzuki: The Most Ancient Shrine of Japan':

> Already I can hear a heavy sound, as of surf, within the temple

court; and as we advance the sound becomes sharper and recognizable – a volleying of handclaps. And passing the great gate, I see thousands of pilgrims before the Haiden, the same huge structure which I visited last night. None enter there; all stand before the dragon-swarming doorway, and cast their offerings into the money-chest placed before the threshold; many making contribution of small coin, the very poorest throwing only a handful of rice into the box. Then they clap their hands and bow their heads before the threshold, and reverently gaze through the Hall of Prayer at the loftier edifice, the Holy of Holies, beyond it. Each pilgrim remains but a little while and claps his hands but four times; yet so many are coming and going that the sound of the clapping is like the sound of a cataract.[6]

Although Satow had visited the Ise Shrines which were supposed to be far more sacred and popular than Izumo, he neither cared about 'thousands of pilgrims', nor listened to the clapping hands 'like the sound of a cataract'. He says:

In some cases, however, the oratory is a mere shed on four uprights; before this the worshipper bows his head, clapping his palms together, but not uttering an audible prayer. The brief ceremony concluded, he throws a few copper coins on the matted floor, and takes his departure.[7]

This accurate but peculiarly lifeless description of a typical shrine presents a striking contrast to Hearn's vivid sketch:

Mothers would bring their children to my threshold, and teach them to revere me saying, 'Bow down before the great bright God; make homage to the Daimyōjin.' Then I should hear the fresh soft clapping of little hands, and remember that I, the ghost and god, had been a father.

Daily, I should hear the plash of pure cool water poured out for me, and the tinkle of thrown coin, and the pattering of dry rice into my wooden box, like a pattering of rain; and I should be refreshed by the spirit of the water, and strengthened by the spirit of the rice.[8]

Hearn tried to focus his eyes on the people's belief – the common people of Japan who had naturally believed in Shinto and whose presence the learned member of the Asiatic Society so scornfully ignored.

Hearn felt scorn only for them who were trying to 'mock the conviction of forty millions of people' and 'prove the faith absurd' without looking at the fact 'that millions of people during thousands of years have worshipped their great dead before such yashiro – that a whole race still believes those buildings tenanted by viewless conscious personalities.'[9] He triumphantly concluded his essay by saying:

> But to have seen Kitzuki as I saw it is also to have seen something much more than a single wonderful temple. To see Kitzuki is to see the living centre of Shintō, and to feel the life-pulse of the ancient faith, throbbing as mightily in this nineteenth century as ever in that unknown past whereof the *Kojiki* itself, though written in a tongue no longer spoken, is but a modern record. . . Buddhism has a voluminous theology, a profound philosophy, a literature vast as the sea. Shintō has no philosophy, no code of ethics, no metaphysics; and yet, by its very immateriality, it can resist the invasion of Occidental religious thought as no other Orient faith can. . . Indeed the best of our scholars have never been able to tell us what Shintō is. To some it appears to be merely ancestor-worship, to others ancestor-worship combined with nature-worship; to others, again, it seems to be no religion at all; to the missionary of the more ignorant class it is the worst form of heathenism. Doubtless the difficulty of explaining Shintō has been due simply to the fact that the sinologists have sought for the source of it in books: in the *Kojiki* and *Nihongi*, which are its histories; in the *Norito*, which are its prayers; in the commentaries of Motoori and Hirata, who were its greatest scholars. But the reality of Shintō lives not in the books, nor in the rites, nor in commandments, but in the national heart, of which it is the highest emotional religious expression, immortal and ever young.[10]

Using similar words and phrases, Hearn, too, acknowledged that some essentials of religion were wanting in Shinto. However, he did not find it empty and jejune. He flatly denied what his best friend and other authorities had said about Shinto and blessed its 'immateriality' as the most effective barrier against 'the invasion of Occidental religious thought'.

But what does he mean by the word of 'immateriality'? Why is it a merit rather than a fatal defect? And finally, where does his extraordinary confidence come from (for he had been in Japan less than half a year)? To avoid theological arguments, which, I suppose, most of us are not interested in, I set only one question: How could he appreciate Shinto to such an extent at Kizuki?

Although all that Shinto possesses may be that mysterious 'immateriality', two things are always 'material' or at least visible there; – the people and the Great Shrine of Kizuki itself. Shinto may have no set of dogmas, no sacred book, and no moral code, but it certainly has an uncountable number of worshippers and shrines through which he could learn something about the ways of the gods. Chamberlain and the other Japanologists in the Meiji era failed to understand it partly because they refused to see the people and missed something at shrines, – something that was vital to its appreciation.

Hearn could appreciate the beauty of the unornamented style of the pure Shinto shrine from the beginning and was impressed by its great size and solidity and the majesty of the approaches under successions of colossal torii. Again this was not the case with the other Japanologists. Hearn wrote:

> Effacing colours and obliterating distances, night always magnifies by suggestion the aspect of large spaces and the effect of large objects. Viewed by the vague light of paper lanterns, the approach to the great shrine is an imposing surprise – such a surprise that I feel regret at the mere thought of having to see it tomorrow by disenchanting day: a superb avenue lined with colossal trees, and ranging away out of sight under a succession of giant torii, from which are suspended enormous shimenawa, well worthy the grasp of that Heavenly-Hand-Strength Deity whose symbols they are. But, more than by the torii and their festooned symbols, the dim majesty of the huge avenue is enhanced by the prodigious trees – many perhaps thousands of years old – gnarled pines whose shaggy summits are lost in darkness. Some of the mighty trunks are surrounded with a rope of straw: *these trees are sacred*. The vast roots, far-reaching in every direction, look in the lantern-light like a writhing and crawling of dragons.[11]

Satow gave his explanation for the origin of those sacred trees. Unlike Hearn's impressionism, it sounds very logical and analytical, but was in fact deeply distorted by the modern rationalism.

The temple grounds are usually surrounded by a grove of trees, the most common among which is the cryptomeria, a useful timber tree. These plantations were originally intended to supply materials for the repair or re-erection of the building, but in many cases their great antiquity causes a sacred character to be attributed to the older trees, which are then surrounded by a fillet of straw rope, *as if they were tenanted by a divine spirit.*[12]

Besides the worship of the sacred trees, it seemed to him, every architectural feature of Shinto shrines showed its primitiveness and inferiority:

> Pure Shin-tō architecture does not admit of any external decoration, as such, being applied to the temple in the shape of carving or colouring. It should preserve the traditional form of the primeval Japanese hut, of which it was, historically speaking, a mere adaptation.[13]
>
> In early times the dwellings of the people who inhabited these islands were constructed of young trees, with the bark on, fastened together with ropes made of rush, perhaps with the tough shoots of the wisteria, and thatched with grass. In modern buildings the uprights stand upon large stones, laid on the surface of the earth, but this precaution against decay had not occurred to the ancients, who planted the uprights in holes dug in the ground.[14]
>
> It is commonly said that Shin-tō must be a singularly pure form of paganism, since its temples contain no images. . . A possible explanation of the absence of images or pictorial representations of the deity may be that in the earlier stage of Shin-tō, and previous to the introduction of the arts in conjunction with Buddhism, the Japanese people were ignorant of sculpture and painting.[15]
>
> The architecture of the Shintô temples is derived from the primeval hut, with more or less modification in proportion to the influence of Buddhism in each particular case. . . All the buildings which form part of the two temples of Isé are constructed in this style, so disappointing in its simplicity and perishable nature.[16]

More articulate and eloquent was Chamberlain's disappointment in his first edition of *Things Japanese*:

To the student of Japanese history and religion, the word Ise is
in itself a magnet. But it may be a question whether the
ordinary tourist would be repaid by going out of his way to
visit the temples of a creed which binds itself to the severest
architectural simplicity – white pinewood and a thatch of
rushes, no carvings, no paintings, no images, nothing but an
immense antiquity, and even that only in the sense of historic
continuity; for immemorial custom decrees that the two
shrines shall be razed to the ground and rebuilt every twenty
years in precisely the same style.[17]

Was this really intended to be an advice to the ordinary
tourist? Perhaps you can notice that his rhetoric, particularly
counting out the things that are wanting at Ise, rather than
paying attention to the things that are there, has much in
common with his bitter criticism of Shinto. Apparently the
disappointment was his, not of the naive tourist. So he repeats
the warning in his *Handbook for Travellers in Japan*:

It should be premised that the interest of the trip to Ise is
chiefly antiquarian. Without going so far as to say, with a
disappointed tourist, that 'there is nothing to see, and they
won't let you see it', we may remind intending travellers of the
remarkable plainness of all Shintō architecture, and add that
the veneration in which the shrines of Ise are held is such that
none but the priests and Imperial personages are allowed to
penetrate into the interior. The rest of the world may only
peep through the outer gate.[18]

The Great Shrines of Ise were stripped of their last merit,
the greatness in terms of size and scale, by another British
Japanologist. W.G. Aston wrote in 1905:

The Shinto shrine is by no means so costly an edifice as its
Buddhist counterpart. The hokora, as the smaller shrines are
called, are in many cases so small as to be easily transportable in
a cart. Even the great shrines of Ise are of no great size and of
purposely plain and simple construction. In 771 a 'greater
shrine' had only eighteen feet frontage.[19]

This was all he had to say about Ise Shrines in his *Shinto*, the
first and even now the most influential book on the subject
written in English. There was not much of disappointment
here because he had expected nothing. He was a great admirer

of Satow and Chamberlain.

The prestige of those three British scholars was so high that it was very difficult for anyone to discover a good thing about Ise. Brave and innocent as she was, Isabella L. Bird, one of the first female globe-trotters, who visited Ise shrines in 1878, could not find anything to add to what her fellow countrymen had told her except the beauty of the camphor groves.

The camphor groves alone are well worth a visit, for they are gloriously beautiful; but no beauty of nature or sunshine can light *the awful melancholy of the unutterable emptiness* of the holiest places of Shintô.[20]

It is sufficient to describe the Gekû shrine, which is exactly copied from the Naikû. Both stand in the midst of ancient cryptomeria, each stately tree in Shintô fancy worthy to be a god, but it is camphor groves, the finest in Japan, covering the extensive and broken grounds with their dark magnificence, which so impress a stranger with their unique grandeur as to make him forget *the bareness and meanness* of the shrines which they overshadow.[21]

Passing through stately groves by a stately road, and under a second massive torii, the visitor reaches the famous Gekû shrine, and, even in spite of Mr Satow's realistic description, is stricken with *a feeling of disappointment*, for he is suddenly brought up posts, which are just over 9 feet high, being planted at distances of 6 feet, the intervals being completely filled up with closely fitting and very heavy planking laid horizontally.[22]

Within this stands the shôden or shrine of the gods, and on the right and left two treasuries. The impression produced by the whole resembles that made upon the minds of those who have made the deepest researches into Shintô—*there is nothing, and all things, even the stately avenues of the Gekû, lead to NOTHING.*[23]

Having followed Shintô to its centre at Isé, the *bare* wooden building, which is the kernel of the Gekû enclosure, and the Shintô 'Holy of Holies', assumes a very special interest; but here, again, there is *nothing but disappointment*, for the shôden only contains four boxes of unpainted wood, furnished with light handles, resting on low stands, and covered with what is said to be white silk.[24]

Poor Isabella, perhaps you would like to pity her who went

through all kinds of hardships as a lone traveller and found nothing but disappointment at Ise. I should say, however, she did not have to come a long way when all she expected to see was just another Westminster Abbey.

Now let me quote a passage from Hearn's essay entitled 'A Living God' for I believe this is the finest description of the Shinto shrines ever written in English, and by examining it we may discern Hearn's unique way of understanding Shinto:

> Of whatever dimension, the temples or shrines of pure Shintō are all built in the same archaic style. The typical shrine is a windowless oblong building of unpainted timber, with a very steep overhanging roof; the front is the gable end; and the upper part of the perpetually closed doors is wooden lattice-work–usually a grating of bars closely set and crossing each other at right angles. In most cases the structure is raised slightly above the ground on wooden pillars; and the queer peaked façade, with its visor-like apertures and the fantastic projections of beam work above its gable-angles, might remind the European traveller of certain old Gothic forms of dormer.[25]

For the first time we are told by the European traveller that the Shinto shrines are not so disappointingly simple. He found the overhanging roof *very steep*; the façade *queer peaked*; the projections of beamwork *fantastic*; the front doors *perpetually closed*; the apertures *visor-like*. The visor for what? Undoubtedly he was alarmed at the appearance of the unknown form as if he met a fully armed alien warrior, beautifully exotic and dangerous. *Unpainted* would be the only word which reminds us of the three scholars, but he was too careful to leave it unexplained:

> There is no artificial colour. The plain wood soon turns, under the action of rain and sun, to a natural gray, varying according to surface exposure from the silvery tone of birch bark to the sombre gray of basalt.[26]

You must notice that instead of 'unpainted' he now chooses the phrase 'no artificial colour', which clearly suggests less primitive backwardness than unflinching will and natural purity. 'Rain', 'sun', 'birch' and 'basalt' also highlight the natural beauty of 'the plain wood'. At last the European traveller discovered the fact that the Shinto shrine is closer and friendlier to nature than the Western or Buddhistic counterparts are:

> So shaped and tinted, the isolated country yashiro [shrine] may seem less like a work of joinery than a feature of the scenery, – a rural form related to nature as closely as rocks and trees – a something that came into existence only as a manifestation of Ohotsuchi-no-Kami, the Earth-God, the primeval divinity of the land.[27]

What he has captured here is not a mere impression of the country shrine, but the whole ideal of Shinto,–the essence of the religion. The shrine seems to him a manifestation of Ohotsuchi-no-Kami, and this Japanese Gaia represents the land, one of the four elements of nature. The shrine, the god, and nature – each of them has close affinities with others. In fact, they were so close that it was difficult for him to make a clear distinction, and they are one in the eyes of the native people.

Why could Hearn alone perceive this Japanese idea of 'the Holy Trinity' through the shrine? One of the reasons would be his keen poetic perception. But it did not help very much for he confessed the difficulty to catch the feeling of the Shinto shrines in his letter to Amenomori, one of his closest Japanese friends, who wrote his recollections of Hearn after his death in 1905:

> When making studies on Shinto shrines he wrote to me, – 'You understand, of course, how difficult it is for a foreigner to convey to Western minds the feeling of these things as they impress *him*. On the other hand, he *cannot* convey the feeling of the Japanese mind, because he has not experienced it. He can only guess or imagine.'[28]

The crucial difference between Hearn and the other Japanologists was not in their natural abilities, but in their attitudes and stances. Hearn alone managed to 'convey the feeling of the Japanese' simply because he alone tried to 'guess or imagine'. He alone tried as the others did not because he alone believed the Shinto shrine was worth doing so. He wrote in the same essay:

. . . and when you remember that millions of people during thousands of years have worshipped their great dead before such yashiro – that a whole race still believes those buildings tenanted by viewless conscious personalities – you are apt also to reflect how difficult it would be to prove the faith absurd. Nay! in spite of Occidental reluctances – in spite of whatever you may think it expedient to say or not to say at a later time about the experience – you may very likely find yourself for a moment forced into *the attitude of respect* towards possibilities. Mere cold reasoning will not help you in the opposite direction. The evidence of the senses counts for little: you know there are ever so many realities which can neither be seen nor felt, but which exist as forces – tremendous forces. Then again you cannot mock the conviction of forty millions of people while that conviction thrills all about you like the air – while conscious that it is pressing upon your psychical being just as the atmosphere presses upon your physical being.[29]

Samuel Brown said: 'All essentials of a religion are wanting in Shintôism, and it is difficult to see how it could have been denominated a religion at all.' Chamberlain wrote: '. . . Shintō so often spoken of as a religion, is hardly entitled to that name. . . It has no set of dogmas, no sacred book, no moral code'. Oddly enough, professing to analyze a religion, both of them completely ignored the most essential part of a religion, which was, as Hearn told us, not dogma and moral, but '*Kokoro* (heart)'.[30] With millions of people who have truly believed in it for hundreds of years, it should have been denominated a religion. However different it seems to be, one should not try to prove it absurd by applying some irrelevant foreign criterion. Hearn simply tried to appreciate and enjoy the difference. He was so careful and respectful of the difference that he became uncomfortable with some English words:

Why certain architectural forms produce in the beholder a feeling of weirdness is a question about which I should like to theorize some day: at present I shall venture only to say that Shintō shrines evoke such a feeling. It grows with familiarity instead of weakening; and a knowledge of popular beliefs is apt to intensify it. We have no English words by which these queer shapes can be sufficiently described – much less any language able to communicate the impression which they make. Those Shintō terms which we loosely render by the words 'temple' and 'shrine' are really untranslatable; – I mean that the Japanese ideas attaching to them cannot be conveyed by translation. The so-called 'august house' of the Kami is not so much a temple, in the classic meaning of the term, as it is a haunted room, a spirit-chamber, a ghost-house; many of the lesser divinities being veritable ghosts – ghosts of great warriors and heroes and rulers and teachers, who lived and loved and died hundreds of thousands of years ago. I fancy that to the Western mind the word 'ghost-house' will convey, better than such terms as 'shrine' and 'temple', some vague notion of the strange character of the Shintō miya or yashiro – containing in its perpetual dusk nothing more substantial than symbols or tokens, the latter probably of paper. Now the emptiness behind the visored front is more suggestive than anything material could possibly be. . .[31]

Strikingly similar comments were made later by a German architect who visited the Great Shrines of Ise. It was, however, in 1933. Hearn, Bird and the three British Shinto scholars were dead or dying and people did not care for them very much. The Meiji era was far behind and a new age was coming. The Japanese military victories over China and Russia, and the participation in the First World War changed the attitude of the European travellers towards Japan dramatically: they were now willing to discover the Japanese architectural beauties and religious values.

Born in Königsberg in 1880, Bruno Taut was a fairly well-known architect of modernism in Europe when the Nazi party took over power and he decided to exile himself by going to Japan at the invitation of the Association of Japanese Architects. He stayed there for three-and-a-half years and was fascinated by the Japanese traditional architecture. Perhaps he was the first European architect that lived in Japan and devoted his time not to teaching Western design, but to studying the Japanese one. Fortunately or unfortunately it was the age of nationalism. His studies on the Japanese architecture, translated and published only in Japan, were enthusiastically received both by the public and academic. In his books, however, he bestowed his unqualified praise on only two of its classical masterpieces; the Katura-Rikyu Palace in Kyoto and the Great Shrines of Ise. His remarks on Ise would be another example of how to appreciate Shinto:

> There seems to be little difference between the Outer Shrine of Ise [Geku] and an ordinary Japanese farmhouse with its projections of beamwork roofed with straw. Some would say that is why Ise represents the Old Japan. However, if you look at it more closely, they differ very much in many respects: its fresh timber – taintless cypress wood of the finest quality has a light brown colour and sometimes shines as brightly as silver; the inimitably precise construction of all the buildings and fences belonging to the edifice; the unpainted virgin wood has a bracing purity in harmony with the ground covered with clean pebbles. . . Without any foundation the Shrine stands solidly and majestically with its pillars deep in the earth. . . This is the House of the gods which the ideal of Shinto made built in strict conformity with nature. . . We don't know its origin, nor the name of the first designer. Indeed such a masterpiece could have come down only from the heaven just like the first Emperor himself. . . So pure and so exquisite are the composition and the construction. . . This is not a religion from the Western point of view. But who cannot be forced into the attitude of respect towards the Ise Shrines![32]

Almost forty years earlier Hearn had made the same discoveries. Both of them, the poet and the architect, could enjoy the colour of unpainted timber and note that the Shinto shrine was not a reproduction of the primeval hut. They clearly saw it represented not only a simple natural beauty, but also the ideal of Shinto, – the closer affinities among men, gods and nature. When Hearn praised 'the immateriality of Shinto' as the most effective barrier to 'the invasion of Occidental religious thought', he surely meant this universal intimacy. They can be intimate because their gods force nothing to men, no set of dogmas, no sacred book, and no moral code, and men communicate with them, or rather feel their existence simply by stepping into the holy ground. Who can decline such an attractive offer? And who has to? You do not have to be even a Shintoist to get it; it is so simple, so subtle, and so unconscious. Hearn was right. The very immateriality of Shinto is the secret of its survival into this material age.

After World War II, Shinto was strangely and erroneously identified with fascism and militarism. In addition to the oppressive measures by the occupation forces, Japanese intellectuals, speaking for either the US or USSR, wrote millions of nasty things about it. The rhetoric and argument of those British Shinto scholars revived. Hearn was ostracized as the pro-Japanese writer. People became more shy or reluctant to speak up, especially to the outside world, although they still loved, as Hearn had seen a half century ago, their local and family gods and never stopped making their pilgrimages to the national shrines such as Ise and Izumo. Shinto was once again hidden by the harsh verdicts and once again the European traveller had to 'discover' it.

★ ★ ★

In May 1974 seventy-two-year-old André Malraux visited the Nezu Museum in Tokyo and saw one extraordinary picture:

> Je pense à la *Cascade de Nachi*, l'un des plus célèbres paysages primitifs du Japon. . . Une falaise verticale, de face. Des cassures plates de rochers plats, sur des arbres plats. Au centre, une autre roche plate barre la cascade, à côté d'un pin vert sombre. Une crête, un astre confus, le minimum de ciel. De haut en bas du tableau vert et brun, la cascade blanche tombe en s'élargissant, glaive d'une civilisation inconnue. Le rouleau déployé, je pense: Ameratsu – la déesse-mère du Japon, la divinité des eaux, des colonnes de pins, du soleil; et dont descend l'empereur. Cette eau verticale, qui tombe de deux cents mètres, est fixe.[33]

According to the Japanese professor who guided him, Malraux said to his wife, 'Here in this picture the cascade is none other than a god, a god as the supernatural in nature, a god as the spiritualized nature.' After a moment he whispered to himself, 'There is no such spiritualization in the West.'[34] When he marvelled at the divinity of the cascade, he certainly discovered the native ways of gods, –Shinto. In fact, the Cascade of Nachi has been worshipped as the chief god of the Great Shrine of Kumano-Nachi for hundreds of years and the cascade itself makes the essential part of the shrine.

At the end of the month he made a pilgrimage to the Great

Shrines of Ise. What impressed him most was not the architecture, but those gigantic cypress trees that surrounded the whole place. He said to the Japanese scholar, 'Can you see the cascade as a huge cypress tree? After all they represent one and the same esprit; that is the eternal intercourse between high and low, communication between heaven and men.' 'Both these trees and the cascade are alive, and our eyes are turned upwards by their vertical lines. This could never happen in our cathedrals with their supporting columns.'[35] Those words would reappear with slight modifications in his final edition of *Anti-Mémoires*. Again, the artist succeeded in finding out the closer affinities between men, gods and nature.

★   ★   ★

We have examined three cases of understanding Shinto. All of them – Hearn, Taut and Malraux – happened to be artists with no academic background of Japanology, yet somehow managed to appreciate Shinto and got deep insight into the native religious values. I am not trying to say, 'See what the artists have done. And despair, you scholars.' For their success, I should think, depended more on their unique ways of approaching Shinto than their personal abilities. Then what is the difference between the former professional approaches and the later amateur ones?

The British scholars began their Shinto studies by translating the ancient religious texts and were deeply disappointed with the results. They had expected to find a sacred book of Shinto, a consistent system of moral and dogma. They got, however, bits of fact and fancy contradicting each other, legends, traditions, prayers and songs. They wanted to have a Shinto Bible so that they could commune with the native gods by reading it. That was the way they did in England. The gods in this land, however, rarely speak up and have very little to say. They have silently lived for thousands of years in this land, by the rivers or deep in the woods, sometimes loved, sometimes feared by people, just like an element of nature.

It seems to me that their trying to reach the gods by reading, only through the medium of written words, was a Christian way rather than a philological approach. Philology does not require such a single-mindedness. In the quest for a Japanese Bible their 'biblicism' somehow turned into the greatest obstacle to its appreciation and their excellent knowledge of the language helped them only to find what was lacking in it. We can understand now why their harsh verdict was almost word-for-word identical with the one given by Samuel Brown, one of the first missionaries in the Meiji period who did not have any expertise on the subject.

Hearn, Taut and Malraux could not read Japanese. Therefore they had no intention to discover the *logos* of Shinto. One thing was possible for them; to look at the shrine and perceive 'the ways of gods' as they were. At this point their artistic sensibilities helped a great deal. They had their own prejudices, too. They were all obsessed with finding something uniquely Japanese, as most travellers were so. They were ready to welcome anything exotic: different manners, different people and even different gods.

However, what they saw in Shinto was not just all exotic. They found, as they repeatedly told us, an interreligious truth that people do care for their own gods in their own ways and have every right to do so. Ironically those three British scholars, Satow, Chamberlain and Aston, who had so earnestly tried to find a universal value in Shinto, ended up denying this right and truth.

Hearn's contributions to Shinto were amazing and beautiful. He was virtually the first Westerner who appreciated it so fully, and the only one who explained it so beautifully. Most literary critics, both Japanese and Western, have missed this point for a long time because they have never dreamed of the enormous difficulties he had in appreciating it. Shinto is just one example. Take up any subject on Japan, and you will find a similar accomplishment in his writings, the same sort of pioneer work, which deserves much more of our attention and praise.

14

LAFCADIO HEARN'S INTERPRETATION OF JAPAN

Paul Murray

Lafcadio Hearn was profoundly influenced by religion, morality and scholarship. These factors, together with certain convictions and/or prejudices, informed his vision of Japan. Among these convictions was an unshakeable belief in the virtue of the common man; in Japan he believed that this was in inverse proportion to his degree of Westernization. Another important factor was Lafcadio's failure to master the Japanese language and so his contribution was of a different order to that made by his great scholarly contemporaries – Satow, Aston, Chamberlain – although it could be claimed that his extensive field-work in the area of Meiji customs and folklore constitute a considerable body of scholarship, albeit of a different nature to that of the men just mentioned.

Many people will be surprised that I describe Hearn as a man deeply concerned with religion. Because he abandoned Christianity in his youth, he is generally thought of as anti-religious; in fact, he was deeply concerned with – one might say obsessed by – religion, philosophy and the supernatural in his life and writing. In the decade prior to his arrival in Japan, Lafcadio had immersed himself in Buddhism as well as Herbert Spencer's 'synthetic philosophy'; his attempt to reconcile the two was an important impulse in bringing him to Japan. When he got there, the experience of encountering a living

Buddhism enthralled him.

His scholarship preconditioned him, however, not just to delight in Buddhism, but to accept a second and to him new religion, Shinto. He had absorbed the work of the French historian, Fustel de Coulanges, whose book, *La Cité Antique*, linked the religious practices of classical Greece and Rome with the ancient religion of the hearth. Hearn believed that in Shinto he had found the Japanese equivalent, a means of relating Japan to the classical world as well as of differentiating it from contemporary Western culture.

He also believed that an understanding of its religion was essential to the comprehension of any society and, in *Japan: An Attempt at Interpretation*, his late attempt to codify his views, he set out, overtly, to interpret Japan through religion. However, the majority of chapters in his first book on the country, *Glimpses of Unfamiliar Japan*, published ten years earlier in 1894, were also concerned with religion and the supernatural. So, too, was much of the writing sandwiched in between: for example, *In Ghostly Japan*, which appeared in 1899, could just as easily have been called 'In Buddhist Japan'.

Hearn's moral outlook permeated all his work on Japan. Stated simply, he did not believe, unlike Basil Hall Chamberlain for example, that might was right; on the contrary, he distinguished between the West's material superiority, then overwhelming, and what he saw as its moral inadequacy. He had been sceptical about the civilizing mission of Western imperial expansion from his earliest Cincinnati journalism and this turned into downright hostility in his Japanese work.

If we turn from his outlook to examine Hearn's life in Japan we can see that it falls into four main sections, reflected in his books, even if there is not an exact chronological match. Firstly, there was a year spent in Matsue, 1890-91, mirrored in *Glimpses of Unfamiliar Japan*; then three years in Kumamoto, 1891-94, represented by *Out of the East*; two years in Kobe, 1894-96, which produced two books, *Kokoro* and *Gleanings in Buddha Fields*; the remainder of his life, 1896-1904, was spent, reluctantly, in Tokyo where he wrote a further eight books.

In my view, Hearn's early interpretative Japanese work, done between his arrival in 1890 and his move to Tokyo in

1896, was generally his best. It was distinguished by an insistence on seeing Japan from a Japanese perspective and explaining it to his Western audience in these terms. This differentiated him from most of his contemporaries – and I include here such notable scholars as Basil Hall Chamberlain, Ernest Satow and William George Aston – as well as many who have written of Japan since. Furthermore, I see his vision as double-edged, illuminating Japanese culture on the one hand and, on the other, providing a critique of what he perceived to be the West's shortcomings.

Many will see him as a one-dimensional malcontent, a man who despised his own civilization, perhaps because of the unhappy circumstances of his childhood, when he fell between the stools of various cultures, Greek, Irish and English. Certainly his childhood was traumatic, and he never had a sense of belonging, to the Greek world of his mother, to the Protestant Irish world of his father, or to the Roman Catholic world of the great-aunt who brought him up. While this may have helped generate the undeniably neurotic – and artistic – elements in his personality, Hearn's upbringing left him without that sense of the righteousness of his own culture which characterized many of his contemporaries, and this in turn preconditioned his approach to Japan. It resulted in the paradox that Hearn, the life-long prototypical and determined outsider, should have attempted to see Japan with an insider's eye.

One could discern elements of his alienation from mainstream Western culture in his early American work: the portrayal of Tahiti, for example, as a paradise destroyed by the intrusion of Western capital and religion. In Cincinnati, he identified with suffering and the underdog, from dumb beasts in the slaughterhouses to the condemned at the end of a rope, from the outcasts of Bucktown, the city's vice quarter, to the negro culture of the riverside levee. Much the same pattern could be seen in his focus on the Creole cultures of New Orleans and the West Indies and his immersion in the world of French culture when he was in the United States.

The interpretation of Hearn as an iconoclastic misfit leaves out of account, however, Hearn's rapid progress from youthful radicalism to a trenchant conservatism while still a young man. In New Orleans he came to see political developments from the old slave-owners' perspective; in the West Indies this led him to adopt condescending attitudes towards the region's negro population.

Looked at in terms of the dynamics of his own development, therefore, it might not have been a great surprise if Hearn had adopted patronizing attitudes towards Japan, similar perhaps to those evident in *Madame Chrysanthème*, that novel of 1880's Nagasaki by Pierre Loti, a literary icon and correspondent of Hearn's. The fact that he did not was primarily due, I think, to his belief that he had found there a traditional society, at the same point on the evolutionary scale as classical Greece and Rome, morally and spiritually superior to the world from which he had come. In other words, his conservatism, which produced one reaction in the West Indies, produced a fundamentally different one in Japan.

Hearn's political views could occupy a lecture in themselves but I would summarize them by saying that he rejected contemporary Western notions of *laissez-faire*, not from the viewpoint of socialism, which he abominated, but from the perspective of a traditionalist who believed that the collectivism of pre-capitalist societies could provide a morally superior form of existence. He also saw that Japan was being shaped into a new world power, a process which clearly was not in train in the West Indies. Finally, there was an elusive emotional chemistry between a man for whom the supernatural seemed to weave in and out of everyday life and a culture which gave him the sensation of being in a world of mysteries and living gods, with a 'delicious ghostliness' closer and more real than the mortals around him.

★   ★   ★

'The Japanese Smile', an outstanding essay in his first book, *Glimpses of Unfamiliar Japan*, provides in microcosm the essence of Hearn's reaction to Japan; the views he formed at that stage did not change over the years in their essentials. The inspiration lay in a visit paid by Lafcadio to the open port of Kobe after spending three years in a Japanese environment. By living in the interior for the bulk of his first four years in Japan he had developed a triangular perspective, balanced between the traditional society of the interior, the West, and the Westernized world of the Treaty Ports. Viewed through this prism, he was now able to view the reactions, and the interaction, of Japanese and foreigners with a fresh eye. Struck by their mutual incomprehension, he took the differing nature and purposes of the smile in the cultures of East and West to illustrate the gulf between them:

> If the Japanese are puzzled by English gravity, the English are, to say the least, equally puzzled by Japanese levity. The Japanese speak of the 'angry faces' of the foreigners. The foreigners speak with strong contempt of the Japanese smile. . .[1]

The Japanese smile, was often taken as a sign of heartlessness by Westerners who did not understand that it was, in fact, the outward aspect of the regulation of the expression of feeling in Japanese society; by contrast, Western facial expressions seemed unnaturally grave to the Japanese, who did not comprehend the role of the smile in disguising emotions, especially aggression, among Occidentals. To Hearn, the differing nature and purposes of the smile illustrated the mutual incomprehension which arises from mistaken assumptions of universality of cultural norms.

Surveying the process of modernization, and accepting its necessity – Japan, he said, could have attempted no less – Hearn still felt that many of the fine traditional qualities of the Japanese race were being lost or coarsened. At the same time, he believed that the Japanese could distinguish between Western material superiority and Western morals and he was optimistic that Japan would be able to assimilate Western civilization while preserving its 'peculiar modes of thought and feeling'.[2] On the other hand, he was critical of what he saw as a lack of originality and metaphysical speculation in the Japanese character and admitted missing aspects of Western life while living in the interior.

We can see in this essay that Lafcadio had not, as some have imagined, turned away from the modernizing world of Meiji Japan to shut himself off in an arcane purity in the interior. He was in fact concerned with the dynamics of change in Meiji society from the beginning. Even that wonderful literary confection, 'My First Day in the Orient', also in *Glimpses of Unfamiliar Japan*, achieves much of its effect from the juxtaposition of the wonders of the new civilization with the disagreeable symbols of Westernization; you may have Hokusai's own figures walking about but they are passing ugly new European buildings; the shop of Buddhist images is next to the shop selling American sewing-machines; the exotic streets are lined with telegraph poles; there may be infinite hand-built variety in crafts but there are also machine-made products to meet vulgar foreign demand; Japanese trees may be lovely but they have to be protected against the vandalism of foreign tourists; he may have been describing Japanese Yokohama but he had come from the European quarter. In other words, right from his very first essay on Japan, Hearn was dealing with the process of modernization and, indeed, much of the effect of his description of the traditional derives from this consciousness on the part of the reader.

In the wider context, he was concerned with Japan's relationship with the West and was in a sense interpreting the two worlds to each other. This is true of 'The Japanese Smile', to which I have already referred, as well as a number of important essays in his early books, especially 'Jiujutsu' and 'Of the Eternal Feminine' in *Out of the East*; 'The Genius of Japanese Civilization' in *Kokoro*; and, 'About Faces in Japanese Art', in *Gleanings in Buddha Fields*.

In 'Jiujutsu' the martial art was used as a metaphor for the manner in which Japan dealt with the outside world, of using an opponent's superior weight and strength against him. He formulated a distinction in the Japanese approach between imitation and assimilation; Japan had taken only what she needed from the West and nothing was borrowed for purely imitative reasons:

> Those who imagine the Japanese to be merely imitative also imagine them to be savages. As a fact, they are assimilative and adoptive only, and that to a degree of genius.[3]

By taking only what she needed materially from the West and rejecting those aspects of Western culture not of practical use in building up her strength, Japan was practising a form of

national jiujutsu on the Western powers. Hearn contradicted
Sir Harry Parkes' prediction that Japan would become a
'South American republic'; 'the fierce heart of Old Japan' was
beating too soundly for that.[4] For a man allegedly living in
fairyland, this essay seems to me to be a superb analysis of
Japanese *realpolitik*.

Also published in *Out of the East*, 'Of the Eternal Feminine'
took as its theme the contrasting sexual attitudes of East and
West and how these could lead to mutual misapprehension;
this is of especial interest given Hearn's belief in – and practice
of! – sexual freedom when he lived in the West. Now he took
the view that much of Western literature, based on the idea of
romantic love, was incomprehensible to a Japanese imbued
with filial piety, the basis of society; in the Orient, affection
had to be subordinated to duty, especially to the parents. Not
alone did he try to make his Western readership see Japan
from a Japanese point of view, he told them that if they wished
to understand the Orient, they must study the Occident's life
and thought from the Oriental perspective. By deconstructing
the certainties of their own culture, in particular the ideal of
the Eternal Feminine, all pervasive in the West but unknown
in the ancient East, the Westerner could come to appreciate
the values of the East. Basil Hall Chamberlain wrote that it was
'quite the best thing ever written on Japan'.[5]

Hearn's double vision of East and West was, if anything,
even more in evidence in 'The Genius of Japanese
Civilization' in *Kokoro*, the first of his two Kobe books.
Here he perpetrates a type of jiujutsu by luring his Western
reader into a false sense of security with an outline of the two
cultures with which he would be comfortable: Japan could not
match the epic scale of the ultimate expressions of European
culture, from medieval cathedrals to Verdi and Wagner.
Having made this concession, Hearn then denounces the
'hard, grim, dumb' utilitarianism of a Western city, and
opposes it with the suppleness and polymorphic malleability of
Japanese life. The West built for permanence, Japan for
impermanence; he challenged the Western assumption that
stability is necessary for progress; Japan had demonstrated that
enormous development was possible without any stability at
all:

Uniformly mobile, and thus uniformly impressionable, the nation has moved unitedly in the direction of great ends.[6]

It was the absence of 'egotistical individualism' and the teachings of Shinto and Buddhism which had enabled Japan to act as a collective whole and thus 'preserve its independence against prodigious odds'.[7]

The common worker in the West was, he said, less free than his Japanese counterpart, a fascinating concept even today. He linked the ancient civilization of Japan with its 'capacity to threaten Western manufacturers'.[8] Building on this social vision in another essay, Hearn predicted that the future competitiveness of Japanese industry would be based on the aesthetic superiority of her culture, rather than cheap labour; in fact he saw an essential truth which has been vindicated in our own generation: 'The art-genius of a people may have a special value against which all competition is vain.'[9]

He even predicted what has in fact happened since the Second World War, that Japan's place in the world would be established by commercial rather than military means.[10] I note that a key claim made for Sir George Sansom by Gordon Daniels was that, in the 1930s, he saw that Japan was 'rapidly passing out of the imitative phase and is developing into a powerful industrial and commercial state';[11] without disrespect to Sansom, it can be said that Hearn had foreseen this four decades earlier. By contrast, Basil Hall Chamberlain was confident in 1904 that the West had little reason to fear Japanese economic competition.[12]

The theme of art was continued in 'About Faces in Japanese Art', published in his second Kobe book, *Gleanings in Buddha Fields*. The last in the series of great essays which completed Hearn's early, interpretative, phase in Japan, it was, incidentally, inspired by a paper presented to the Japan Society in London: rebuking the Japanese Minister to the Court of St James for comments made on that occasion, when he drew attention away from Japanese art to the triumphs of the Sino-Japanese War, Hearn warned that Japan's future industrial prosperity would depend on the 'conservation and cultivation of the national art sense'. Indeed, the ability to supply the armaments for the war in China was due to 'the commercial results of that very art sense'. Japan would have to rely on her 'aesthetic faculty, even in so commonplace a field of industry as the manufacture of mattings; for in mere cheap production she will never be able to undersell China'.[13]

More generally, while the essay was essentially a comparison of popular Japanese and Western art, it also explored Lafcadio's long-standing interest in the ways in which the respective cultures expressed their aspirations. The detailed realism of a contemporary Western engraving was compared unfavourably with the suggestiveness of popular Japanese art:

> A common Japanese drawing leaves much to the imagination,– nay, irresistibly stimulates it,– and never betrays effort. Everything in a common European engraving is detailed and individualized. Everything in a Japanese drawing is impersonal and suggestive. The former reveals no law: it is a study of particularities. The latter invariably teaches something of law, and suppresses particularities except in their relation to law.[14]

Hearn made the imaginative leap of trying to study Western facial expressions through Oriental eyes; the result, as might be anticipated, was distinctly unflattering.[15]

I should say at this point that Hearn's relationship with Japan, while always respectful, was also ambiguous; indeed, it was so complex that it caused the Japanese writer, K.K. Kawakami, to wonder if Hearn was a lover or hater of Japan.[16] However, the underlying unity of vision which united the five great essays I have mentioned was a determination to make his Western audience see Japan from a Japanese perspective and a willingness to juxtapose Western norms with their Japanese counterparts in a way which deflated an automatic assumption of superiority on the part of the Westerner. In the 1905 edition of *Things Japanese*, Basil Hall Chamberlain said of Hearn's early work:

> Never perhaps was scientific accuracy of detail married to such tender and exquisite brilliancy of style. . . Lafcadio Hearn understands contemporary Japan better, and makes *us* understand it better, than any other writer, because he loves it better.[17]

Despite an almost Oriental tendency towards self-depreca-tion, Hearn had a very clear vision of his own position in the contemporary field of Japanology:

> The difference between myself and other writers on Japan is simply that I have become practically a Japanese – in all but knowledge of the language; while other writers remain foreigners, looking from outside at riddles which cannot be read except from the inside.[18]

Hearn's Tokyo period may have given him the material for a further eight books but, with the exception of *Japan, an Attempt at Interpretation*, his focus turned away from the overtly interpretative. Having explored Shinto in considerable depth in his early books, the balance now swung back to Buddhism and his long-standing interest in reconciling it with Western science.

A second great preoccupation of these later years was the supernatural. All his life, his mind and consciousness had been permeated by horror but now it steadily increased until it became the predominant ingredient in the books which he published at the rate of about one a year. His mature, simplified, prose style admirably suited these translations of *kwaidan*, or traditional ghost stories, and it is for these that he is primarily remembered in Japan today. A third significant element in the later books was the autobiographical, the public laying bare of his Dublin childhood experiences so traumatic that they remained vivid in his consciousness.

This is not to assert that Hearn had nothing further to say about Japan. Quite the contrary but, with one great exception, he was now content to illuminate specific aspects of Japanese life without the consciously interpretative purpose which had marked his finest earlier work.

That exception was, of course *Japan: an Attempt at Interpretation*. A view has grown up that having been written just before his death in 1904, it represented a kind of late flowering, a welcome infusion of realism into the work of a writer who hitherto had been wholly unrealistic; to some it was even a form of *mea culpa*. This was expressed by the British diplomat, Frank Ashton-Gwatkin, in his novel, *Kimono*, written under the pseudonym, John Paris: here

Hearn's books were described as opium visions of a fairyland which had never existed and it was claimed that he had learned nothing about Japan until, in a state of disillusionment, he wrote *Japan: an Attempt at Interpretation* at the end of his life.

It will be obvious from what I have said so far that I do not agree with this rubbishing of Hearn's work prior to the *Attempt at Interpretation*. Indeed, I see the *Attempt* as organically linked with the early Japanese work although in some vital respects it actually represents a regression in the accuracy of his analysis.

The organic link to his earlier work was, of course, Shinto which he had earlier come to see as the embodiment of the Japanese spirit. In *Japan: an Attempt at Interpretation*, Shinto is again seen as the bedrock of Japanese society, the religion which embodied the Hearn concept of respect for the ancestors – historically, of course, ancestor worship was actually grafted on to the older, animistic, roots of Shinto – which Lafcadio shaded into the concept of the rule of the dead, satisfying the demands of Herbert Spencer's evolutionary philosophy and blending with the growing hold which the *kwaidan* had on his mind.

The structure and coherence of *Japan: an Attempt at Interpretation* is especially impressive coming from an author whose previous work had been seriously lacking in architectonic ability. It also has the superficial attraction that, rather than having to search through a dozen books of disparate material where even the individual essays often lack cohesion, the *Attempt at Interpretation* offers a neat summary in one structured volume.

Contrary to appearances, however, Hearn had not suddenly been graced with architectonic ability out of the blue; the structure of *Japan: an Attempt at Interpretation* was largely borrowed: about half the chapter headings come from Fustel de Coulanges' *La Cité Antique*.[19] Furthermore, the fundamental objective of de Coulanges' book, to show that the institutions of ancient Greece and Rome were based on popular religious beliefs, stemming specifically from the cult of the dead, was applied to Japan by Hearn, something for which he was later taken to task by his Irish contemporary,

W.G. Aston. One needs, however, to exercise caution in entering this rather arcane area of scholarship: his influence on Hearn is controversial among de Coulanges scholars, with the modern view being more sceptical of the extent of that influence.[20]

Another scholarly input came from the familiar figure of Herbert Spencer. Between his all-embracing evolutionary structure and Hearn's adaptation of de Coulanges to fit into it, Lafcadio developed a theory that Japanese civilization was at the same stage of development as the West had been at in the millenium before Christ. The result was to some extent a negation of Hearn's earlier view that Japan was *sui generis* and should not be evaluated in relation to the norms of the West. Under Spencer's influence, Hearn had become deeply pessimistic about the future, developing Orwellian visions of universal subjection under the sway of industrial combines and socialism. He now decided that the group structure of Japanese society rendered it incapable of democracy and that its future competitiveness would depend on the expansion of Western-style individualism. Not that he had changed his views on the baleful influence of the West; he reiterated at great length the destructive potential of Christianity for Japanese society and the need to keep Western capital at bay.

While one could say that Hearn may have departed somewhat from his earlier insistence on seeing Japan from a Japanese perspective and was now instead imposing the straitjacket of Western philosophical orthodoxy, this is only half the story; paradoxically enough, many of the ideas infusing the *Attempt at Interpretation*, as well as some of his earlier work, had been in circulation in Japan for some time before. The Confucian scholar, Yasui Sokken had, in his 1875 book, *Bemmō* or *Exposure of Falsehood* expounded the view that Christianity was incompatible with the ethical notions of ancestor worship, filial piety, and loyalty to superiors which were fundamental to the Japanese polity. Similarly, the Buddhist scholar, Inoue Tetsujirō, a colleague of Hearn's at Tokyo University, had written of a conflict between the state and Christianity. Certain Buddhist sects had been teaching the compatibility of Buddhism with modern science. And if Hearn declared that he worshipped Spencer, he was not alone:

in the words of Sir George Sansom, 'the gospel of most intellectuals in Japan was the gospel of Herbert Spencer'.[21] The *Attempt at Interpretation* was, therefore, in some respects the least accurate of Hearn's major interpretative statements on his adopted country – it has been called his worst book on Japan[22] – though it was a unique fusion of contemporary Western and Japanese ideas.

* * *

Having looked at Hearn's interpretation of Japan, it might now be useful to see how it is regarded today. Professor Hirakawa of Tokyo University has commented:

> Hearn's writings are today so discredited among American Japanese specialists that if a young student quotes Hearn sympathetically, he is almost certain to be criticized by his academic advisers and considered a belated romanticist unfit for serious scholarship. There is, however, no problem at all with quoting the authoritative Chamberlain.[23]

It might be interesting to look briefly at Basil Hall Chamberlain and see how this figure, who seems to be carved out of a scholarly Mount Rushmore, really does compare with Hearn. This is particularly appropriate as, his scholarly achievements notwithstanding, it is as an interpreter of Japan, through his book, *Things Japanese*, that Chamberlain is now primarily remembered. Also, the two men were exact contemporaries.

Their views on Japan had points of similarity as well as difference. Both accepted the necessity of Meiji modernization to ward off what they saw as predatory Western powers and both were contemptuous of Christian missionary activity when used as an agency of imperial expansion. Hearn, however, accepted the validity of indigenous Japanese culture and, accordingly, regretted the process of change. Chamberlain, by contrast, saw 'civilized white men on the one hand' opposed by a Japan emerging from 'Asiatic semi-barbarism' on the other, needing to prove her fitness to be brought into the 'family of Christian nations'[24] and he had no doubt that 'European ways' were superior 'materially and intellectually'.[25] To Hearn, the Westernization of Japan represented a moral and societal regression; in Chamberlain's view it became more civilized as it became more Westernized. He was blunt in his dismissal of Japanese philosophy,[26] literature,[27] and music.[28] Thus, the fundamental dividing line between the two men was Hearn's insistence on seeing Japan in its own terms and Chamberlain's equal insistence on a Western perspective.

It is inconceivable that Hearn would have written much of Chamberlain's *Things Japanese*: for example, the chapter on 'English as She is Japped', with its extended mockery of Japanese malapropisms in English, sounds very like an anthology of anecdotes swapped over dinner in a foreigner's club, an environment frequented by Chamberlain but shunned by Hearn.[29] These differences in viewpoint are to be expected: Chamberlain remained essentially within a Western environment in Japan; Hearn, by contrast, was seen by his fellow Westerners as having 'gone native', living a mainly Japanese lifestyle, avoiding them as much as he could. Chamberlain was fiercely loyal to the Treaty Ports' Western inhabitants; his fury at the British Government for what he regarded as a diplomatic humiliation over the Anglo-Japanese agreement of 1894 was due mainly to his indignation at the prospect of foreign residents having to submit to the rule of Japanese law.[30]

It was this issue more than any other which revealed the incompatibility of Hearn's and Chamberlain's views on Japan. Hearn's insistence on seeing the treaty revision from Japan's point of view infuriated Chamberlain, who wrote:

> But surely these are not the lines on which to judge a treaty between a great Western state and that two penny half-penny Brummagem imitation of one which these frock-coated officials have made of Japan.[31]

In other sections of *Things Japanese*, Chamberlain underlined these sentiments by emphatic approval of 'gunboat diplomacy' to be administered by Western powers to a Japanese Government which, if it showed 'dread and dislike' of 'high-handed policy' would quickly come to see that it was 'founded in reason'.[32]

The two men were also fundamentally opposed on the merits of Shinto, a highly political subject in the context of the time. Chamberlain, a sturdy rationalist in the nineteenth-century tradition, believed that Shinto was being fraudulently re-invented as a new religion of loyalty and patriotism by an illiberal and obscurantist Japanese bureaucracy which dared not allow the light of freedom and scientific thought to be shed on their furtive enterprise.[33]

The differences between the two men continued posthumously. Within a few years of Hearn's death, his reputation was engulfed in the most acrimonious controversy, with former friends prominent on both sides. Among other things, he paid a heavy price for having ignored the taboos of his time, particularly on the coloured question in the United States.

Chamberlain played a particularly destructive role in undermining Hearn's reputation as an interpreter of Japan. Professor Hirakawa has documented the progressively more negative entries on Hearn contained in the later editions of *Things Japanese* and related them to Chamberlain's unhappy circumstances, particularly the shame of having his brother, Houston Stewart Chamberlain, achieve notoriety as a Nazi theorist.[34] By the 1939 edition, he was writing that Hearn's life had been a succession of dreams which had turned into nightmares; that, awakening from his dream of Japan, he realized he had taken a false step; the Japan he had described could only have existed in his own imagination, and so on.[35] At this stage, Chamberlain's language had taken on echoes of *Concerning Lafcadio Hearn*, the attempted comprehensive demolition job which another erstwhile friend, George Gould, had written a few years after Hearn's death in an effort to salvage his own reputation.[36] There were echoes also of Frank Ashton-Gwatkins's negative views.

As well as his unhappy personal circumstances, I think that Chamberlain may have been responding to the darkening international mood as the world prepared for war. Hearn was then out of tune with the times; the man who had extolled the charms of a new ally and rising world power at the end of the nineteenth century was not the man for the Manchurian crisis, the Second World War, or its aftermath. Indeed, Arthur Kunst has written that

> ... the Great Pacific war with Japan in the 1940s seemed for a time to have obliterated Hearn from the American consciousness, a kind of guilt over a youthful infatuation. The misleading notion of Hearn as a spokesman for Japan left him without literary defences when Japan and things Japanese became enemy.[37]

Yet, it was at this time that Hearn may have exercised his greatest influence. In 1945, General MacArthur accepted the argument of a memorandum prepared by Brigadier General Bonner Fellers that the Showa Emperor should not be prosecuted for war crimes. As a young college undergraduate, Fellers had been persuaded to study the writings of Lafcadio Hearn by a Japanese Quaker woman, Yuri Isshiki. When Fellers arrived in Japan in 1945, both Isshiki and her friend, Michiko Kawai, a leader of the anti-war movement, presented him with arguments against prosecution of the Emperor. Within a few weeks, Fellers submitted his memorandum to MacArthur. Quite what influence Hearn's writings exercised on Feller's decision may never be precisely disentangled, but it seems fair to assume that Hearn's interpretation of Japan, with its emphasis on Shinto, and the importance of the Emperor in that system, at least played a role in conditioning Fellers to accept the logic of the arguments put to him in 1945.[38] The fact that Fellers became a close personal friend of Lafcadio's son, Kazuo, and paid homage at his grave underlines this point.

Now that the memory of international antagonisms earlier in the century are fading in history, we can, I hope, see dispassionately the merits as well as the failings of a man who, in addition to being an artist of enduring merit, was arguably the finest of a talented generation of early interpreters of Japan. Indeed, the tide may already be turning: within the last few years, Francis King, novelist and Hearn anthologist, has claimed in *The Spectator* to have learned more from Hearn's *Attempt at Interpretation* than anything else on Japan[39] and the Tokyo Bureau Chief of the *Financial Times* has commented that Hearn's 'Jiujutsu', 'invites an obvious moral for anyone negotiating with Japanese business or government'.[40] Few

people of his era tried harder to promote mutual understanding between East and West and he remains worth reading
for his penetrating analysis of Japan, as enduring as the magic
of his prose.

NOTES & REFERENCES

Chapter 1 SUKEHIRO HIRAKAWA Rediscovering Lafcadio Hearn

1. George Hughes, 'An Irish Version of Lafcadio Hearn' in *Comparative Literature Studies*, Vol. 33 No. 1 (Penn State Press, 1996):82.
2. Arthur Kunst, *Lafcadio Hearn* (New York, Twayne Publishers, 1969): 126.
3. Basil Hall Chamberlain's book *Things Japanese* (1905 edition) is still available in paperback; however, the publishers changed the title to *Japanese Things* (Rutland, Vermont and Tokyo, Charles E. Tuttle Co). In this edition there is no article entitled 'Lafcadio Hearn', although there are a lot of references to Hearn and his books.
4. George Sansom gave a talk in Japanese on B. H. Chamberlain (1850–1935), shortly after his death in a reunion held in Tokyo commemorating 'the dean of Western Japanologists'. See Hirakawa: *Yaburareta yūjō* (Tokyo, Shinchō-sha, 1987):22. The book deals in detail with the relationship between Chamberlain and Hearn.
5. Edmund Gosse writes as follows in his book *Silhouettes*, p226: 'These lectures are marked by an almost naïve simplicity. We seem to be returning in them to the infancy of criticism, where everything is good or bad, beautiful or ugly. But this does not detract from their merit, which depends on their freshness, their artless enthusiasm, and also on the vigour with which impressions independently made on the enthusiasm of the lecturer are passed on to his audience.'
6. Richard Bowring, 'An Amused Guest in All: Basil Hall Chamberlain' in Sir Hugh Cortazzi & Gordon Daniels ed., *Britain and Japan* (Routledge, 1991):128–136.
7. Muramatsu S., *Reikon no tankyūsha Koizumi Yakumo* (3-1-1, Toro, Shizuoka-city, Shizuoka Shinbun-sha, 1994).
8. All the original Japanese stories used by Hearn and preserved in Toyama University library are reproduced in Hirakawa S., ed., Koizumi Yakumo, *Kaidan kidan* (Tokyo, Kōdansha [gakujutsu-bunko], 1990):357–462. The original Japanese stories of *Yasōkidan* which Hearn used for the recreation of 'The Story of Kwashin Koji' and for that of 'The Story of O-Tei' are also reproduced in it.

9. *Lafcadio Hearn: Japan's Great Interpreter*, ed., by Louis Allen & Jean Wilson (Sandgate, Folkestone, Kent, Japan Library Ltd., 1992):282–308.
10. Marguerite Yourcenar, *Oriental Tales*, trans. by A. Manguel (New York, Farrar Strauss Giroux, 1985).
11. For the original French story, see Marguerite Yourcenar, *Nouvelles Orientales* (Paris, Gallimard):24–25.
12. 'A strange red scarf' is of course suggestive of Ling's blood when his head was cut off.
13. See Roy Andrew Miller, *The Japanese Language in Contemporary Japan* (American Enterprise Institute for Public Policy Research, 1977) and his article in *Journal of Japanese Studies* Vol. 3 No. 2 (1977). As for my rebuttal, see Hirakawa, 'In Defense of the "Spirit" of the Japanese Language', *Journal of Japanese Studies* Vol. 7 No. 2 (1981):393–402.
14. It is also true that in the official Confucian mileu the existence of ghosts and spirits is neglected. That attitude is reflected in the following passage: 'the Master never talked of prodigies, feats of strength, disorders or spirits' (*Analects*, BKVII, CHXX). In China it is in the unofficial world that ghost stories flourished.
15. See the beginning of *Kojiki, Records of Ancient Matters*, trans. B.H. Chamberlain (Rutland Vermont & Tokyo, Charles E. Tuttle Co. 1981):15.
16. Part III dealing with 'the animistic world of Kwashin Koji' was originally presented to the UBC conference on *Nature and Selfhood in Japanese Literature*. As for my more detailed discussion on the subject, see Hirakawa and Tsuruta ed., *Animizumu o yomu* (Tokyo, Shinyōsha, 1994):64–108.
17. See Hirakawa's introduction to Paul Murray, *A Fantastic Journey, the Life and Literature of Lafcadio Hearn* (Sandgate, Folkestone, Kent, Japan Library Ltd., 1993).
18. Ueda Akinari, *Ugetsu monogatari: Tales of Moonlight and Rain*, trans. Leon Zolbrod (Rutland Vermont & Tokyo, Charles E. Tuttle Co.).
19. As Dominic Cheung had treated 'The Ghost-Wife Theme in China, Japan and Korea' in *Tamkang Review*, Vol. XV, pp151–174, I wrote for the same academic journal Vol. XVIII, pp187–198, the article 'Was She Really Reconciled?' in order to open new American perspectives by including Hearn's and feminist interpretations of the same story. While many Western scholars were in favour of the feminist interpretation referred to, most Chinese scholars were decidedly against it.
20. Sōseki Natsume, *Sanshiro*, trans. J. Rubin (University of Washington Press):183–184. I made a slight modification as to the English title of *gaikoku kyōshi*. I believe 'foreign professor' or 'foreign lecturer' fits better the high position *gaikoku kyōshi* occupied through the Meiji years than 'foreign instructor' used by Rubin.
21. Sōseki's 'Third Night' in its relation with Hearn's retold story of Mochida-no-ura legend is treated in detail in Hirakawa, *Koizumi Yakumo—seiyō dasshutsu no yume* (Tokyo, Shinchōsha, 1981):63–111.
22. Sōseki Natsume, *Ten Nights of Dream*, trans. A. Ito & G. Wilson (Rutland Vermont & Tokyo, Charles E. Tuttle Co):27–28.
23. Lafcadio Hearn, *Kwaidan*, présentation by Denise Brahimi (Paris, Librairie Minerve, 1988)

24. Soseki Natsume, *Ten Nights of Dream*, trans. A. Ito & G. Wilson:29–30.
25. Ibid:30.

Chapter 2 EARL MINER Hearn and Japan: An Attempt at Interpretation

1. Citations of Hearn's work refer to the 'Koizumi Edition' of *The Writings of Lafcadio Hearn*, 12 vols. (Cambridge, MA: Houghton Mifflin, 1922), vol. 8 for the titles given. Subsequent references will be given as *Writings* by volume and, where necessary, page numbers.
2. Detroit: Wayne State University Press, 1964; hereafter cited as Yu. Yu gives a well balanced account, understandably treating Hearn's writings about Japan most thoroughly, but he does also discuss Hearn as author from his earliest extant story.
3. *Koizumi Yakumo to Kamigami no Sekai* (Koizumi Yakumo and the Realm of Divinities; Tokyo: Bungei Shunjū, 1988), hereafter referred to as Hirakawa.
4. Santa Barbara, Ca: Ross-Erikson; hereafter cited as Rexroth. Kenneth Rexroth is named as its author; no claim is made for the editing other than that the selections are taken from the *Writings*.
5. Lafcadio Hearn, *Writings from Japan* (Harmondsworth, Mddx: Penguin, 1984). King provides an introduction as well.
6. For example, she has edited (in English and Japanese) *The Ernest F. Fenellosa Papers* in the Houghton Library at Harvard University, 3 vols. (Tokyo: Museum Shuppan, 1982–87). For Kodama, see *American Poetry and Japanese Culture* (Hamden, CN: Archon, 1984).
7. See Bloom, *The Anxiety of Influence* (New York: Oxford University Press, 1973), and his elaboration in later boks. Claudio Guillén's earlier *Literature as System* (Princeton: Princeton University Press, 1971), chs. 1 and 2, seems closer to describing the process in which Hearn was involved. Other issues will be remarked on subsequently.
8. See my *Japanese Tradition in British and American Literature* (Princeton: Princeton University Press, 1958), pp. 66–96.
9. That translation is not present in the second edition of 1891. It is present in the fifth edition of 1905, a date more than five years earlier than Pound's interest in *nō*. Because the Princeton libraries do not have the third and fourth editions, I cannot say just when the translation was added.
10. The Fenellosa manuscript is privately possessed by Mr Omar Shakespeare Pound, Pound's son.
11. *The Japanese Tradition*, p. 91. The actual letters are held by the rare books department at the University of California, Los Angeles, in a collection bearing my name.
12. *Writings*, 1, x.
13. Many things have been said about Hearn's command of Japanese, some assuming full command and others full ignorance. For samples of his writing in Japanese to his wife, see Hirakawa, 96–100. The level is perhaps that of a mature student of second-year Japanese. Something more will be said of this in another context.
14. The word recurs; e.g., see *Writings*, 1, 367.

15. *Letters from Basil Hall Chamberlain to Lafcadio Hearn*, ed. Kazuo Koizumi (Tokyo: Hokuseido Press, 1936), p. 16.
16. Quoted from Rexroth, p. x, who does not cite his source.
17. Versions of the story go back as far as the *Man'yōshū*. Hearn's version is 'The Dream of a Summer Day', *Out of the East, Writings*, 7, 3–23. As mentioned, the retelling of Japanese stories is a distinct feature of Hearn's later career.
18. 'Of the Eternal Feminine', *Out of the East, Writings*, 7, 65.
19. Basil Hall Chamberlain, *Things Japanese* (London and Kobe: Kegan Paul and Thompson, 1927), a reprint of the 1905 edition, with two appendices added. I do not see that Chamberlain ever expressed any change of view on the arts, although he does quote sometimes the more favourable opinions of W. G. Aston.
20. For a clear and enthusiastic account of Hearn's *Japan*, see Yu, p. 195–204.
21. The book has seven illustrations (including the frontispiece), of which only the last – showing the red gate of the University of Tokyo – is not religious.
22. *Japan, Writings*, 12, 456–57. The ellipsis marked in Hearn's own, but I have also broken there (p. 456) and next picked up by quoting the final words of the book.
23. *Japan*, 196–216; see also the appendix, 459–64. The first and, I believe, still most complete account of Hearn's attempt to unite Buddhism and Spencerian evolutionary thought was that of Paul Elmer More, 'Lafcadio Hearn', *Shelburne Essays* (New York and London: Putnam, 1905). See also my *Japanese Tradition*, 87–96.
24. *Japan*, 456. This quotation is out of immediate context but fits into the larger context of the concluding pages.
25. Yu seems inclined to the view that Hearn combined West and East: see his concluding pages, 285–87. I find those pages finally more appealing than proved.
26. When in elementary school in Sapporo, my wife (whose ancestry is not Japanese) had to endure taunts from classmates: 'Foreigner! Beak-nosed foreigner!' ('Gaikokujin! Hana taka gaikokujin!'). Japanese have had corresponding racial insults to bear, but this recollection may serve to illustrate the domestic conversation *chez* Koizumi about the husband's nose.
27. *Life and Letters of Lafcadio Hearn*, ed. Elizabeth Bisland, 4 vols. (Boston and New York: Houghton Mifflin, 1923), 1, 140. There is also Chamberlain's account, appearing in *Things Japanese* at least as early as the 1905 edition, which reaches a climax in the following: 'Lafcadio Hearn understands contemporary Japan better, and makes *us* understand it better, than any other writer, because he loves it better.' That is well said, and the close of the remarks are revealing on other grounds: 'Our only quarrel is with some of Lafcadio Hearn's judgments:—in righting the Japanese, he seems to us continually to wrong his own race. . . However, Europe is well-able to take care of herself; and if this be the price demanded for so great a gift to literature and ethnologic science, we at least will pay it uncomplainingly' (65). Chamberlain unwittingly delineates, with exactitude, himself as well as Hearn.

Chapter 3 GEORGE HUGHES Lafcadio Hearn: Between Britain and Japan

Works cited

Behdad, Ali. *Belated Travelers: Orientalism in the Age of Colonial Dissolution.* Durham: Duke UP, 1994.

Cortazzi, Sir Hugh and Gordon Daniels. *Britain and Japan 1859–1991: Themes and Personalities.* London: Routledge, 1991.

Enright, D.J. *The World of Dew.* London: Secker and Warburg, 1955.

Gould, George M. *Concerning Lafcadio Hearn.* Philadelphia: George W. Jacobs, 1908.

Hearn, Lafcadio. *Glimpses of Unfamiliar Japan.* 1894. Rutland, Vermont: Charles E. Tuttle, 1976.

—. *Shadowings and A Japanese Miscellany. Works,* Vol. X. Boston: Houghton Mifflin, 1922.

—. *The Life and Letters of Lafcadio Hearn,* ed. Elizabeth Bisland. Boston: Houghton Mifflin, 1906.

—. *The Japanese Letters of Lafcadio Hearn,* ed. Elizabeth Bisland. London: Constable, 1911

—. *Veiled Letters from Lafcadio Hearn,* ed. Kaoru Sekita. Tokyo: Yushodo P, 1991.

Hirakawa, Sukehiro. *Koizumi Yakumo to Kamigami no Sekai.* Tokyo: Bungei shunju, 1988.

Keene, Donald. *On Familiar Terms: A Long Journey Across Cultures.* New York: Kodansha, 1994.

Kennard, N.N. *Lafcadio Hearn.* New York: D. Appleton, 1912.

King, Francis. Introduction. *Writngs from Japan.* By Lafcadio Hearn. Harmondsworth: Penguin, 1984.

Lewis, Wyndham. *Time and Western Man.* London: Chatto and Windus, 1927.

Murray. Paul. *A Fantastic Journey.* Folkestone: Japan Library, 1993.

Nishi, Masahiko. *Rafukadio Haan no Mimi.* Tokyo: Iawanami Shoten, 1993.

Noguchi, Yone. *Lafcadio Hearn in Japan.* Tokyo: 'Ars' Bookshop, 1923.

Ota, Yuzo. *Rafukadio Haan.* Tokyo: Iawanami Shoten, 1994.

Paris, John. [Frank Ashton-Gwatkin]. *Kimono.* London: W. Collins, 1921.

Plomer, William. *Paper Houses.* London: Hogarth Press, 1929.

Rhys, Jean. *Sleep It Off Lady.* 1976 Harmondsworth: Penguin, 1979.

Stevenson, Elizabeth. *Lafcadio Hearn.* 1961. New York: Octagon Books, 1979.

Tinker, E.L. *Lafcadio Hearn's American Days.* New York: Dodd, Mead & Co, 1924.

Thomas, Edward. *Lafcadio Hearn.* London: Constable and Co, 1912.

Transactions and Proceedings of the Japan Society. Vol. VI, 1902–3; Vol XVI 1917–8.

Webb, Kathleen, M. *Lafcadio Hearn and His German Critics.* New York: Peter Lang, 1984.

Chapter 4 GEORGE HUGHES Lafcadio Hearn and the Fin de Siècle

Works cited

Baudelaire, Charles. *Oeuvres Complètes: Les Fleurs du Mal,* ed. F.-F. Gautier. Paris: Nouvelles Revue Francaise, 1918.

Cott, Jonathan. *Wandering Ghost: The Odyssey of Lafcadio Hearn.* New York: Alfred A. Knopf, 1991.

Douglas, Mary. *Purity and Danger: An Analysis of Concepts of Pollution and Taboo.* London: Routledge and Kegan Paul, 1966.

Gould, George M. *Concerning Lafcadio Hearn.* Philadelphia: George W. Jacobs and Co, 1908.

—. *Biographic Clinics.* Vol IV. Essays concerning the influence of visual function, pathologic and physiologic, upon the health of patients. Philadelphia: P. Blakiston's Son & Co, 1906.

Hearn, Lafcadio. *A Japanese Miscellany.* 1901. *Writings of Lafcadio Hearn* vol X. Boston: Houghton Mifflin Co, 1922.

—. *An American Miscellany,* ed. Albert Mordell. 2 vols. New York: Dodd, Mead and Co, 1924.

—. *Essays in European and Oriental Literature,* ed. Albert Mordell. New York: Dodd, Mead and Co, 1923.

—. *Gleanings of the Writings of Lafcadio Hearn,* ed. The Hearn Society. 2 vols. Tokyo: Yushudo, 1990.

—. *Interpretations of Literature,* ed. John Erskine. New York: Dodd, Mead and Co, 1920.

—. *Japan: An Attempt at Interpretation.* 1904. Boston: Houghton Mifflin Co, 1923.

—. *Kotto.* 1902. Rutland: Tuttle, 1972.

—. *On Art, Literature and Philosophy,* ed. R. Tanabé et al. Tokyo: Hokuseido P, 1932.

—. *Out of the East.* 1897. Boston: Houghton Mifflin Co, 1922.

—. *The Japanese Letters of Lafcadio Hearn,* ed. Elizabeth Bisland. London: Constable, 1911.

—. *The Life and Letters of Lafcadio Hearn,* ed. Elizabeth Bisland. 2 vols. Boston: Houghton Mifflin Co, 1906.

—. *Veiled Letters from Lafcadio Hearn,* ed. Kaoru Sekita. Tokyo: Yushudo P, 1991.

Gilman, Richard. *Decadence: The Strange Life of an Epithet.* New York: Farrar, Strauss and Giroux, 1979.

Hennegan, Alison. 'Personalities and principles: aspects of literature and life in *fin-de-siècle* England', *Fin de Siècle and its Legacy,* ed. Mikulas Teich and Roy Porter. Cambridge: Cambridge UP, 1990.

Kozumi, Kazuo. *Father and I.* Boston: Houghton Mifflin Co, 1935.

Murray, Paul. *A Fantastic Journey: The Life and Literature of Lafcadio Hearn.* Folkestone, Kent: Japan Library, 1993.

Nordau, Max. *Degeneration.* (Translated from Second Edition of the German Work) London: William Heinemann, 1896.

Pater, Walter. *The Renaissance: Studies in Art and Poetry.* 1893. Oxford: Oxford UP, 1986.

Pierrot, Jean. *The Decadent Imagination.* 1880–1900. (Trans. Derek Colman) Chicago: U of Chicago P, 1981.

Showalter, Elaine. *Sexual Anarchy: Gender and Culture at the Fin de Siècle.* London: Bloomsbury, 1991.

Stevenson, Elizabeth. *Lafcadio Hearn.* New York: Octagon Books, 1979.

Symons, Arthur. *The Symbolist Movement in Literature.* London: William Heinemann, 1899.

Tinker, E.L. *Lafcadio Hearn's American Days*. New York: Dodd, Mead and Co, 1924.

Yeats, W.B. *The Secret Rose, Stories by W.B. Yeats: A Variorum Edition*, ed. Phillip L. Marcus et al. Ithaca: Cornell UP, 1980.

Yu, Beongcheon. *An Ape of Gods: The Art and Thought of Lafcadio Hearn*. Detroit: Wayne State UP, 1964.

Chapter 5 GEORGE HUGHES Entering Island Cultures: Synge, Hearn and the Irish Exotic

Works cited

Barthes, Roland. *Le degré zéro de l'écriture*. 1953 Paris: Seuil, 1972.

Bourgeois, Maurice. *John Millington Synge and the Irish Theatre*. London: Constable, 1913.

Buisine, Alain. *Tombeau de Loti*. Lille: Atelier National de Reproduction des Thèses, 1988.

Bushrui, S.B. Ed. *Sunshine and the Moon's Delight: A Centenary Tribute to John Millington Synge*. Gerrard's Cross: Colin Smythe and American University of Beirut, 1972.

Edwards, Osman. 'Some Unpublished Letters of Lafcadio Hearn', *Transactions of the Japan Society*. XVI. 1917–8.

Greene, D.H. and E.M. Stephens. *J.M. Synge 1871–1909*. Revised Edition. New York: New York University P., 1989.

Grene, Nicholas. *Synge: A Critical Study of the Plays*. London: MacMillan, 1975.

Hearn, Lafcadio. *Glimpses of Unfamiliar Japan*. 1894. Rutland, Vermont: Tuttle, 1976.

—. *On Art, Literature and Philosophy*, ed. Ryuji Tanabe et al. Tokyo: Hokusaido P, 1932.

—. *The Japanese Letters of Lafcadio Hearn*, ed. Elisabeth Bisland. London: Constable, 1911.

—. *Veiled Letters from Lafcadio Hearn*, ed. Kaoru Sekita. Tokyo: Yushodo P, 1991.

Kiberd, Declan. *Synge and the Irish Language*. London, MacMillan, 1979.

Loti, Pierre. *Aziyadé* 1879 Collection Folio. Préface de Claude Martin. Paris: Gallimard, 1991.

—. *Le mariage de Loti*. Paris: Safrat, 1990.

—. *Madame Chrysanthème*. 1887. Paris: Flammarion, 1990.

Moura, Jean-Marc. *Lire l'Exotisme*. Paris: Dunod, 1992.

Segalen, Victor. *Essai sur l'Exotisme*. Paris: Fata Morgana, 1978.

Synge, J.M. *Collected Works* ed. Robin Skelton. (Plays ed. Ann Saddlemyer; Prose ed. Alan Price) Gerrards Cross: Colin Smythe, 1982.

—. *The Aran Islands*. 1907. London: Penguin, 1992.

Chapter 6 GEORGE HUGHES W.B. Yeats and Lafcadio Hearn: Negotiating with Ghosts

Works cited

Amenomori, Nobushige. 'Lafcadio Hearn, the Man'. *Atlantic Monthly*. 96. 1906.

Donoghue, Denis. *The Third Voice*. Princeton: Princeton UP, 1959.

Ellmann, Richard. *Yeats: The Man and the Masks*. Harmondsworth: Penguin, 1979.

Goldman, Arnold. 'Yeats, Spiritualism and Psychical Research', *Yeats and the Occult*, ed. G.M. Harper. London: Macmillan, 1976.

Hearn, Lafcadio. 'Among the Spirits', *Cincinnati Enquirer* (Jan. 25, 1874).

—. *Gleanings in Buddha Fields*. 1897. Rutland: Tuttle, 1971.

—. *Glimpses of Unfamiliar Japan*. 1894. Rutland: Tuttle, 1976.

—. *Japan: An Attempt at Interpretation*. 1904. Rutland: Tuttle, 1956.

—. *Japanese Letters of Lafcadio Hearn*, ed. Elisabeth Bisland. London: Constable, 1911.

—. *Kokoro*. 1896. Rutland: Tuttle, 1972.

—. *Kwaidan*. 1904. Rutland: Tuttle, 1972.

—. *Lectures on Shakespeare*, ed. I Inagaki. Tokyo: Hokuseido P, 1928.

—. *Life and Letters of Lafcadio Hearn*, ed. Elisabeth Bisland. 2 vols. Boston: Houghton, Mifflin, 1906.

—. *Life and Literature*, ed. John Erskine. New York: Dodd, Mead, 1921.

—. *On Art, Literature and Philosophy*, eds. R. Tanabe et al. Tokyo: Hokuseido P, 1932.

—. *On Poetry*, eds. R. Tanabe et al. Tokyo: Hokuseido P, 1934.

—. *Oriental Articles*, ed. I Nishizaki. Tokyo: Hokuseido P, 1939.

—. *Out of the East*. 1897. Rutland: Tuttle, 1972.

—. *Shadowings*. Boston: Little, Brown, 1900.

—. *Spirit Photography*. ed. P.D. Perkins. Los Angeles: John Murray, 1933.

Kutch, Peter. ' "Laying the Ghosts"? – W.B. Yeats's Lecture on Ghosts and Dreams.' *Yeats Annual* 5 (1897).

Oppenheim, Janet. *The Other World: Spiritualism and Psychical Research in England 1850–1914*. Cambridge: Cambridge UP, 1985.

Murray, Paul. *A Fantastic Journey: The Life and Literature of Lafcadio Hearn*. Folkestone, Kent: Japan Library, 1993.

Taylor, Richard. 'Assimilation and Accomplishment: Nō Drama and An Unpublished Source for *At the Hawk's Well*.' *Yeats and the Theatre*, Ed. R. O'Driscoll et al. London: Macmillan, 1975.

Takahashi, Yasunari. 'The Ghost Trio: Becket, Yeats and Noh.' *The Cambridge Review*. Dec. 1986.

Vendler, Helen. *Yeats's Vision and the Later Plays*. Cambridge, Mass: Harvard UP, 1963.

Waley, Arthur. *The Nō Plays of Japan*. 1921. Rutland: Tuttle, 1972.

Worth, Katharine. *The Irish Drama of Europe from Yeats to Becket*. London: Athlone P, 1986.

Yeats, W.B. *Explorations*. London: Macmillan, 1962.

—. *Letters of W.B. Yeats*, ed. Allan Wade. New York: Macmillan, 1955.

—. *Mythologies*. London: Macmillan, 1955.

—. *The Celtic Twilight*. 1893. Bridport : Prism Press, 1990.

—. *The Classic Noh Theatre of Japan*. 1917. New York: New Directions, 1959.

—. *The Collected Letters of W.B. Yeats III*, ed. John Kelly and Ronald Shuchard. Oxford: Clarendon P, 1994.

—. *The Variorum Edition of the Plays of W.B. Yeats.* ed. Russell K. Alspach. London: Macmillan, 1966.

Chapter 7 LOUIS ALLEN Lafcadio Hearn and Ushaw College

1. Vera McWilliams, *Lafcadio Hearn,* New York, 1946, repr. 1970, p. 39.
2. D. Milburn, *A History of Ushaw College,* Ushaw, 1964, p. 57.
3. Milburn, op. cit., pp. 170–174; E. Towers, D. D., 'The Revolt at Ushaw, 1842', *Ushaw Magazine,* LV (1945) pp. 1–29.
4. Milburn, op. cit., p. 176.
5. V. McWilliams, *Lafcadio Hearn,* p. 44.
6. Wrote a contemporary, Joseph Corbishley, later to become President of Ushaw, 1909–1910.
7. V. McWilliams, op. cit., pp. 39–40.
8. Wrote another ecclesiastical eminence, from the later comfort of a canonry.
9. V. McWilliams, op. cit., p. 40.
10. *Lafcadio Hearn: Containing Some Letters from Lafcadio Hearn to His Half-Sister, Mrs Atkinson,* New York, 1912.
11. Letter to Basil Hall Chamberlain, 2 October 1984, in *Japanese Letters of Lafcadio Hearn,* ed. E. Bisland, London and New York, 1911, p. 388.
12. Ibid.
13. Stevenson, op. cit., p. 15.
14. Stevenson, op. cit., p. 14.
15. *Life and Letters of Lafcadio Hearn,* London and New York, 1906, pp. 26–32.
16. *Life and Letters of Lafcadio Hearn,* I, pp. 27–28.
17. Ibid., p. 29.
18. *Life and Letters,* p. 30.
19. Ibid., pp. 31–32.
20. Stevenson, op. cit., p. 21.
21. Prefect General 1845–1854, Vice President 1877–1878, President 1878–1885.
22. *Japanese Letters of Lafcadio Hearn,* 11 July 1893 and 31 October 1893; p. 135, p. 187.
23. *Life and Letters,* Vol. I, pp. 32–33.
24. V. McWilliams, op. cit., p. 41.
25. 'They rose every morning at 5.30, Sundays included, and attended the Mass celebrated daily by the Procurator at six in St Joseph's (then known as the Maid's Chapel), so as to be able to make all the beds and dispose of all the slops in the rooms and dormitories while the staff and students were engaged in their prayers and Masses. I suppose they had a break of some kind for breakfast, but they were back upstairs cleaning the rooms and galleries as soon as we were in class or otherwise out of the way. Many of them who worked in the kitchen or laundry or sewing-room we never saw, much less spoke to.' L.L. McReavy, 'Recollections of an earlier Ushaw', *Ushaw Magazine,* No. 249, Vol. LXXXVIII, June 1977, p. 13.
26. Nina H. Kennard, *Lafcadio Hearn: Containing Some Letters from Lafcadio Hearn to His Half-Sister, Mrs Atkinson,* New York, 1912, p. 12.
27. Ibid., pp. 13–14, in Stevenson, op. cit., p. 8.

28. E. Bisland ed. *Life and Letters of Lafcadio Hearn*, Vol. I, p. 10–11.
29. L. Hearn, *Out of the East*, London, Cape, 1927, pp. 22–23.
30. cf. J. Scott, 'The Game of Cat', *Ushaw Magazine*, II, 1893, pp. 19 et seq.
31. Stevenson, op. cit., p. 24.
32. Stevenson, op. cit., p. 25.
33. Stevenson, op. cit., p. 74.
34. Letter to Basil Hall Chamberlain, 6 March 1894, *Japanese Letters of Lafcadio Hearn*, pp. 268–270.
35. *Japan: An Interpretation*, p. 371.
36. Ibid.,
37. Ibid., pp. 371–372.
38. Stevenson, op. cit., p. 265.
39. Letter to Basil Hall Chamberlain, 4 February 1893, *Japanese Letters of Lafcadio Hearn*, pp. 47–48..
40. Charles Hearn died of malaria at Suez on the return journey from India on 21 November 1866. Lafcadio had by then been in Ushaw for three years, and had another year to go.
41. *Japanese Letters of Lafcadio Hearn*, pp. 48–49.
42. Ibid.
43. *Life and Letters of Lafcadio Hearn*, p. 34.
44. 'Recollections of an Earlier Ushaw', *Ushaw Magazine*, June 1977, No. 249, Vol. LXXXVIII, p. 3.
45. D. Milburn, *A History of Ushaw College*, Ushaw, 1964, p. 282, n.44.
46. Vol. L., pp. 17–38.
47. Ibid., p. 33.
48. Why 'consequently' is far from clear.
49. Ibid., p. 34.
50. *Exotics and Retrospectives*, London, 1905, p. 177.
51. Vasey, op. cit., p. 35.
52. London, Cape, 1942, p. 44.
53. She writes on 30 May 1908.

Chapter 8 ALAN ROSEN Hearn and the Gastronomic Grotesque

1. The dedication reads: 'To my kindest and truest friend Mrs M. Courtney – by whose generous care and unselfish providing I recovered that health of mind and body without which no literary work can be accomplished.'
2. See *Two Years in the French West Indies*, in *The Writings of Lafcadio Hearn* (Boston and New York: Houghton Mifflin, 1922), Vol. IV, pp. 55–56. Hereafter this edition will be cited as *Works*.
3. Other articles include, in The Cincinnati *Enquirer*, 'Beer' (4/26/73), 'A Dish of Soup' (10/19/73), 'Soup Houses' (12/10/73), 'Cunning Confectioners' (9/12/75), '. . . The Mysteries of Fruit Preserving' (9/19/75), and 'Talk With a Butter Man' (1/14/77).
4. Edward L. Tinker, *Lafcadio Hearn's American Days* (London: John Lane, The Bodley Head Ltd., 1925), p. 181.
5. 'The Raven passeth Its time thusly: In the morning it riseth with the Sun and

drinketh a cup of coffee and devoureth a piece of bread. . . Then It goeth to a Chinese restaurant, where It eateth an amazing dinner, –Its bump of ALIMENTATIVENESS being enormously developed.' *Letters from the Raven,* (New York: Brentano's, 1907), p. 71. Mrs Page Baker writes this about Hearn's visits to Grand Isle with her husband: 'The waiters were not efficient; and it was one of Mr Baker's self-imposed tasks to see that his friend got enough to eat. He ate as much as two men, and it was not always easy to keep the waiters up to the mark in supplying his wants.' *Lafcadio Hearn's American Days,* p. 364.

6. The phrase 'Period of the Gruesome' was coined by Dr George Gould in his early biography, *Concerning Lafcadio Hearn,* Philadelphia: George W. Jacobs and Co., 1909.

7. Article written by Hearn for the *Enquirer.* I am indebted to Jon Hughes for this reference in his introduction to *Period of the Gruesome: Selected Cincinnati Journalism of Lafcadio Hearn* (Maryland: University Press of America, 1990).

8. Hearn's research for 'Greeks, Jews and Cannibals' may well have sparked his interest in the differences between Jewish and Gentile attitudes towards eating, animal slaughter, and blood – which became the subject of 'Haceldama'.

9. *Period of the Gruesome,* p. 192.

10. Less than a year after 'Haceldama', Hearn wrote another article about blood-drinking called 'A Slaughter-House Story – About One Who Drank Three Glasses of Blood, and Went Blind' for the Cincinnati *Commercial,* 26 July 1876. In it, Hearn reworks many of the graphic details of blood-drinking presented in 'Haceldama' while discussing with perfect scientific detachment the problems of parasites and coagulation. Text is from Hughes, *Period of the Gruesome,* pp. 238–40.

11. Here perhaps is the origin of the image of self-cannibalism which reappears in Hearn's later work as a metaphor for the artist.

12. 'The Creole Doctor', reprinted in *Occidental Gleanings by Lafcadio Hearn,* Vol. 2, collected by Albert Mordell (New York: Dodd, Mead and Co., 1925), pp. 204–05.

13. *Works,* Vol. II, p. 220.

14. This is also one of the early instances of what Carl Dawson calls Hearn's 'lifelong love of naming' in *Lafcadio Hearn and the Vision of Japan* (Baltimore: Johns Hopkins University Press, 1992), p. 63.

15. See *Two Years in the French West Indies,* 'A Midsummer Trip to the Tropics', *Works,* Vol. III, p. 44, and 'Martinique Sketches', *Works,* Vol. IV, pp. 56–66.

16. Quoted from Tinker, pp. 78–79.

17. *Occidental Gleanings,* Vol. 2, pp. 263–64.

18. *Works,* Vol. XV, pp. 172-73.

19. *Works,* Vol. XIV, pp. 223–24.

20. Kazuo Hearn Koizumi, *Re-Echo* (Idaho: Caxton Printers, 1957), p. 80.

21. *Re-Echo,* p. 115.

22. *Re-Echo,* p. 121–22. Hearn most likely knew the story either directly from the Volsunga Saga in the Poetic Edda or from William Morris's version, 'The Story of Sigurd the Volsung and the Fall of the Niblungs' (1876).

23. 'In the Prose Edda it is told how Thor, accompanied by Loki and Thjalfi, after various misadventures arrived at Utgard to visit King Skrymir [king of the

giants]. . . Thor and his companions undergo a whole series of mystifications culminating in a series of matches at the giants' castle, when Loki is defeated at eating, Thjalfi at running, and Thor himself had failed to empty a drinking horn in three draughts, to lift more than one leg of a cat from the floor, and to win a wrestling match with an old woman. The following day on their departure Skrymir explains that Loki was defeated by Logi – meaning fire; Thjalfi by thought; that the drinking horn was connected with the sea, and that Thor's prodigious draughts had lowered the sea levels around the northern coasts. . .; that the cat was Jormungard, the Midgard serpent, the lifting of whose leg had caused vast earthquakes all over the world; while the old woman was Elli, or old age, with whom no one could struggle. When Thor in a fury at having been deceived turned round to strike the giant, everything disappeared.' *Everyman's Dictionary of Non-Classical Mythology,* compiled by Egerton Sykes (London: J.M. Dent & Sons, 1977), p. 197.

24. Letter to Mrs Courtney, 28 August 1884, from Grand Isle, reprinted in Tinker, *Lafcadio Hearn's American Days,* p. 217. In several letters, Hearn described the details of his current food situation to her, praising or criticizing the local fare.
25. 'Feed Hungry Ghosts' is the literal meaning of 'Se-ga-ki', the Buddhist rites for the repose of the dead.
26. Cited from *Lafcadio Hearn's American Days,* pp. 40–41.
27. Letter to Chamberlain (13 April 1893) *Works,* Vol. XV, p. 397.
28. Letter to Mitchell McDonald, (April 1898), *Works,* Vol. XV, p. 114.
29. Koizumi Kazuo, *Father and I: Memories of Lafcadio Hearn* (Boston: Houghton Mifflin, 1935), p. 164.
30. Koizumi Setsuko, *Reminiscences of Lafcadio Hearn* (Boston: Houghton Mifflin, 1918), pp. 44–45.

Chapter 9 NAOKO SUGIYAMA Lafcadio Hearn's *Youma*: Self as Outsider

1. Barbara Christian, *Black Women Novelists: The Development of a Tradition, 1892–1976,* (Westport, Conn.: Greenwood Press, 1980).
2. 'Some Poems about Insects', in *Interpretation of Literature Vol. II,* (New York: Dodd, Mead and Company, 1915), p. 262.
3. Basil Hall Chamberlain's criticism that Hearn 'saw details very distinctly while incapable of understanding them as a whole' comes to mind. Basil Hall Chamberlain. *Things Japanese: Notes on Various Subjects Connected With Japan* (1980; 6th ed. London: Kegan Paul, Trench, Trubner. 1939), 296.

Works Cited:
Chamberlain, Basil Hall. *Things Japanese: Notes on Various Subjects Connected With Japan* 1980. 6th ed. London: Kegan Paul, Trench, Trubner. 1939.
Christian, Barbara. *Black Women Novelists: The Development of a Tradition, 1892–1976.* Westport: Greenwood Press, 1980.
Hearn, Lafcadio. 'The Race Problems in America'. In *Editorials from Kobe Chronicle.* Tokyo: Hokuseido. 1960, pp. 34–39.
—. 'Some Poems about Insects'. In *Interpretation of Literature.* Vol II. New York: Dodd, Mead and Company, 1915, pp. 238–271.

—. *Youma.* In *The Writings of Lafcadio Hearn* IV. Boston, 1922; rpt. Kyoto: Rinsen Books, 1973, pp. 261–371.
—. *The Writings of Lafcadio Hearn.* Boston, 1922; rpt. Kyoto: Rinsen Books, 1973. Vols. XIV and XV.
Scholes, Robert. 'The Left Hand of Difference'. *Textual Power: Literary Theory and the Teaching of English.* New Haven: Yale UP, 1985.

Chapter 10 HIROMI KAWASHIMA Travel Sketches of Lafcadio Hearn

1. Letter to H. E. Krehbiel in 1886, in *Life and Letters of Lafcadio Hearn*, ed. Elizabeth Bisland, vol. XIII of *The Writings of Lafcadio Hearn* ([n. p.], Rinsen Book Co., 1973), p. 374.
2. Letter to George M. Gould in 1887, in *Life and Letters of Lafcadio Hearn*, vol. XIV of *The Writings of Lafcadio Hearn*, p. 20.
3. Letter to Jerome A. Hart in January 1883, in *Life and Letters of Lafcadio Hearn*, vol. XIII of *The Writings of Lafcadio Hearn*, p. 242.
4. *Stories from Pierre Loti*, ed. Albert Mordell (Tokyo: Hokuseido Press, 1933), p. 218.
5. *Ibid.*, p. 220.
6. *The Writings of Lafcadio Hearn*, vol. V, pp. 72–73.
7. *Ibid.*, pp. 93–97.
8. Letter to W. B. Mason on 30 July 1892, in *Japanese Letters of Lafcadio Hearn*, ed. Elizabeth Bisland, vol. XVI of *The Writings of Lafcadio Hearn*, p. 281.
9. Letter to B. H. Chamberlain on 18 February 1893, in *Life and Letters of Lafcadio Hearn*, vol. XV of *The Writings of Lafcadio Hearn*, p. 383.
10. Letter to B. H. Chamberlain on 2 February 1894, in *Japanese Letters of Lafcadio Hearn*, vol. XVI of *The Writings of Lafcadio Hearn*, p. 115.
11. Letter to B. H. Chamberlain on 7 March 1894, in *Japanese Letters of Lafcadio Hearn*, vol. XVI of *The Writings of Lafcadio Hearn*, pp. 147–48.
12. Letter to B. H. Chamberlain on 12 December 1892, in *Life and Letters of Lafcadio Hearn*, vol. XV of *The Writings of Lafcadio Hearn*, pp. 346–47.
13. Letter to B. H. Chamberlain on 10 June 1893, in *Japanese Letters of Lafcadio Hearn*, vol. XV of *The Writings of Lafcadio Hearn*, p. 435.
14. Letter to B. H. Chamberlain on 18 February 1893, in *Japanese Letters of Lafcadio Hearn*, vol. XV of *The Writings of Lafcadio Hearn*, p. 383.
15. *The Writings of Lafcadio Hearn*, vol. XIII p. 46.

Chapter 11 YOKO MAKINO Hearn's 'Yuki-Onna' and Baudelaire's 'Les Bienfaits de la Lune'

1. *The Writings of Lafcadio Hearn*, (Boston: Houghton Mifflin, 1922) XI, 227.
2. *Writings of Lafcadio Hearn*, XI, 231.
3. *Writings of Lafcadio Hearn*, VI, 337–38.
4. *Writings of Lafcadio Hearn*, XV, 378.
5. 'Studies on Extraordinary Prose', *Interpretations of Literature*, ed. John Erskin (New York: Dodd, Mead & Co., 1915) II, 84.

6. *Writings of Lafcadio Hearn*, II, 312.
7. *Writings of Lafcadio Hearn*, II, 312.
8. *Writings of Lafcadio Hearn*, II, 23–30.

Chapter 12 YUZO OTA Lafcadio Hearn: Japan's Problematic Interpreter

1. Lafcadio Hearn, *Letters from the Raven*, ed. Milton Bronner (New York: Boni Books, 1907), p. 133.
2. Obituary in the 29 September 1904 issue. Quoted from a clipping in the possession of the Department of English of Tokyo University. All citations from newspaper articles and other newspaper materials, such as advertisements, in this paper are based on clippings in the possession of the same Department.
3. The 29 January 1905 issue. The reviewer's name is George Hamlin Fitch.
4. Edited by Louis Allen and Jean Wilson and published by Japan Library Ltd at Sandgate, Folkestone, Kent.
5. Letter of 3 November 1902 to Mrs Wetmore, *Veiled Letters from Lafcadio Hearn Preserved by Shunzo Kuwabara*, ed. Kaoru Sekita (Tokyo: Yushodo Press Co., Ltd., 1991), pp. 427–48.
6. See *Gleanings of the Writings of Lafcadio Hearn*, ed. the Hearn Society, II (Tokyo: Yushudo Press Co., Ltd., 1991), 278–80.
7. As quoted in Kajitani Masayuki, 'Yakumo yukari no hito', *Herun*, No. 5, Yakumokai, 1967, p. 11. The recipient's name is Tamaki Akihide.
8. Letter to Elizabeth Bisland, *The Life and Letters of Lafcadio Hearn*, ed. Elizabeth Bisland (Boston and New York: Houghton, Mifflin and Company, 1906) [Hereafter cited as *Life and Letters*], II, 3.
9. *The Japanese Letters of Lafcadio Hearn*, ed. Elizabeth Bisland (1910; rpt. Wilmington, Delaware: Scholarly Resources, Inc., 1973) [Hereafter cited as *Japanese Letters*], p. 313, quoted in my paper, 'Lafcadio Hearn and Basil Hall Chamberlain', *Asian Cultural Studies*, Tokyo, International Christian University, Special Issue No. 3, 1992, p. 66, where you will find a few other quotations from Hearn's letters showing that his enthusiasm for Japan did not last.
10. Letter to Ellwood Hendrick of Matsue, 1891 in *Life and Letters*, II, 61.
11. Nobushige Amenomori, 'Lafcadio Hearn, the Man', *Atlantic Monthly*, October 1905, p. 520.
12. Nina H. Kennard, *Lafcadio Hearn* (1912; rpt. Washington, N.Y.: Kennikat Press, 1967), p. 278.
13. It was reviewed by Kiyoshi K. Kawakami in the 30 May 1926 issue.
14. Quoted from an obituary in the 8 October 1904 issue of *Commercial* [Bangor, Me.].
15. Letter to Mitchell McDonald, *Life and Letters*, II, 356. I have already touched on Hearn's own negative evaluation of *Glimpses of Unfamiliar Japan* in 'Lafcadio Hearn and Basil Hall Chamberlain', p. 72.
16. Letter of 17 April 1993, *Japanese Letters*, p. 82.
17. *Japanese Letters*, p. 84.
18. *Life and Letters*, II, 407–08.
19. The review appeared in the 14 October 1894 issue.

20. See a clipping in the possession of the Department of English of Tokyo University.
21. See my paper 'Western Interpreters of Japan and their Visions' which I presented at the Thirteenth Congress of International Comparative Literature Association held in Tokyo in 1991 (scheduled to be published in 1995 in v. 6 of its Proceedings). I have commented on Hearn's love of Old Japan also in 'Lafcadio Hearn and Basil Hall Chamberlain', p. 67.
22. I already hinted at this in 'Western Interpreters of Japan and their Visions'.
23. *Life and Letters*, II, 192.
24. *Things Japanese* (Tokyo: The Hakubunsha, 1890), p. 353.
25. In the 17 August 1931 issue (evening edition) of the *Tokyo Nichi Nichi Shimbun*.
26. *Glimpses of Unfamiliar Japan* (1894; rpt. Rutland, Vermont & Tokyo: Charles E. Tuttle), pp. 676–81.
27. *Life and Letters*, p. 258.
28. *Japanese Letters*, pp. 120–21.
29. *Glimpses of Unfamiliar Japan*, p. 687.
30. *Life and Letters*, p.258.
31. *Japanese Letters*, p.227
32. An advertisement in the 31 August 1930 issue of the *Tokyo Asahi Shimbun*.
33. Ibid.
34. Koizumi Kazuo, *Chichi Koizumi Yakumo* (Tokyo: Koyama Shoten, 1950), p. 6.
35. See clippings in the possession of the Department of English of Tokyo University.
36. Its clipping is found in a scrap book the possession of the Department of English of Tokyo University.
37. *Japanese Letters*, p. 325.
38. Lafcadio Hearn, *Kokoro* (1896; Rutland, Vermont and Tokyo: Charles E. Tuttle, 1972), p. 152.
39. *Life and Letters*, II, 271.
40. *Some New Letters and Writings of Lafcadio Hearn*, ed. Sanki Ichikawa (Tokyo: Kenkyusha, 1925), p. 203.
41. Used by Hasegawa Minokichi in his announcement of the planned publication of the complete works of Lafcadio Hearn in Japanese translation, The *Tokyo Asahi Shimbun*, 4 May 1926.
42. *Life and Letters*, II, 493.
43. See clippings in the possession of the Department of English of Tokyo University.
44. *Life and Letters*, II, 399. See ibid., II, 341 and 398–99 for Hearn's discussion of his limitations as a writer.
45. I have already commented on this both in 'Lafcadio Hearn and Basil Hall Chamberlain' and 'Western Interpreters of Japan and their Visions'. See, especially, 'Lafcadio Hearn and Basil Hall Chamberlain', pp. 68–70.
46. Hearn's rejection of the idea of racial equality is most clearly evident in an article titled 'The Race Problem in America' written in Japan during his brief affiliation with the *Kobe Chronicle*. In this article, Hearn says, for example: 'Those who knew the character of the African race had nothing to do with the irrational legislation made on its behalf after the time of emancipation,–the

conferring of universal suffrage upon millions ignorant as cattle, and the constitutional amendments declaring them entitled to all privileges of citizenship, and the special laws punishing refusal to acknowledge their rights to such privileges. Those who did not know, or who did not care, about the negro race made these laws. . .' (Lafcadio Hearn, *Editorials from the Kobe Chronicle*, ed. Makoto Sangu [Tokyo: The Hokuseido Press, 1960], p. 36)

47. Lafcadio Hearn, *Japanese Miscellany* (1901; rpt. Rutland, Vermont & Tokyo: Charles E. Tuttle, 1954), p. 222.

48. *Life and Letters*, II, 227.

49. 'Lafcadio Hearn and Basil Hall Chamberlain', p. 71.

50. Review of *The Sacred Tree, Being the Second Part of the Tale of Genji*, by Lady Murasaki, translated by Arthur Waley. *Dial*, July 1926, 80.

51. Arthur Waley, 'Notes on Translation', in *Madly Singing in the Mountain: An Appreciation and Anthology of Arthur Waley*, ed. Ivan Morris (London: George Allen & Unwin, 1970), p. 156. See also Waley's comment on how he translated Ukon's speech on p. 154 of the same article.

52. Lafcadio Hearn, *Glimpses of Unfamiliar Japan* (1894; rpt. Rutland, Vermont & Tokyo: Charles E. Tuttle, 1972), p. 18.

54. *Glimpses of Unfamiliar Japan*, p. 398.

55. *Glimpses of Unfamiliar Japan*, p. 389.

56. Baelz, p. 62.

57. *Out of the East*, p. 92.

58. In fact, he came to suspect as much even before finishing his essay. In his letter of 25 June 1893 Hearn confided to Chamberlain: 'After writing one hundred pages of MS. (about) on the Eternal Feminine, I suddenly find myself checked by doubts of a very serious kind. I read your 'Classical Poetry' over again today; and I find so many sweet thoughts in those poems that I fear my argument about the absence of the love-element from Japanese romance (except as the love of dancing girls, etc.) must be all wrong' (Elizabeth Bisland, *The Japanese Letters of Lafcadio Hearn* [1910; rpt. Wilmington, Delaware, Scholarly Resources Inc., 1973], p. 125). 'Of the Eternal Feminine' in *Out of the East*, however, shows little evidence that Hearn modified his argument because he had come to suspect that it was 'all wrong'. He also continued to talk about the deficiency of the sexual instinct of the Japanese. For example, in his letter to Chamberlain of February 1895, he writes: 'I am now convinced. . . that the deficiency of the sexual instinct (using the term philosophically) in the race is a serious defect rather than a merit, and is very probably connected with the absence of the musical sense and the incapacity for abstract reasoning' (*Life and Letters*, II, 209–10). These facts make us doubt his intellectual probity.

59. *Japan: An Attempt at Interpretation* (1904; rpt. Rutland, Vermont & Tokyo: Charles E. Tuttle, 1956), pp. 9–10.

60. Ibid., p. 10.

61. I already suggested this explanation for Hearn's popularity in Japan in 'Lafcadio Hearn and Basil Hall Chamberlain', p. 72.

62. Those readers who would like to see a fuller examination of Lafcadio Hearn and his work undertaken by me along the lines suggested by this paper are

referred to my book (written in Japanese) *Rafukadio Haan* (Tokyo, Iwanami Shoten, 1994) on which this paper is partially based.

Chapter 13 MASARU TODA The Western Appreciation of Shinto: Lafcadio Hearn, Bruno Taut and André Malraux

1. B.H. Chamberlain, *Things Japanese* (2nd ed., London and Yokohama, 1891), 374–77.
2. B.H. Chamberlain, *Things Japanese* (1st ed., London and Yokohama, 1890), 173.
3. The following discussion is quoted from E.M. Satow, 'The Shintō Temple of Isé' *Transactions of the Asiatic Society of Japan*, vol. 2 (1874), 135–39.
4. The italics are mine.
5. B.H. Chamberlain, (ed.), *A Handbook for Travellers in Japan* (3rd ed., London and Yokohama, 1891), 350.
6. *Writings of Lafcadio Hearn*, vol. V (Boston and New York, 1922), 218–19.
7. E.M. Satow, (ed.), *A Handbook for Travellers in Japan in Central & Northern Japan* (2nd ed., London and Yokohama, 1884), 64.
8. *Writings of Lafcadio Hearn*, VIII, 8.
9. *Writings of Lafcadio Hearn*, VIII, 5.
10. *Writings of Lafcadio Hearn*, V, 242–43.
11. *Writings of Lafcadio Hearn*, V, 212–23. The italics are mine.
12. Satow, *A Handbook for Travellers in Japan in Central & Northern Japan*, 64. The italics are mine.
13. Satow, *A Handbook for Travellers in Japan in Central & Northern Japan*, 65.
14. Satow, *A Handbook for Travellers in Japan in Central & Northern Japan*, 65.
15. Satow, *A Handbook for Travellers in Japan in Central & Northern Japan*, 63–64.
16. Satow, 'The Shintō Temple of Isé' 118–19.
17. Chamberlain, *Things Japanese*, 1st ed., 173.
18. Chamberlain, *A Handbook for Travellers in Japan*, 3rd ed., 245.
19. W.G. Aston, *Shinto: The Way of the Gods* (London, 1905), 223–26.
20. Isabella L. Bird, *Unbeaten Tracks in Japan* (London, 1900), 437–37. The italics in the following quotations are mine.
21. Bird, *Unbeaten Tracks in Japan*, 438.
22. Bird, *Unbeaten Tracks in Japan*, 439.
23. Bird, *Unbeaten Tracks in Japan*, 440.
24. Bird, *Unbeaten Tracks in Japan*, 440.
25. *Writings of Lafcadio Hearn*, VIII, 3.
26. *Writings of Lafcadio Hearn*, VIII, 3.
27. *Writings of Lafcadio Hearn*, VIII, 3–4.
28. Nobushige Amenomori, 'Lafcadio Hearn, the Man' *Atlantic Monthly*, vol. 96 (1905), 511.
29. *Writings of Lafcadio Hearn*, VIII, 5. The italics are mine.
30. *Writings of Lafcadio Hearn*, VII, 264.
31. *Writings of Lafcadio Hearn*, VIII, 4–5.
32. Translated by the present author from the Japanese version: Bruno Taut, *Taut*

no Nikki (Tokyo: Iwanami, 1975), 253–57. The original German diary is not available.

33. André Malraux, *L'Intemporel*, vol. 1 (Paris, 1976), 205.
34. Tadao Takemoto, *Malraux Nihon eno Syogen* (Tokyo: Bijutsukoron, 1978), 358. Translated by the present author.
35. Takemoto, *Malraux Nihon eno Syogen* 385–88. Translated by the present author.

Chapter 14 PAUL MURRAY Lafcadio Hearn's Interpretation of Japan

1. Lafcadio Hearn, *Glimpses of Unfamiliar Japan*, Houghton Mifflin Company, Boston, 1894; reprinted by Charles E. Tuttle Company, Inc, Rutland, Vermont, and Tokyo, 1976, 657
2. *Glimpses of Unfamiliar Japan*, 676
3. Lafcadio Hearn, *Out of the East*, (Houghton Mifflin Company, Boston, 1897), Reprinted by Charles E. Tuttle Company, Inc. Rutland, Vermont, and Tokyo, 1972, 202
4. *Out of the East*, 236 & 225
5. *More Letters from Basil Hall Chamberlain to Lafcadio Hearn*, compiled by Kazuo Koizumi, Hokuseido Press, Tokyo, 1937, 163
6. Lafcadio Hearn, *Kokoro*, (Houghton Mifflin Company, Boston 1896), Reprinted by Charles E. Tuttle Company, Inc. Rutland, Vermont, and Tokyo, 1972, 36
7. *Kokoro*, 35–7
8. *Kokoro*, 30
9. *Kokoro*, 54–5
10. *Kokoro*, 145
11. Gordon Daniels, 'Sir George Sansom (1883–1965)', in Sir Hugh Cortazzi and Gordon Daniels (ed), *Britain and Japan 1859–1991, Themes and Personalities*, Routledge, London and New York, 1991, 280
12. Basil Hall Chamberlain, *Things Japanese*, Fifth Revised Edition, London, J Murray; Yokohama, Kelly and Walsh Ltd, 1905; reprinted in paperback as *Japanese Things*, by Charles E. Tuttle, Co., Rutland, Vermont and Tokyo, 1971, 249 (This edition is hereafter referred to as *Things Japanese*)
13. Lafcadio Hearn, *Gleanings in Buddha Fields*, (Houghton Mifflin Company, Boston, 1897), Reprinted by Charles E. Tuttle Company, Inc. Rutland, Vermont, and Tokyo, 1971, 100–101
14. *Gleanings in Buddha Fields*, 113–4
15. *Gleanings in Buddha Fields*, 121–3
16. 'Lafcadio Hearn – Lover or Hater of Japan: Concerning Some Newly Discovered Letters', *Japan*, San Francisco, Vol 15, 1926
17. *Things Japanese*, 65
18. MSS Hearn letter to Horace Scudder, 28/8/95, Kobe; Middlebury College, Middlebury, Veermont, USA
19. Fustel de Coulanges, *La Cité Antique*, 17th edition, Librairie Hachette, Paris, 1900; *The Ancient City: A study of Religion, Laws, and Institutions of Greece and*

Rome, Fustel de Coulanges, translated from the French by Willard Small, Lee & Shepard, Boston, Lee, Shepar, & Dillingham, New York, 1874, 3–7

20. See Bernard Grasset, *Les intellectuels et l'avènement de la troisième république, 1871–1875*, Paris, 1931, and Jane Herrick, *The Historical Thought of Fustel de Coulanges*, The Catholic University of America Press, Washington DC, 1954, 117, for contrasting views

21. G.B. Sansom, *The Western World and Japan, A Study in the Interaction of European and Asiatic Cultures*, (1950), Charles E. Tuttle Company, Vermont & Tokyo, 1977, 478

22. Sukehiro Hirakawa, 'Lafcadio Hearn's "At a Railway Station". A Case of Sympathetic Understanding of the Inner Life of Japan', paper given at the Woodrow Wilson International Centre for Scholars, Smithsonian Institute, Washington D.C., 19/7/1979; published in *Lafcadio Hearn: Japan's Great Interpreter. A new anthology of his writings 1894–1904*, Louis Allen & Jean Wilson (ed), Japan Library, Sandgate, Kent, 1992, 302–8

23. Sukehiro Hirakawa, 'Supplementary Comment on the Lafcadio Hearn Paper', paper given at the Woodrow Wilson International Centre for Scholars, Smithsonian Institute, Washington D.C., 19/7/1979: published in *Lafcadio Hearn: Japan's Great Interpreter. A new anthology of his writings 1894–1904*, Louis Allen & Jean Wilson (ed), Japan Library, Sandgate, Kent, 1992, pp. 302–8

24. *Things Japanese* 489

25. *Things Japanese* 237

26. *Things Japanese* 368

27. *Things Japanese* 295

28. *Things Japanese* 339

29. *Things Japanese* 137–146

30. *Things Japanese* 488–497

31. *Letters from Basil Hall Chamberlain to Lafcadio Hearn*, compiled by Kazuo Koizumi, Hokuseido Press, Tokyo, 1936, BHC to LH, 8/9/1894, Miyanosita, 112–4

32. *Things Japanese* 361–2

33. 'The Invention of a New Religion', Appendix published in *Things Japanese*, 531–544

34. Sukehiro Hirakawa, 'Who Was the Great Japan Interpreter, Chamberlain or Hearn?', paper read to *Perspectives on Japonisme, The Japanese Influence on America*, An International Conference at Rutgers, May 13–14, 1988

35. Basil Hall Chamberlain, *Things Japanese*, 6th Edition Revised, Kegan Paul, Trench, Trubner & Co, 1939, 295–8

36. George M Gould, MD, *Concerning Lafcadio Hearn*, with a bibliography by Laura Stedman, George W Jacobs and Company, Philadelphia, 1908

37. Arthur E. Kunst, *Lafcadio Hearn*, Twayne Publishers Inc., New York, 1969, 126

38. Mutsuo Fukushima, 'MacArthur Aide May Have Saved Emperor From Trial', *Daily Yomiuri*, 4/1/1993

39. *The Spectator*, 1/1/1994

40. *Financial Times*, The FT Review of Business Books, 15/3/94

LIST OF CONTRIBUTORS

Louis ALLEN
Formerly of the School of Modern European Languages, Durham University, United Kingdom

Sukehiro HIRAKAWA
Professor Emeritus, University of Tokyo, Japan

George HUGHES
Department of Literature, University of Tokyo, Japan

Hiromi KAWASHIMA
Tōyō Gakuen University, Chiba, Japan

Yoko MAKINO
Seijō University, Tokyo, Japan

Earl MINER
Princeton University, New Jersey, USA

Paul MURRAY
Irish Foreign Service

Yuzo OTA
Department of History, McGill University, Montreal, Canada

Alan ROSEN
Kumamoto University, Kumamoto, Japan

Naoko SUGIYAMA
American Studies, Saitama University, Urawa, Japan

Masaru TODA
Kobe University, Kobe, Japan

INDEX